THE WAY WE ATE

THE WAY WE ATE

Pacific Northwest Cooking, 1843-1900

JACQUELINE B. WILLIAMS

WSU PRESS

Washington State University Press
PO Box 645910
Pullman, WA 99164-5910
(800) 354-7360

Washington State University Press, Pullman, Washington 99164-5910
© 1996 by the Board of Regents of Washington State University
First printing 1996

Cover illustration courtesy Museum of History and Industry, Seattle, #15117.

Library of Congress Cataloging-in-Publication Data
Williams, Jacqueline B.
    The way we ate : Pacific Northwest cooking, 1843-1900 / Jacqueline
B. Williams.
        p.   cm.
    Includes index.
    ISBN 0-87422-137-4 (cloth).—ISBN 0-87422-136-6 (pbk.)
    1. Cookery—Northwest, Pacific—History.   2. Frontier and pio-
neer life—Northwest, Pacific.   3. Kitchens—Northwest, Pacific—
Equipment and supplies—History.   I. Title.
TX715.W7244   1996
641.59795—dc20   96-21942
                                                                      CIP

Washington State University Press
Pullman, Washington 99164-5910
Phone: (800) 354-7360
Fax: (509) 335-8568

To the men and women who kept the diaries and wrote the letters, and to their families who saved these precious pieces of our history.

Contents

Foreword

by Ruth Kirk

PUT YOURSELF IN A WRITER'S place and add a willingness to research exhaustively and an urge to imbue history with a sense of immediacy. What single theme could you build around to both present the past and assure the empathy of readers today? The answer is easy—and Jackie Williams has found it. Food. *The Way We Ate* draws us in. Young and old, then and now, we all savor good food, hope for it, and strive one or another to find it.

Jackie starts her tale with the home itself, the physical structures settlers built after they had stepped from their covered wagons and around-the-Horn sailing ships into the new life they traveled so far to find. She gives us the architectural distinction between log cabins and log houses, the former built with timbers left round, the latter with squared timbers carefully fitted at the corners. The account reminds me of traveling around Whatcom County years ago with Michael Sullivan, at the time county historic preservation officer and now heading cultural resource planning for the City of Tacoma. Michael showed us four eras of log construction represented by examples scattered about the countryside. Some stood isolated and empty, others still lived in and loved. (To easily see such houses for yourself, visit Ferndale's Pioneer Park, a collection of actual cedar houses brought together for preservation and exhibit. Or in western Washington, stop at the John R. Jackson cabin north of Toledo, 1845, or the Obadiah McFadden cabin in Chehalis, 1859. In eastern Washington, visit the Olmstead Place east of Ellensburg or the Perkins cabin in Colfax, both built in the 1870s.

The first era of log construction is largely represented by rude little cabins that a man working alone could build. The second began as families started arriving and several men could combine forces to build with cedar slabs far too heavy to be handled alone. Their tools still were limited to little more than a felling ax, broad ax, hand ax, froe, and crosscut saw. By the 1890s, however—the third era of log construction—tool kits had expanded to include augers, chisels, jack planes, draw knives, and assorted saws for specialized uses. Houses became more elaborate, some with second stories, many with floor plans shaped as T's or L's or E's. The fourth era began as milled lumber became readily available and solid, hand-built cedar houses received fashionable cladding, some even with curlicue gingerbread as a final touch.

Of course, not all early homes followed this classic, almost stereotypical progression. In 1852 when James Swan—later renowned as a judge, Indian agent, collector, and writer—arrived at Willapa Bay he brought with him zinc plates to use for building a house, a not uncommon type of construction. Pattern-book architecture also arrived in the Northwest early on, a design approach to building that is just as the term implies, home plans to be picked from a book, a pioneering *Sunset Magazine* approach but with full-scale drawings available along with suggestions for building materials and notes on ideal interior decoration and garden plantings. Examples of pattern-book houses included the country-Gothic officers' row at the 1856 army post of Fort Simcoe, west of Yakima, and Hoquiam's Castle, an elaborate Queen Anne, turreted mansion built in 1897 for a Grays Harbor timber baron. After the railroad arrived in the 1880s, Washingtonians also had pre-cut houses sold through the Sears Roebuck catalog, and Washington lumber went into pre-cut houses sold beyond the Northwest region. A Chehalis milling company manufactured houses for an Iowa mail order firm and window frames for Montgomery Ward. The home of the milling company's owner, Osmer Palmer, still stands.

Within the homes of these varied ilk, our early cooking and eating took place. Kitchens, in the dictionary sense of "a room specially set apart and equipped for cooking food," were not a part of the simplest cabins, nor were stoves. Single rooms with open hearths sufficed at first. On the overland trail, cooks had plied their art with iron skillets and Dutch ovens set over hot coals. They continued such cookery in their homes, pleased to have a chimney for the smoke to go up. Many had lightened their wagons by jettisoning stoves. On arrival, some did not have even a chimney at first. Among the many quotes given us in the pages of *The Way We Ate* are the words of Steilacoom's Mrs. M.E. Shorey: "There was not a cook stove in the town that could be purchased, so the cooking had to be done over an outdoor fire beside a big stump." Matches, Jackie Williams tells us quoting a Grand Mound settler, came in a "block of wood split length-wise into about 100 sticks" or as China matches sold "1,200 in a bunch."

Readers with gray hair will find their own memories triggered by such mentions, and younger readers will hear again the voices of parents and grandparents. In my case, living with my park ranger husband in the odd houses set in beautiful places that characterized the immediately post-World War II National Park Service, cooking was with kerosene, oil, coal, wood, and bottled gas. It is the wood stove at El Morro, in New Mexico, that I remember most fondly. Louis offered our four-year-old son a penny a load to bring in stove wood, but in time Bruce wearied of the arrangement and suggested reversing roles: he paid his father to bring in wood until his pennies were gone, then resumed the chore himself—a first, rudimentary lesson in economics all because of a wood stove.

Other than the utensils and fire, cooking, of course, also necessitated a water supply. In western Washington, Jackie Williams tells us, Grand Mound settler Anna Maria James wrote to her sister: "We are blessed with the most beautiful springs of water I ever saw, one of which will be enclosed in our door yard."

In contrast, an 1880s Spokane pioneer reminisced, "Father had not dug a well yet, so my oldest brother, Rouse, aged seven and a half years, and I used to take horses to water about one mile away to another homestead that had a well. We tied all the empty syrup cans to the saddle to fill with water and take back home, that was twice a day and cold, to draw water from a well with a pail and rope."

Early mentions of food storage and preservation also figure into the tale this book tells, fodder again for personal memories among all readers who grew up emptying the drip pans of back-porch ice boxes and sucking on chips from the fifty-pound blocks carried from delivery truck to house by icemen wielding huge tongs. Chilled food and drink seems universally appealing. The Hudson's Bay Company actually leased glaciers in Alaska to entrepreneurs, who shipped ice to San Francisco, at the time in the midst of its post-gold rush boom. The young Ulysses S. Grant, while a brevet captain quartermaster at Fort Vancouver, also shipped ice to San Francisco, hoping to net enough to pay off gambling debts. His ice came from the Columbia River, which then frequently froze over in winter. Unfortunately, his ice melted en route south and provided the future Civil War general and president of the United States with additional loss rather than a solution to debt—another rudimentary lesson in economics.

Lava caves near The Dalles, Jackie Williams tells us, were also a commercial source of ice; almost-perfect insulation of the porous rock there maintained ice from winter seepage. She quotes *The Commercial Age*, which commented that "a dearth of ice is a sad calamity to bar-rooms and butter plates," then added that ice packed by mule to the steamboat landing thirty-five miles from the caves underwent a 50 percent loss, "which might be greatly reduced by more careful packing."

By the 1870s, the harvesting of natural ice dwindled as commercially frozen ice became widespread (although ranchers continued to use lava caves for storing butter and cheese prior to shipping them to market). Washington can even claim the pioneering manufacture of dry ice; watch for an abandoned, mission-style building at a public fishing area on the river bank a mile and a half east of the small town of Klickitat. There this new form of refrigeration was developed, drawing on deep wells that provided abundant natural carbon dioxide.

Ice. Water. Stoves. Kitchens. Cabins. In *The Way We Ate* we also find dozens of recipes and instructions: How to Make Tough Beef Tender; How to Freshen Yeast that Has Become Bitter; Sauer Kraut ("Spread washed cabbage leaves to cover the bottom of a barrel..."); Fourth of July Pudding; Wedding Cake ("15 eggs well beaten, 1½ pounds butter..."). We read about churning butter—a contrast with our present-day fat-free spreads and sprays—and about how to "put down" eggs in a crock filled with two gallons of water, a half pint of "good salt," and a piece of unslaked lime the "size of a teacup"—also a contrast for the cholesterol-conscious who have turned to simulated eggs pre-beaten and packaged in what look ironically like cream cartons.

In this book we read, too, of parties. Local papers reported "jolly times of music and dancing" across the state, from the Election Ball held on November 16, 1868 in Olympia, where "supper [was] furnished by the ladies," to a fete at the Colfax Hotel detailed in the December 12, 1879 *Palouse Gazette*. That account ends, "In the fullness of our stomach[s] we thank Mrs. James Ewart for that nice Christmas dinner."

So, too, we thank Jackie Williams. Her book is filled with painstaking documentation and immediacy. *Bon appetite!*

Preface

In the last chapter of my book, *Wagon Wheel Kitchens: Food on the Oregon Trail*, I wrote that "once the emigrants reached their destination, their troubles were not over....Making it through their first winter was one more hazard for the weary emigrants." Yet make it they did. The tired and often destitute settlers who planned to make the Oregon country their home unpacked their wagons and continued to bake, broil, stew, and fry. Nearly empty larders did not prevent women from serving meals to their families. How pioneers stocked their pantries and filled their cellars adds another story to the early history of the Pacific Northwest.

Trying to describe and document kitchen problems facing settlers during the first fifty-plus years of settlement in the Pacific Northwest presented several dilemmas. Generalizing about foodways in the rapidly developing Pacific Northwest cannot be done. Simply giving dates and places would not be sufficient. Just because one family in Oregon City had a well-stocked pantry in 1850 does not imply that all settlers did. Somehow I needed to convey the similarities and differences between homesteaders who farmed on fertile land with adequate water and families who watched their crops dry up in summertime when the rains forgot to fall. I had to explain that everyone had to preserve food for winter, but wealthier families might have the resources to purchase glass jars for their preserves while less fortunate ones had to reuse old kerosene cans. I wanted to tell the reader about the many tasks involved in cooking, yet dispel the idea of grim-faced pioneer women who never left the kitchen. And finally, I had to accurately retell the stories pieced together from pioneers' letters and diaries without adding my twentieth-century voice and biases to the interpretation.

Perhaps a brief description of the region where pioneers built their new homes will explain some difficulties inherent in such a survey. When emigrants rode into Oregon country in 1843 they found a land of varied geography, consisting of coastal plains, large forests, high mountains, inland rivers, and arid, semi-desert lands. Comprising the present states of Oregon, Washington, and parts of Idaho, Montana, and Wyoming the area is further separated by the Cascade chain of mountains.

The boundaries changed when Congress created Oregon Territory in 1848, Washington Territory in 1853, Idaho Territory in 1863, and Montana Territory in 1864. By 1859 Oregon achieved statehood and in 1889 Washington and Montana were admitted as states with Idaho following in 1890.

The communities west of the Cascade mountains generally have a temperate climate. In the settlement years vast forests of towering trees decorated the landscape. An 1869 publication touting the advantages of Marion County, Oregon, noted: "There are many springs and spring branches bubbling up, and cutting through the various portions of the country." East of the mountains the summer is hot and dry, the winters cold, and there are few trees. Where one settled had a major impact on how one lived. Homesteading in the treeless lands east of the Cascade mountains meant that the farmer and his wife had to worry about finding water and preventing the animals from freezing in the winter. Those who settled in certain parts of the Willamette Valley worried about too much rain swelling the rivers and spoiling the harvest.

The region's remote location and absence of good roads also contributed to the availability of food in different locations. Unless one lived near accessible rivers, getting supplies often meant a slow, difficult trip over muddy roads that seemed constructed from twisted tree roots. Until territorial legislatures appropriated money for adequate roads, moving goods in the interior required great fortitude. As noted in *The Washington Pioneer* on December 17, 1854, "the business of this place has been seriously retarded this season, in consequence of the almost impassable state of the road....both our business men and farmers are well aware."

Since access to goods and an adequate water supply made homemaking easier, the first pioneers established communities along the Columbia, Cowlitz, and Willamette rivers. Towns grew where the boats docked and mills could find power to turn the wheels that ground the flour. The Willamette Valley became the first area of urban growth in the Pacific Northwest. In the 1860s, when many homesteaders were just starting out in log cabins, the Willamette Valley had thousands of framed homes.

Disparities in family income, the year of arrival, the rapid development of consumer products after 1860, and the overall economy also added to the problem of describing the settler's kitchen. Better stoves and more choice in cooking implements may have changed the way a financially well-off woman baked and broiled, stewed and simmered, but they would not have helped her poorer neighbor who cooked in front of a fireplace. In some instances families who "scraped by" lived next door to ones who had a stove which held a reservoir filled with hot water. In 1845 pioneers living close to Fort Vancouver or The Dalles had a better chance of obtaining flour and sugar than those who settled around Ford's Prairie (Centralia area). Well-stocked shelves with a variety of goods in 1865 in Portland or Seattle did not mean pioneers homesteading in the rural areas could count on the same varied inventory.

Though I have included a variety of perspectives, this study is not all-inclusive. I have tried to help readers understand that not all families found shortages of food, but when they did, the adaptations and substitutions described in the text are what they might have followed. I have made a conscious effort to show that factory-made utensils and tableware found their way to the Pacific Northwest, but family finances and good roads determined whether a family purchased them.

The Way We Ate is divided into chapters that highlight kitchens, obtaining water, stocking the pantry, cooking methods, special foods, and holiday celebrations. It follows the pioneers from the early years when so often their own shelves, along with merchants' shelves, lacked basic ingredients such as flour, sugar, and coffee; when smoldering logs in a fireplace stood in for a stove; when water had to be hauled from a stream or well—to the time when railroads made it possible for Pacific Northwest cooks to pick and choose from the latest ingredients and implements.

Along the way, *The Way We Ate* tells how coarse, unbolted flour changed to fine white; a simple box stove turned into a cooking range with ornamental tiles and warming ovens; and kitchen cabinets replaced open shelves. As early settlers reminisce about long ago days in the Oregon Territory, we hear of pie fillings made with beans or sheep sorrel instead of fruit, a yellow tomato masking as a fig, sweeteners concocted from watermelon and corn cobs, and the delicacies served at the many balls when emigrants danced the nights away.

A glimpse into the days that pioneer cooks spent in the kitchen offers an understanding of the many tasks involved in preparing meals. In the days before most homes had sinks, running water, and refrigerators, a cake on the menu meant starting from scratch—raising chickens to obtain eggs; churning cream into butter; and butchering a pig in order to render fat into lard (shortening).

In writing this story I have used letters, journals, diaries, and business records found in university, museum, and historical society archives. Oral histories, conversations with descendants of pioneers, nineteenth-century newspapers, and magazines fill in the gaps. Newspaper advertisements and business journals have been especially helpful in showing what merchandise was available, where it came from, and oftentimes the price. I have also relied on reminiscences, like those solicited by the Works Projects Administration Federal Writers Project, recognizing both the biases and selectivity inherent in such interviews and the fact that the passage of time frequently blurred events. Most archival material came from archives and libraries in Washington state. The settlers' experiences in Oregon and Washington territories were quite similar, however.

When quoting from original sources I have kept "unique" spellings, punctuation, and grammatical idiosyncrasies. Recipes are written as they appeared, complete with inadequate measurements and inadequate directions. The women of yesteryear learned the art of cookery at an early age and did not require detailed recipes. Measurements in standardized cup and spoon sizes did not begin to appear until the end of the nineteenth century. Well into the twentieth century, cookery writers listed butter the size of a walnut, or a teacup full of sugar. Readers wanting to sample Sarah McElroy's recipe for Sally Lunn cake, Horner's sour dough bread, or carrot pudding must do so with the same inadequate measurements, and with the knowledge that nineteenth- and twentieth-century sugar are similar but not the same.

The Way We Ate is not a cookbook that tries to duplicate the foods nineteenth-century housewives so diligently prepared. My purpose is to describe foods and implements that adorned the kitchen shelves, dangled from a string stretched over the stove, or sat on the front burner of the old wood stove. The recipes were chosen to illustrate the kinds of ingredients available and used, cooking techniques such as pickling and fruit drying, and the popularity of certain foods.

Because few diarists left detailed recipes, I often relied on those from the farm and home columns of local nineteenth-century Pacific Northwest newspapers, *Godey's Lady's Book* (a very popular source of information about the home), and popular cookery writers like Catharine Beecher. Other recipes came from early community cookbooks published in Oregon and Washington. Printed after the pioneer period, this type of cookbook contains popular family recipes from earlier years. It is fair to assume that the first settlers baked similar breads and cakes; recipes sent in for organizational cookbooks are old favorites handed down from family and friends.

Charred cooking holes, salmon and halibut bones, grinding stones, and hillocks of oyster and clam shells piled up over hundreds of years confirm the fact that ancient people lived in the Pacific Northwest at least 10,000 years ago. Yet, in spite of this history of an abundance of foods, and scientific evidence of hunting and gathering by native persons who first enjoyed a Pacific Northwest cuisine, I have eliminated the native diet when reporting on tales from Northwest kitchens. The story is important, but since I have only stories left by the non-natives I do not believe I would be giving an accurate account. Foodways of Native Americans in the Pacific Northwest deserves to be told from a native perspective.

I chose to concentrate my research around the era of pioneer cooking that occurred from the time the first large group of wagons rolled into Oregon country in 1843 to just after the Northern Pacific and Great Northern Railroads finally chugged across the mountains to the Pacific Northwest in the 1880s. Pioneers who settled a new area after this time frame are included if their experiences were similar to the first settlers.

By concentrating on these fifty-plus years, I have for the most part eliminated the missionary families who came earlier, and the special foods of ethnic Americans. Many of the pioneers cooked from family recipes that hint of an ethnic or regional background. But I will not focus on special Chinese, German, Irish, Jewish, or Scandinavian cuisines. Most of these large ethnic communities came to the Pacific Northwest at the end of the pioneer period and influenced early twentieth-century cookery more than the nineteenth century. If, however, a pioneer writes that a particular recipe came from her German grandmother, I do try to mention that. Unfortunately, most do not say, and I did not want to guess. Assigning a recipe to a particular culture is very difficult. The proliferation of cookbooks and women's magazines in the last half of the nineteenth century popularized the specialties of ethnic cooking.

What follows is my attempt to add to Pacific Northwest history through a peek into the nineteenth-century kitchen: a cornucopia of culinary tales filled with "all the little particulars."

Jacqueline Williams
Seattle, Washington
June 1996

Acknowledgments

IN THE PROCESS OF researching and writing this book, I have used manuscripts, archives, and special collections at the University of Washington, Washington State Library at Olympia, Washington State Historical Society Library, Seattle's Museum of History and Industry Library, and Oregon Historical Society. I am indebted to the archivists and librarians of those institutions for helping me locate letters, journals, and other materials.

Weldon W. Rau, Dale Rutledge, Minerva Herrett, Tove Burhen, Lucille Wilson, Dr. C.G. Gunter, David James, Mrs. Mary Ann Bigelow, Norma Lou Jones, and Bob Pruitt graciously provided personal memories and treasured family recipes. Julie Eulenberg took the time from her own research to pass on food-related items of historical interest; Erica Calkins, Kathy Mendelson, and Kathleen McClelland answered desperate queries related to food preservation and gardening. And Mary Wright and Nancy Hevly plowed through first drafts to see if my ideas made any sense. To all of them, my heartfelt thanks.

I am especially indebted to David Freece, director of the Cowlitz County Historical Museum, who appreciated the merits of *The Way We Ate* when it was just an idea and passed the information on to Washington State University Press. Keith Petersen, my editor, has earned my profound gratitude for always answering my letters and phone calls and contributing clarity and polish to the thousands of words I sent him. Also at the Press I would like to thank: Tom Sanders, Mary Read, Beth DeWeese, Sharon White, Wes Patterson, Jean Taylor, Arline Lyons, and Jenni Lynn—all of whom played important roles in the production of this book.

Finally, special thanks to my husband, Walt Williams, who spent his vacation time at numerous historical museums, read and corrected countless drafts, and never complained when all I wanted to talk about was Catharine Blaine and Phoebe Judson's trials and tribulations in a hot kitchen. Without his support I could never have written *The Way We Ate*.

Chapter One
First Homes, First Kitchens

"TODAY I TOOK THE THINGS out of the wagon. Emeline washed," Elizabeth Austin wrote on October 9, 1854.[1] That date marked the day she and her family—tired, dusty, and dirty from months of overland travel—finally reached Washington Territory. For Austin and thousands of other emigrants who came to the Pacific Northwest in the second half of the nineteenth century, taking their possessions out of the wagon and washing their grimy clothes marked the end of a difficult journey across prairies, plains, and mountains.

But unpacking did not mean that families could relax. In deciding to settle in an area that lacked houses and well-stocked stores, pioneers knew the importance of building a shelter and restoring their dwindling and sometimes depleted food supplies. Unless friendly neighbors or one's family had already taken up residence and could offer temporary lodging, the job had to be done immediately. Shorter days and gray winter rains would soon turn the fertile soil into a muddy morass. No one had time to rest. Both people and supplies needed a shelter. Besides, after 1850 when the Donation Land Claim offered free acreage to those who lived on the land for four years, putting up a house told your neighbors that you meant to stay.[2]

During the first years of settlement, most families who came to the sparsely developed Pacific Northwest lived in log cabins and continued cooking practices that had fed them on the overland march to the West Coast. Numerous dinners still simmered and baked in a Dutch oven over a hearth fire. The family cook baked the daily bread, if she could purchase flour, and dried fruit—especially apples, which remained a constant ingredient of sweets and savories.

Additionally, pioneers handmade many of their own household goods, grew their own food, often dined on tin plates, and considered themselves lucky if they had a cup of real coffee instead of fake varieties made from parched bran or barley. Isaac Stevens, Washington's first territorial governor, had to live in "a mere shanty" until things settled down and he could build a home from the "immense cedar trees and firs hewn down."[3]

Until they finished their home and more supplies arrived, tents and the prairie schooner continued as shelter. At least one energetic family set up temporary quarters in an old tree stump. However, unlike the old woman who "lived in a shoe...and didn't know what to do," the McAllisters, who came to the Nisqually Valley in 1847, knew just what to do. "Father scraped out the stump [two large stumps side by side] and made a roof, and mother moved in with her six children. She found it very comfortable, the burnout roots making such nice cubby-holes for storing away such things."[4]

During camp outs, burning logs smoldering on the ground continued as a stove because most manufactured cook stoves had been abandoned on the overland trail. But at least for now weary travelers did not have to pack and unpack dishes and supplies every day, or constantly search for fuel and water. Since most early emigrants settled on the west side of the Cascade mountains, a walk into the verdant forests supplied ample amounts of logs, and dippers immersed in sparkling streams filled water buckets with clear water.[5]

Staying put did not eliminate all problems but there were advantages. "I can't hope to explain to you how happy we all were...here we had found a country of beauty...instead of seeing nothing but a long winding train of prairie schooners with a cloud of dust hanging over all, we saw waving grass and vividly green fir trees," Catherine Morris explained when she wrote about the thrill of finally reaching Oregon Territory in 1851.[6]

Not only land separated overlanders from their families who lived in the eastern half of America or the southern states. Especially after the Civil War, those in the East had well-built homes with separate kitchens and dining rooms furnished with kitchen equipment purchased in local "warerooms" that offered a variety of cookware, crockery, cutlery, and table accouterments. They entertained in a grand style, and could easily find fancy ingredients called for in recipes printed in popular women's magazines such as *Godey's Lady's Book*. Middle class families in the Victorian era had money to purchase an array of goods and services that announced to the world that they had "made it."

How long this difference between East and West lasted depended on what years pioneers came to the West, where they settled, and whether or not they had enough money left from their westward journey to buy goods.

Some families might live in the log cabin only a few months; others for several years. Families who came in the late 1850s to urban areas around Oregon City, Portland, Olympia, and Vancouver could pick and choose from a variety of foods and ingredients, purchase a cook stove, and buy daily bread. In contrast to their city sisters, housewives who homesteaded in undeveloped areas and/or had few assets might go for months without flour, while grinding peas for coffee.

First, Cut The Logs

At first, most everyone lived in a one- or two-room log cabin built from timber that the forests supplied free of charge, "very little time being required for the purpose."[7] Early settlers felled logs on their own land, which they would have had to do under any circumstance in order to plant a garden. Like Michael Luark they hoped a "broad tree which we found on the hill above the house [would work] but when it was felled it twisted too much for boards consequently we had to look out for another which we found...but did not get it down till night over took us."[8] If sufficient trees were not accessible, logs, preferably cedar, had to be cut down elsewhere and dragged home.

An average log cabin, approximately twelve feet by sixteen feet up to twenty feet by thirty feet, required approximately 30 to 40 logs for walls. "Imagine a room 12 by 16 feet with an inside chimney a staircase and 3 doors on one side and a work bench occupying the other side beside an endless amount of loose chairs and bits of lumber, books tool boxes and 13 grown persons and you have a faint idea of our circumstances," Luark wrote in his diary on November 25, 1861.[9] Yet despite such discomforts Luark had pleasant memories from that one room. When his family abandoned it for larger quarters, he tacked a copy of a sentimental song, "My Old Log-Cabin Home" to the door. The chorus refrain conveyed his sentiments: "Oh my little cabin dear—Oh how happy we were here...I am going now to leave thee and I'm weeping all the day."

Because trees could be cut with only an ax and were heavy enough to be held together without nails, log cabins could be constructed easily and quickly. Since a well-stocked tool box added unwanted weight to the covered wagon and had to be discarded or left at home, many people ended up in the Oregon Territory with just an ax. John Champion Richardson, who settled around Eugene, Oregon country, in 1846 described an early method of cutting the logs:

We had to go with ax and crosscut saw and hang a boy to each end of that saw and cut the timber into proper lengths and then with maul and wedge split it into what the western man called boards, but Yankees called shakes....We made the boards stay in their places by means of green willows.[10]

Even if pioneers came after commercial establishments in larger cities offered a selection of building material and sawmills turned out thousands of feet of timber for more substantial homes, those who moved to sparsely populated areas continued to build a log cabin for their first home. As late as 1901 the Laurie family, who homesteaded in Okanogan County, "lived in tents for about two months until dad and the boys could build a one-room log cabin."[11] The Lauries, just like the settlers who came before them, obtained logs and cut shingles from timber on their homestead. Only the one-by-twelve boards for flooring came from a sawmill.

Making log cabins without nails was common. If the logs did not line up exactly right, and most did not, settlers filled the interstices with "chinking," usually clay, moss, smaller boards, or half logs. Complaining may have made the settlers feel better but it did not keep out drafts. Catharine Blaine, a minister's wife who taught at the first school in Seattle, described the situation she faced on a cold January day in Seattle in 1854:

> Yesterday the family that had been living in the back room of this house moved out taking their windows with them. By the way, the windows were only factory cloth nailed to the window frames, but they served to keep out some of the cold and their stove helped to warm the house. The two rooms are not wholly separated and the cold wind comes in, making itself disagreeable. Our one room is so open that we can look out through the cracks on every side. It freezes not six feet from the little stove when we have as much fire as we can get into it. You would rightly infer that we are not very comfortable, but we console ourselves with the thought that this will not last long, indeed it is getting warmer already.[12]

Thirty-five years later, when most families had abandoned log cabins for homes built with planed lumber, the financially destitute Higbees faced the same problem. In her autobiography Blanche Higbee commented that the walls of their one-room log cabin in Tekoa, a community in eastern Washington, were:

> So open that in winter I have seen snow drifting in through the cracks and staying piled up in spite of a fire kept going all day. Also the roof leaked. Whenever it rained we had to put empty milk pans under the leaks to catch the water. One day it started to rain on my face as I lay

in bed. I got up and put an open umbrella over the pillow! Joys of pioneering![13]

To add a little insulation, settlers used an assortment of materials to cover the walls. Susanna Slover McFarland Price Ede, who lived near Grays Harbor, recalled sealing their second, larger house "inside with redwood shakes split out of driftwood" found on the beach. They had also found glass packed in a box with straw. The glass went into the windows; the straw provided insulation.[14] Other families nailed boards over cracks, put up Indian mats and quilts or blankets, stuffed flour sacks between cracks, or pasted newspapers over rough walls. Countless pioneers recalled learning to read by "reading the walls."

The log cabins, or what Elwood Evans portrayed in his journal as "one-story frame cabins of primitive architecture," featured few amenities. Filling them up with furniture and supplies made them crowded and comfortless.[15] When John and Margaret Laurie crammed a big wood-burning cook stove, a homemade table large enough to seat eleven, another table holding the family Bible, and homemade beds with trundle beds under them into their one room, "there was scarcely room to walk through the cabin," exclaimed their daughter, Helen Jewett Laurie.[16] To gain some privacy families divided the room. The Chambers family built a two-room log cabin, made the smaller room the kitchen, and curtained off the other room for bedrooms. Large families added extra bedrooms to the log cabins by attaching a lean-to, a structure with a slanted roof attached to the main building.

Pioneers referred to their early homes as log cabins, but historians and architects make a distinction between a log cabin and a log house. Both are defined as folk houses to distinguish them from more formal architectural styles. In a log cabin the timbers were usually left round (unhewed), making it difficult to chink the walls. The one room was sometimes referred to as a *pen*. Cabins may or may not have had window openings.

Constructed from square-hewn logs joined by carefully hewn corner notching, log houses frequently had windows, doors, a fireplace, and stairs to a loft area. Houses with windows on either side of the door and one-room deep developed from the traditional British folk plan called "hall and parlor." When homeowners added a second story and the house remained only one-room deep, the plan followed what architects refer to as the I-house plan. Pioneer builders who had access to sawmills sometimes covered portions of the hand-hewn timbers with posts, studs, and clapboards and added framed additions and porches. Log houses could be quite substantial. The building process usually required at least a month's time. On a typical claim pioneers might first build a log cabin, then a hewn log house, and finally a framed or milled lumber one.[17]

Pioneer women added a variety of decorative touches to give their log cabins a homey appearance. "It was one of the long-to-be-remembered days of my life when we bought some lace curtains for the house [two rooms],"Ann Elizabeth Bigelow happily recalled.[18] Phoebe Judson wrote that "we moved into our rudely built cabin, with scarcely an article to make it look attractive or homelike," but later her husband "put up a few three-cornered shelves in the chimney corner, on which I arranged my china and glass ware, which consisted of three stone china plates, as many cups and saucers, and one glass tumbler."[19]

Cupboards began appearing in American homes in the mid-seventeenth century. Originally "cup boards" were single shelves built to hold cups and other dishes, but they eventually acquired sides, backs, drawers, and shelves enclosed by doors. Designed to fit into corners or stand against a wall, cupboards became all-purpose storage areas in houses built without closets or pantries.

In Lillian Christiansen's kitchen the corner cupboard "held a few ironstone china dishes and what groceries we had."[20] Christiansen lined the shelves with folded newspaper cut into fancy-edged shelf paper. Mrs. D.T. Denny and Mary Hayden made china closets, dressers, and tables from boxes covered with material. Denny used pink calico; Hayden covered hers with unbleached muslin. Oilcloth, even if, like Lillian Christiansen's, "not of pretty design or color," covered kitchen tables. Homemakers appreciated the easy-to-clean surface and cheap price. Wiping up a spill on oilcloth made for less work than laundering linens. In 1856 the Wilson and Dunlap stores in Olympia and Tumwater sold an oilcloth cover for 72¢; a Damask one for $1.50.[21] Actually people covered their tables with whatever material they found. Frequently fringed flour sacks recycled into tablecloths covered the tables.

Putting down decorative coverings over the floors also gave the homemaker an opportunity to add a personal touch. Pioneer residents used several types of material. One clever family scrubbed off the sail of an old vessel and laid it on the floor; another put down coverings of deer hide "with the hair left on and always pointing towards the door so they could be easily swept with a rye grass broom."[22] Pleased that her prized possessions survived the long trip around Cape Horn, Phoebe Judson immediately placed the longed-for carpet over unpolished floors in the parlor (living room). "Must be nice to have a carpet in the front room," commented Kate Polson's sister, Birdie.[23]

Made of hard-packed dirt or crude unplaned logs, floors in the log cabins "never seemed to be clean no matter how many times she swept it."[24] Using gravel, which needed raking to stay clean, as a floor covering in their Chelan County homes, women jokingly asked each other, "Have you done your house raking today?"[25] "Now when I get a broom I shall be made. It is a real pioneer life and how I wish I had some carpet," Lucy Ryan wrote from Sumner in 1875.[26]

The floor logs, called puncheons, were split and laid down with the smooth side on top. To keep floors from rocking when walked on, puncheons were fastened with wooden pins to small logs or "sleepers."[27] Both types of floors required constant cleaning and sweeping to keep them neat. "I scrubbed the floor this morning and this evening I feel very badly," Rebecca Ebey, very much pregnant, recorded in her diary on February 5, 1853.[28]

In 1860 merchants in Steilacoom, Tumwater, and Olympia carried a stock of planed lumber and urged homeowners to replace their rough floors:

> WHO WOULD HAVE A ROUGH FLOOR WHEN they can have a smooth one...Save splinters on your feet and pitch in...Anything that can be eat or used about a lugging camp, taken in exchange. A.J. Miller & Co.[29]

When smooth floors replaced rough boards, housewives beamed with pride. Governor Elisha Ferry and other visiting dignitaries who came for dinner at Fort Nisqually made "Mrs. Huggins happy by admiring the swell floors," observed Edward Huggins. The material, the first matching flooring at Nisqually, came from the Tacoma mill.[30]

To ease the burden of cleaning carpets, a chore particularly disliked by those who had to do the beating, Levant Thompson of Sumner made a deal with his wife. "If you will do [clean] just one room at a time we will beat the carpet. But no beating if you tear up the entire house. There is no place to sit; we are cold with all windows open at once!"[31]

To clean a rug required several onerous tasks. Someone had to carry it outdoors, shake out the dust, hang it up on a clothesline, and then vigorously beat out the remaining dirt. In some homes, fastidious housekeepers laid fresh straw under the cleaned carpet; tacks or nails kept the carpet in place. "The straw would sometimes be so deep that the doors to the room

would open and shut with difficulty."[32] Homeowners often made brooms by peeling "willow made by selecting the wood when it was just right, binding it to the handle with wire, peeling both bark and wood above and below the encasing wire then turning the upper portion down and fastening it all around again."[33]

In the eastern half of the United States middle class dining rooms almost always displayed decorative wall-to-wall carpeting, room-size carpets, or rag rugs. "Furnishings warerooms" offered a variety of designs, from expensive Brussels carpet to plainer ingrain weave. By covering floors in the log cabin kitchen/dining room, pioneers emulated their more urban sisters. "We would like to have you buy for us a good two-ply ingrain carpet, 30 yards....We want a first-rate article. I mean one that will wear," requested Catharine Blaine. Homemakers made their own rag rugs from remnants of household fabrics and clothing. Commenting about hers, Blaine wrote: "My rag rug is about as good as ever. I think much of it but we need another one. We can get binding and tacks here; about the stretcher, I don't know—never saw one, but Mr. B. and I can stretch pretty well." In a later home, she laid the rag rug on the parlor floor.[34] Ella Rodman Church's *How to Furnish a Home* (1881) advised women that a rag carpet was "best for either the kitchen or the dining room."[35]

Hardwood floors replaced cruder surfaces in the 1870s when woodworking machinery simplified the process of planing wood and made it more economical.[36] Adelaide Gilbert in 1891 planned to place fur rugs over stained floors in her new Spokane house. Then as now decorators debated about the floor covering: wall-to-wall carpeting or a decorative rug.

Though most log cabins were simply one or two rooms, there were variations. The Kallock family, five men, two women, and two children, built a sort of duplex, referred to as a Missouri or "saddle bag" house. That is, they joined two cabins to a common middle section, the space between the two being called the dog-trot.[37] Because the family arrived in 1883 when easier travel made it possible to bring larger amounts of personal belongings, they decorated with Brussels carpeting. Harriet Kallock Howard remembered the house as primitive but comfortable:

> We had to live in quite primitive style. The one cabin was quite large, with a fireplace in one end and a hole cut for a door in the other. This was covered with a rubber blanket. As soon as possible the men finished the cabin and built another about sixteen feet from it. They then closed in the space between with split cedar, floor sides and roof. This became our living room, dining room and kitchen with a front door

and window and also a back door....It was really very comfortable when completed.[38]

Until they finished the kitchen, the Kallock women prepared their food and washed dishes on top of an old log that their menfolk had leveled by hewing the top off. Other families mentioned hollowing out logs, filling them with water, and using them to wash dishes. Washing dishes then as now proved a distasteful task. No one had enough soap or hot water, and what soap they had caused rough and red hands. Just about every pioneer woman complained about this aspect of housekeeping.

Elsewhere pioneers expanded the one room hall-and-parlor cabin to the popular story-and-a half, which put bedrooms and storage areas in the upper half. Luark planned for his permanent home to be "octagonal in shape 12 feet sides and two stories high. This plan suits me very well I think."[39] The Swift family, who built on Whidbey Island in 1863, followed a more typical design: "The house is built of logs, a story and a half, two large rooms downstairs as large as your sitting room. The North room we use for our own room, the other is the dining room, and off that are the stairs. We are having added a kitchen, pantry and bedroom."[40]

Later, the Swifts, like other families, enlarged their home. Hattie Swift, Louise Swift's stepdaughter, brought the family up to date on details of the new home:

> On the opposite of the entry is the dining room not now papered or carpeted though it is soon to be papered and is to have an oil cloth on the floor. That has a fireplace, sewing machine, tables, chairs, like we had. A walnut table just like yours, and a bamboo chair like a sofa....The kitchen is very convenient and plenty large enough as are all the rooms. Then there is a large, nice pantry and a bed room besides....Some of the rooms are carpeted and papered but there are some yet to be, as there has been so much to do. Upstairs are four bed rooms.[41]

Oilcloth for floor covering sounds strange, because we think of oilcloth as a slippery material that would be hazardous on floors. But advertisements in the *New York Post* in 1850 indicate that factories turned out heavy, medium, and floor oilcloths for floors, as well as table oilcloths. The floor cloths came in sheets eighteen and twenty-four feet wide. On recommendation of domestic advisors, such as Catharine Beecher, homemakers painted a thinner oilcloth and made it suitable for the floor. The introduction of linoleum in the 1870s usurped oilcloth's role as a floor covering. Before too long, hand-hewn logs turned into saw-cut lumber as the enormous Northwest forests provided timber for rapidly growing towns. With the increase in population, sawmills and other commercial establishments began to offer a variety of building lumber. Starting from the middle of the 1850s, wallpaper, paint, roofing material, glass, nails, and tools regularly appeared in advertisements. Unfortunately ads do not describe inventories so it is difficult to determine the quality or quantity of goods for sale. Wealthier families sometimes bypassed local merchants and ordered directly from business establishments in California or the East Coast.

Having access to milled lumber meant that carpenters could utilize "balloon frame" construction, a technique that made a frame from two-by-four or four-by-four studs held together by machine-cut nails. This technique made it easy to add popular Victorian designs, such as gables, turrets, and arched openings.[42]

Settlers took advantage of the abundant materials available and quickly began to build more permanent homes. A year after arriving at Grand Mound in 1853, Samuel James built a combination log cabin and frame lumber home with six bedrooms, three fireplaces, a very large living room with double glass doors, and a beautiful flower garden in front.[43] Joseph Borst put up a two-story white house with a second-floor balcony in 1865—some say to fulfill a promise he made to Mary in order to entice her to marry him. It had a specially crafted soapstone fireplace in the separate dining room and grained woodwork throughout the house.[44]

George Waunch and his family moved into a "box house" made from milled lumber planks purchased in Tumwater. In this construction the planks, about two inches thick, are set vertically, one beside the next. Each plank is nailed to the sill below and at top to the plate. There are no posts or studs.[45] The Waunches had a "big front room from which five doors swinging on iron hinges led off to the dining room, bedrooms, and kitchen."[46] The McElroy house in Olympia, built in 1869, boasted sitting room, parlor, and dining room downstairs, and four large rooms upstairs. To decorate the rooms, Sarah McElroy, an avid gardener, placed plants in "nearly every room of the house—vines in pots that are up on brackets...hanging baskets from the ceiling...flower stand in the kitchen filled with plants."[47]

In 1856 Willis Boatman built a twenty-four-foot by thirty-foot house with plank siding. It had two main rooms with a fireplace in between and a ten-foot porch along the back wall. Twelve years later Boatman added a new two-story section with two large parlors on either side of a central stair hall and three bedrooms on the second floor. Fireplaces on either end of the home provided heat.[48]

Catharine Blaine sent detailed plans of her second, more permanent home to her family in Seneca Falls, New York. The Blaines came to Puget Sound in 1853. They built this home in Seattle in 1854:

> As yet only the frame of the main part is up. We are living in the wing...this is 13 by 14 feet...At the right hand of the door as you enter is a window, the glass 9 x 12 inches. In the end of the room is another. Opposite the door is another door which will open into the woodhouse when we get one. The pantry and hall doors are as they were laid down in the plan I sent you. In this room we have our bed, stove, two tables, three trunks, four boxes each larger than our trunks, a half barrel of flour, a half barrel of sugar, a firkin of butter, a box of soap, another of candles, a stool for our water pail, another for the wash dish, and a half dozen chairs, besides a rough closet for our dishes, etc....
>
> It would be vain for me to attempt to tell you how I have arranged all these in so small a room, but I have succeeded and we have plenty of room for company.

Mrs. Blaine later wrote that "the house was painted on the outside and is the admiration of the whole town. The people say it is by far the handsomest house in the town, that it looks like a house in the states." She was ecstatic when her household goods, which had been shipped around the Horn, finally arrived: "My carpet is just as *good as new,* if it has had so long a sea voyage. O! goodie! goodie!....The pictures and looking glass came as snugly as you please...we think they will be quite an ornament to our parlor."[49]

Home building took several months. Pioneers added improvements when they had time and money. Luark put up two rooms joined by a middle section in January, 1863 then added "two partitions in the back part of the house and laid the floors...finish[ed] the roof on the South sides" and "put up the stove in the kitchen" in November. Then just two days before Christmas he "cut out a Fireplace [in] the west front room and got the Fireplace of clay fairly begun yesterday. Today we finished and put up a plank Chimney while at it the women laid a hearth of Cult's stone." Later he hung doors, put on a porch, dug a cellar, and placed stone in the fireplace "where the dried [mortar] had been removed."[50]

When building their new more modern homes, Northwest builders, just like other Americans, used advice from popular plan books. These plans or patterns from books by architects, such as Andrew Jackson Downing's *Architecture of Country Houses* (1850), A.J. Bicknell's and William Comstock's *Victorian Architecture: Two Pattern Books* (1873), George

E. Woodward's *Victorian Architecture and Rural Art* (1867), and Palliser, Palliser & Palliser Co.'s *American Cottage Homes* (1878) provided full-scale drawings of houses, suggestions for building material, and advice on interior decoration and gardens. Whether the homeowners or carpenters wanted a design for a modest working man's cottage or a country villa, they had only to write the publishers, mail-order house plan companies (Sears and Roebuck; Montgomery Ward), or popular magazines such as *Godey's Lady's Book* to receive a full set of drawings. Indeed between 1846 and 1898 *Godey's Lady's Book* published 450 model house designs.[51]

By the end of the century builders utilized new and improved building methods when constructing homes in the Pacific Northwest. Adelaide Gilbert's 1891 home featured a square hall with a fireplace and round bay windows. For sitting, a parlor with a "colored glass transom," a separate dining room, and plastered walls "finished in grey plast sand finish instead of white (hard finish)." The house came closer to idealized middle class suburban homes than the newspaper walls and cloth-covered windows in hastily constructed log cabins. Grand new homes announced that large areas of Oregon and Washington had become just as modern, just as sophisticated as the rest of the country.

A Room Set Apart

The dictionary defines kitchen as "a room specially set apart and equipped for cooking food." Typical log cabins provided no "room set apart," but pioneers made available a place for cooking food. That "kitchen" could be a corner of the common living areas in the small log cabin or in an attached lean-to.

Kitchen activity in a one- or two-room log cabin centered around the fireplace, which provided a source of heat and light as well as a place for baking bread or simmering savories. Even if families had a cook stove, some hearth cooking continued because early stoves were small and did not have reliable ovens. A wood table, frequently fitted with a drawer, did double duty as a surface for preparing and serving meals.

A bucket or tub held the water supply. If the house or kitchen space had room, a dry sink served this purpose. The forerunner of the kitchen sink, this utilitarian piece of furniture ranged in style from a simple shallow bowl lined in tin to a low cupboard fitted with a zinc- or tin-lined wash bowl. The cupboards usually contained a shelf for storing buckets.

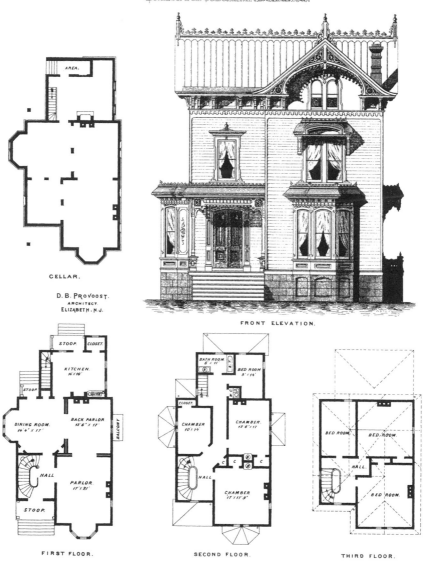

DESIGN FOR SUBURBAN RESIDENCE.

AREA.

CELLAR.

D. B. PROVOOST.
ARCHITECT.
ELIZABETH . N.J.

FRONT ELEVATION.

STOOP.   CLOSET.

KITCHEN.
14' X 16'

STOOP.

DINING ROOM.   BACK PARLOR.   BALCONY
14' 6" X 17'   13' 6" X 17'

HALL   PARLOR.
17' X 21'

STOOP.

FIRST FLOOR.

BATH ROOM
6' X 11'   BED ROOM
8' X 14'

CLOSET.

CHAMBER   CHAMBER.
10' X 14'   12' 6" X 17'

HALL

CHAMBER.
17' X 17' 9'

SECOND FLOOR.

BED ROOM.   BED ROOM.

HALL.

BED ROOM.

THIRD FLOOR.

Scale of Elevation ⅛ *inch = one foot, Plans* 1/16 *inch*

An 1870s pattern-book designed home with detailed plans. Settlers used these plans to build stylish homes with machine-milled lumber that came in a variety of shapes and forms. *A.J. Bicknell and William T. Comstock, Victorian Architecture: Two Pattern Books, 1873. Reproduced by American Life Foundation, 1976.*

Residents stored staples in bags or barrels haphazardly placed on the floor or in an upstairs loft. Surveying her rooms at the rear of her husband's drugstore in Whatcom County, Ella Higginson saw "where a 'cubby hole' revealed a sack of potatoes, a half empty sack of sugar with the top tied in a knot, a sack of flour, one of onions and a five gallon can of coal-oil."[52]

Pioneers built what they could afford and what would be most useful for their family. In the John and Margaret Keck family a platform above the beds stored "flour in 100-pound bags and sugar."[53] And the William and Anne Grahams, who lived on Lopez Island, attached a storage room to the log cabin. "It [the room] had double built walls filled with sawdust to keep out cold in winter and heat in summer. He built shelves all around this room."[54]

Most log cabin homeowners simply chose the largest space for their kitchen items. Captain Samuel and Lurana Percival turned one corner of their one-room home into a kitchen and another into a storeroom.[55] Lillian Christiansen's family used a portion of the bedroom/dining room, the largest room in their two-room cabin.[56] Ann Elizabeth Bigelow followed these trends and cooked and slept in the living room which "consisted of seven chairs, a table, two bedsteads, a cook stove and a [heating] stove."[57]

Before merchants began to stock furniture or, as often the case, before finances became available for purchasing supplies, settlers designed and constructed their own furniture and implements. Depending on the skill of the carpenter, this might run the gamut from a simple open-shelf cabinet to a well designed hutch. Writing to her grandmother that "what furniture I have as you want to know," Lucy Ryan told her, "I have a cook stove, one half dozen chairs, and we will make our own table."[58] A table made by Jane Pattison may not have been typical, but it does show how to make a functional piece of furniture with very little material. "I bored auger holes in the boards of the floor in which we fixed two upright sticks cut from the woods; on these I put some boards, letting one end extend out through a crack between the logs and so we had a table."[59]

On the other hand, the dining room table and kitchen table with a drawer for cutlery made by pioneer craftsman Nathaniel Orr used well-seasoned lumber and employed a lathe. Orr fashioned the furniture in Steilacoom for his wife.

Handmade kitchen implements, or those recycled from household articles, beat batter and folded in egg whites. It did not take too much skill to carve stir sticks and spoons out of a small piece of wood. Lillian Christiansen recalled that her mother fashioned a steamer by punching holes in the bottom of a tin kettle, then set that over a kettle of boiling water.[60] Punching a large tin full of holes and nailing it to a flat piece of wood made a crude but useful grater.

Empty cans took on a second life when Julia Gilliss, an army wife stationed at Fort Dalles, Oregon, filled them with wild flowers. "They look quite pretty covered over the top with moss, which grows in perfection on the rocks."[61] Other families, who may have been more practical, followed *The Washington Standard's* March 14, 1874 advice for turning cans into utensils:

> When cans empty and dry invert them in hot coals in the stove for half a minute...until solder melts and loosen the remaining top of can; then strike it off, smooth off bits of solder, and you have a very convenient cooking utensils...If there are tin shears at hand...the can may be made into passable scoops.

Thrifty homemakers also turned tin tubes into apple corers—small ones for crab apples; a larger size for the standard variety. Empty bottles took on a second calling as glasses. Michael Luark left detailed directions for this procedure in his diary entry of January 5, 1865:

> Fasten something around the bottle with a straight edge where it is to be cut in two, a leather strap will answer then pass a stout cord twice around the bottle. let one person take hold of each end and pull alternately each way as fast as possible while another holds both ends of the bottle keeping the cord as straight as it will bear until the bottle becomes quite hot under the cord then let another dash on a little cold water just as the cord is removed and before you are aware of it you have in one hand a glass tumbler and in the other a glass candlestick.[62]

Cooks beat egg whites until stiff with a swizzle stick, a variation of a wire whisk. In Kittitas Valley they made the whisk by trimming shoots growing in a circle about a thin tree branch, "leaving a circle of stems three or four inches long. In the hand of a skilled cook, a swizzle stick would whip eggs at a furious speed," recalled Leta May Smith.[63] In 1859, Wilson and Dunlap, Olympia merchants, sold egg whips for 37¢. Egg beaters similar to the ones in use today did not come on the market until 1870, when the Dover Company of Boston received a patent for a rotary egg beater. Since then, some variation of a mechanical egg beater has been assured a space in every kitchen drawer.

Increased amounts of goods and an array of all the accouterments of modern living that American manufacturers produced required "a room set apart for cooking," plus a separate pantry or "buttery." Set apart areas in the parlor were no longer adequate. Stoves, sinks, and finally refrigerators demanded special spaces; canned goods, dishes, and cookware needed shelves. Also, with more and more cookery writers urging the American housewife to create multiple-course meals that required elaborate presentation, busy housewives needed space to do their chores as well as feed their families.

To accommodate this growth, architects and builders included plans for kitchens and pantries in their building designs. From the simplest design of turning a small lean-to kitchen into a separate room, to plans envisioning a large room with a range and fixtures for hot and cold water, builders only had to look to pattern books for the latest in kitchen design. A well appointed kitchen, placed at the back of the house so cooking odors and kitchen noises would not offend family and guests, should be "well lighted, and arranged for the especial convenience of the housekeeper, with everything needful at hand—closets, dresser, and range (with hot and cold water), store-room and scullery," G. Woodward wrote in *Woodward's Architecture and Rural Art*, 1867.[64]

In addition to the range and sink, the well-equipped, ideal kitchen contained shelves and/or free-standing cabinets for displaying dishes, cookware, and decorative items, a table or other flat surface for chopping, mixing, and kneading, and an adjoining pantry for storing staples and preserved foods. A boiler built into the stove and/or a common household kettle set on a burner kept water hot. Scrubbed clean, whitewashed, and plastered walls, sparkling window glass, and clean swept floors let the neighbors know a skillful housekeeper kept house. Beecher advised her followers that "if parents wish their daughters to grow up with good domestic habits, they should have...a neat and cheerful kitchen." In wealthy families, maids cleaned dishes and washed dirty pots and pans in a special room or scullery hidden away from the rest of the household.

In the Pacific Northwest the same trends occurred. As pioneers acquired stoves and sinks, they too needed a special room to cook and serve meals. It is probably safe to say that kitchens resembled those in the rest of the country. That is, the home had a special room, usually at the back of the house, with a stove, a place for water, and shelves for cookware and other supplies. Nettie Beirels, granddaughter of pioneer Mattilda Glover Jackson, described one variation:

> Although the house was frame, the kitchen was made of a mass of bricks put together in a rather irregular fashion creating shelves and crannies, all used for some purpose...Pegs were driven between the

bricks in places on which to hang various cooking utensils. It was furnished with a long sturdy dining table covered with a durable, dark oilcloth with a white and gold pattern, a highbacked wooden bench running the length of the table, a large cupboard for food, and a work table and a long wooden sink fitted at one end with cleverly contrived, wooden cross bars to serve as a drain board.[65]

In the Borst house built in 1865 in Centralia, the floor plan followed plans from pattern books. The kitchen was in the back of the house and was entered by a side door. Behind the kitchen and entered by another door a cooling room housed staples and preserved food. Mary Borst had a stove and at some point the family installed a sink.

A free-standing, factory-made kitchen cabinet belonging to Mary Borst resembles the Baker's cabinet that became popular in the 1890s. In that cabinet the top half had shelves for dishes and bins for flour and sugar. The lower half contained shelves and drawers with a flat surface in the middle for kneading, chopping, and rolling pastry.

The Craine home in Issaquah also had a kitchen in the back of the house. "At the back of the house was a lean-to for a very large kitchen....We even had a sink in the kitchen and running water which came from a spring right out of the mountains." The fact that this large kitchen had a sink indicates it must have been fairly modern. Bessie Craine bragged that in 1889 her home had the first plastered walls in the Squak Valley (Issaquah).[66] Placing a kitchen at the back of the house kept the living areas cooler. Some called them "summer kitchens."

The Northwest kitchen, just as those in the Eastern states, began changing after the Civil War for several reasons. For one thing, domestic reformers, like Catharine Beecher and her sister Harriet Beecher Stowe, began a campaign advising American women how to maintain a traditional home in a modern context. Toward this end, the sisters, in *The American Woman's Home,* gave detailed methods for the most efficient way to organize a kitchen. Many people used their plans as a guide, picking and choosing what suited individual needs.

> The flour-barrel just fills the closet, which has a door for admission, and a lid to raise when used. Beside it is the form for cooking, with a molding-board laid on it; one side used for preparing vegetables and meat, and the other for molding bread....
>
> Under the cook-form are shelves and shelf-boxes for unbolted wheat, corn-meal, rye, etc. Beneath these, for white and brown sugar, are wooden can-pails, which are the best articles in which to keep these constant necessities....A small cooking-tray, holding pepper, salt,

GEER'S IMPROVED CHERRY STONER.
Images of new inventions were a constant feature in *Scientific American. May 14, 1870.*

dredging-box, knife and spoon, should stand close at hand by the stove.[67]

In addition, technological advancement after the Civil War led to mass production. Manufacturers turned out a variety of household furnishings and new products, such as processed canned goods, commercial yeast, baking powder, ground coffee, mechanical cooking implements, and factory made kitchen furniture. Indeed, the "direct mercantile response to calls for kitchen reform was to create innumerable utensil novelties, all in the ostensible interest of saving labor for women," even though the new gadgets and appliances often made extra work.[68]

Switching from cooking in the fireplace to cooking on a stove and abandoning ice houses for refrigerators created a need for different kitchen spaces. When fireplaces ceased to be the focal point of cooking, designers had freedom to create different cooking work places and storage areas. A free-standing cook stove could be placed almost anywhere.

Finally, railroads arrived in the Pacific Northwest in the 1880s and made it easier to bring the latest merchandise from east to west. Homemakers now selected from a variety of retail goods and needed a new kitchen to accommodate all these new necessities.

A kitchen cabinet called a Baker's Table, advertised locally in 1879, showed that merchants understood that manufacturing and selling modern kitchen designs boosted revenue. Very quickly they incorporated Catharine Beecher's suggestions into their furniture. The advertisement states that Bowdoin's rotary top kitchen cabinet table is "emphatically a new departure in work tables....Within the body of the table are compartments for Flour and Meal and all ingredients and utensils used in mixing."[69]

By the 1890s cabinet tables acquired a top with shelves that might be enclosed. "[I]t should have two wide closets below and three narrower ones above, with a row of drawers at top of lower closets. Here should be kept all pots and kettles, sauce-pans, waffle-irons, kitchen crockery, tins, etc., all arranged and grouped together so as to be convenient for use," advised the author of *Practical Housekeeping*.[70]

At the turn of the century furniture companies turned out several models, one of which, the Hoosier Kitchen Cabinet, went on to national fame. First appearing in 1899, early Hoosiers were built entirely by hand. By 1903 the company standardized parts in order to manufacture more furniture. These very efficient cabinets included spice containers and metal flour sifters as well as special bins for flour and sugar, several sizes of drawers, and a work table.

Peering into a nineteenth century Northwest kitchen, one might see a pie-safe filled with freshly baked bread, cheese, cakes, or a pie. Ruby Chapin Blackwell recalled that in 1884 in Tacoma their pie-safe sat on the back porch.[71] Initially known as a "safe," this tin-paneled food storage unit has been defined as a "ventilated cupboard used for food and kitchen storage." Carpenters inserted the ventilated portion, made of punched tin with punctured holes, into the doors or sides of the safe. Holes created a decorative pattern, kept insects out, and let air in. To keep ants away, homemakers positioned the safe away from walls and placed the legs in cups of water or kerosene. Safes came in a variety of sizes and were mass produced and nationally marketed by the time many Northwest pioneers set up housekeeping.[72] A cheese-safe and meat-safe, synonyms for pie-safes, are listed in the 1884 inventory of McDonald and Schwabacher, Washington Territory merchants.[73]

But pie-safes protected food only before it appeared on the table. To keep mosquitoes and other flying insects away during mealtimes, "the more careful housewives kept the table covered with mosquito netting until serving time, when it was the duty of some girl in the family to stand with a green sprig from a tree or a fly swatter made from stashed newspapers fastened to a stick and wave the flies away."[74] Manufactured screens for doors and windows did not appear until the late 1870s.[75]

In addition to storing food and implements in free-standing cabinets, homemakers kept supplies in an adjoining pantry. Lined with shelves, this separate room usually contained bins for flour and sugar, oil, spices, some canned goods, and pots and pans. Nathaniel Orr lined his pantry with shelves and separated it from the kitchen. He placed a work table in the room. Larger pantries might have a second sink for washing up and/or preparing foods, such as jams and jellies. Before small packages replaced bulk buying and canned goods eliminated dried ears of corn and home-made preserves, pantries contained all the provisions for a well-run kitchen.

When Adelaide Sutton Gilbert built her new home in 1891, her pantry shelves and cupboards were a far cry from the "three-cornered shelves in the chimney corner" Phoebe Judson used as a showplace for her much loved bric-a-brac. Gilbert wrote:

> My pantry is a "daisy" 12 by 5 ft. In one end is a long cupboard from floor to ceiling glass doors above. Then a long work shelf running from one end to the other and across one end below at the left six little drawers and four big ones, two open shelves under the work shelf in front of where you are supposed to stand at the right four bin—then another cupboard. This is all under work shelf then above at right are open shelves reaching to ceiling then opposite kitchen door room for ice box.[76]

Long-time Pacific Northwest homemakers watched their homes grow from one-room to multiple-story dwellings and saw kitchens expand from a space to a room. Those families with resources to build a larger home most likely included a separate dining room. Taking advantage of the new technology women could, by the late nineteenth century, prepare and serve meals with style.

Chapter Two
Water: One Unfailing Luxury

"WE SELECTED OUR BUILDING place, close to the timber, by a spring of crystal water, making sure of one unfailing luxury should we be deprived of all others," commented Phoebe Judson.[1] "We are blessed with the most beautiful springs of water I ever saw, one of which will be enclosed in our door yard," Anna Maria James wrote to her sister when the James family settled at Grand Mound, Oregon Territory, in 1852.[2]

Settlers knew the importance of choosing a site with close proximity to water. Water is essential for gardening, farming, and animals as well as being an important ingredient in cooking. No kitchen can be without it.

East of the Cascade mountains, settlers did not echo Judson's and James's praise about the bountiful water supply. Hot, dry summers made finding water a constant problem. Here settlers welcomed winter snows, as they brought moisture to the land. Early residents learned quickly to save and recycle precious water. Living near a creek, where water could be diverted by an irrigation ditch to the gardens and orchards, helped solve the problem. The hottest lawsuits—ditch quarrels—in Kittitas County occurred because of disputes over water rights. The disputes continue to this day.[3]

Before municipal water works supplied homes with water, settlers had to carry it in buckets from the nearest creek, haul it up from a well, save rainwater in a cistern, or fashion a set of pipes that would, with the help of gravity, divert the water from a spring into a storage tank. By the 1880s, in certain areas, water wheels or water motors powered the water through the pipes. Inventors claimed that by using these devices "small streams, which have hitherto been useless for water power, may be applied to impart motion to ...machinery."[4] By the end of the century large hydraulic pumping machines on the Columbia and Willamette rivers furnished irrigation water to farms and cities.

A pioneer family in Klickitat County in 1860 made its wooden pipes by boring the centers of fir poles with two augers of different sizes, and then fitting one into the other.[5] Such a gravity system "could be maddeningly slow," said Mary Ann Bigelow who used this method when she moved into the Bigelow home in 1935 after marrying the grandson of the first Daniel Bigelow.[6]

Settlers had to take a different approach in fetching water for homes built away from streams or springs. In the Methow Valley, the Nickell family dug a hole about three feet deep and three feet across near the back door and waited for a nearby creek to overflow. "The creek kept this hole filled with water, so our supply was nearer than most. We had one big tub in which the family washing was done and everyone took baths," alleged Ellen Moore, one of the daughters. She did not say if the family used that overflowing creek water for cooking.[7]

Often the only way to fill a pail was to walk to the nearest source and carry water home. John Murphy recalled that in Thurston County in the 1850s the "early settlers all procured their water from the common spring which flowed clear, cold and delicious....The housewives would hire the Indians to carry the water for them to supply their daily needs."[8] Grant County pioneers had their water hauled from Willow Springs, and paid one dollar per barrel. The water in the barrels buried near their shacks oftentimes "got green and slimy between fillings."[9] Because farmers in Okanogan built their homes high on a hill so they could look over their land, water in that area often had to be carried uphill—900 feet at one site.

Children fetched and filled the pails in some households. In the Spokane area in 1886 a pioneer recalled:

> Father had not dug a well yet, so my oldest brother, Rouse, aged seven and a half years and I used to take the horses to water about one mile away to another homestead that had a well. We tied all the empty syrup cans to the saddle to fill with water to take back home, that was twice a day and cold, to draw water from a well with pail and rope.[10]

Cans recycled into water buckets provided containers. Carl Wood used ten-pound lard buckets and was happy he only had to carry the water "three-quarters of a mile." To make the trip easier his father built a cart and they hauled "water in six square-gallon coal oil cans."[11]

Next to living by a running stream, a well provided the easiest access to a supply of water. Susanna Ede mentioned that in 1870 near Grays Harbor the family had a "splendid well with two buckets with rope running over a wheel for drawing the water buckets." The well sat to the back of the house near the milk house.[12]

Digging a well meant hard work. Customarily two or more holes had to be started before reaching clean water. Several times Rebecca Ebey recorded in her diary that a neighbor is digging a well and "has no water yet. One person dug 60 feet and finally 'quit it' when he came to dry fine sand." Rebecca and her husband Isaac were among the first families to settle Whidbey Island.[13]

Some pioneers claimed that a forked rod or branch properly used accurately predicted the best place to sink a well. The method—called water witching—certainly worked for the Sidney Hanafords. They dug their well at a spot where the water-witch's branch slowly bent downward. All year they drank and cooked with clear cold water hauled from that well.[14]

Finding water only solved one problem. It did not guarantee clean and drinkable water. Rosa Crawford, who lived in Cowlitz County in 1872, complained that "we have got a well dug near the house it is 33 feet deep but it has got so bad that we cannot drink it. it is supposed to be the mineral under ground."[15]

Charles Splawn of Klickitat County had similar misfortunes. Water in his first well "tasted horribly and smelled worse." On a second digging, better luck led him to find "an artesian well."[16] Artesian wells, claimed Lewis M. Hatch, who lived near Pullman, did not guarantee pure water. In a letter to his mother in 1898 he wrote.

> The water here is the worst that I have tasted since I left Oregon, it comes from an artesian well, is pumped to a reservoir on a hill above the city then comes back to town through mains. Think one thing that ails it is that it stands around too long before it is used.[17]

Additionally settlers had to contend with wells going dry in drought years or the hot summers of eastern Washington; water freezing in the bucket in winter; and keeping water clean and free from debris. When summer heat dried up wells, settlers had to ignore the heat and try again to find water. To coax the last drop out of a well too shallow for dipping, Nela Fleming remembered "taking a bucket and a tin cup and clambering down the rough stone sides....I dipped the small supply of water up with the cup and poured it into the pail....Then someone at the top would hoist the precious burden."[18] No wonder homesteaders tried to build their homes near a creek or stream. In the arid inland areas people recycled the water whenever possible. Dumping used bath and washing water on garden plants was practiced many years before environmentalists made saving gray water a patriotic habit.

Even Adelaide Gilbert, who frequently wrote her mother that their "well water is so nice and soft, and the pump is handy in the kitchen," complained upon learning city water would not reach her home: "they have laid the pipes on a street back of us and way above us—and we are left out tho' some of our neighbors are going before the council tomorrow & petition for it."[19]

Usually connected to wells by a lead pipe, the kitchen pump was one of the earliest mechanical kitchen appliances. "When the water did not come up, a little had to be poured in [the pump] to prime it."[20] Minerva Herrett recalled that "before our small town had running water, my mother used a hand pump to pump from a well."[21]

To keep water fresh, well owners were advised to throw away any water that had been left standing in lead pipes, and to use charcoal to keep the water pure. A note in *The Washington Standard*, July 26, 1873, advocated:

> When drinking water is conveyed into a house through lead pipes, it should always be allowed to run a few moments before using, as this will insure safety from lead poisoning. Old lead pipes are safer as they become incrusted with a scale that is innocuous.

In 1860 when their son, Henry, became ill, the Hallers blamed his sickness on "the water which was brought in lead pipes from a spring in a hollow not far from the garrison [Fort Steilacoom]. Many people were affected by the water."[22]

Even when wells had a lid, which most did, someone had to remember to keep it closed. The John R. Jackson family solved that problem by building a covered entry off of the kitchen. The entry "was to provide a home for the well with its genuine oaken buckets, a combination of large, wooden wheel and well sweep," noted Nettie Beirels, the Jackson granddaughter:

> The bucket was lowered by real labor as the operator pulled down on the rope hand over hand. The weight at the end of the well sweep drew up the filled bucket. The big wheel worked on a wooden shaft and if not kept greased, creaked and groaned its protest.[23]

Sarah McElroy doesn't say if the water came from a spring or a well, but in a letter written to her son in 1878 she provides us a good picture of an early household water system in Olympia, Washington Territory:

For a hot water tank she [a neighbor] only has one of the common hot water boilers in the back of her stove and for cold water she has a large sized barrel...the Chinaman fills the barrel up twice a week and keeps the boiler full at the back of the stove and it is just splendid.[24]

In 1866 in Vancouver, Washington Territory, homeowners purchased iron pipes for steam, water, and gas from Mr. C.H. Myers, a plumber who advertised in *The Vancouver Register,* September 5, 1866. He also sold hot water boilers, marble top wash stands, and force and lift pumps. Similar notices appeared in other territorial newspapers.

Cities also used traditional plans of diverting water from springs via pipes. In Seattle, Henry Yesler built a water supply system for his business in 1854 by fashioning boards from his lumber mill into V-flumes (narrow troughs) and connecting a series of these to the water source miles away. Photographs show the first old system of wooden pipes laid on trestles; later pipes made from twelve-inch fir logs with a two-inch hole bored through the center went underground. Eventually metal pipes replaced wooden ones.[25]

Other cities had to wait longer than Seattle to install a water system. As late as 1880, the village of Spokane Falls water works consisted of a town pump and five-gallon cans filled with water and delivered to businesses and homes on the shoulder of an energetic Indian. He charged from 15 to 20 cents to fill up a sixty-gallon barrel.[26]

As settlements grew people came together and figured out a way to convey water to homes and businesses. However, unlike water companies of today, early ones did not worry about providing pure water. In spite of the fact that typhoid, a water-borne disease, killed people throughout the country, little was known about bacteria or purifying water systems. Larger cities like Seattle did not even begin thinking about a pure water system until 1889; it did not begin treating the water supply until 1911. In rural areas few restrictions existed, even by that late date.[27]

A recipe found in a 1909 Washington cookbook provides an egg dish for those ill with typhoid—a hint that typhoid was still a problem. R. Mildren Purman, M.D., contributed the recipe.

Eggs—Boiled for Typhoid Patients—Warm the egg so the shell will not crack. Put in a pail and pour over it one pint of absolutely boiling water. Cover tightly and stand on table for five minutes. Open, and egg should be creamy and easy to digest.[28]

Storing a Supply of Water

Once pioneers found the precious water, they stored it in pitchers, buckets, barrels, large pots, or whatever container they had. In some homes hollowed-out logs did double duty as buckets or a dish pan to wash dishes. On Anderson Island, resourceful families in the 1880s handmade wash boilers, which held the water for washing, "from the big tins in which the light-house tender *Manzanita* delivered mineral oil for fueling the Eagle Island stake light."[29] Pioneers who preferred soft water might have followed this advice:

> To a barrel full of water put a quart of wood ashes. A sediment will settle to the bottom, leaving the water clear and soft. The ashes can be tied up in a cloth if one is very particular, but the strength will not come out as soon. It is a good way, if it is wanted for washing to get the water ready Saturday, and by Monday morning it is ready for use.[30]

Setting buckets next to fireplaces helped keep water warm. Washstands and wash basins are among the early furnishings for sale in territorial newspapers. "A water bucket and washstand stood near the stove," remembered Harry Sherling.[31] "The water bench and other water buckets with a handy dipper, took the place of the modern sink and water from the faucet. A 'wash pan' took the place of a lavatory basin," Laura House recalled when she described early homesteading in eastern Washington.[32] In June, 1860, Wilson and Dunlap's Daybook listed one dozen water buckets for $3.25; their inventory does not mention the size of the buckets.[33]

If families had a cook stove with a reservoir or boiler built into the stove, they heated the water there; if not a large kettle or bucket filled with water sat on a back burner. "I only had to lift up the iron lid of the reservoir on the front portion and dip out pans full of scalding water," noted an enthralled Mary Borst.[34] Since it was the only place to get warm water, the reservoir tank had to be filled repeatedly. It was the "nearest to automatic hot water in those days."[35]

Standard furnishings in log cabin homes did not include a sink with hot and cold faucets that turned on with a quick twist. These accouterments of modern living came later. Unless someone installed a system for bringing water into the home and then removing waste water, a sink offered no more advantages than a large pan.

Factories in the East started manufacturing sinks in the late 1850s. In expensive homes built in Oregon and Washington Territory, architects and builders included detailed specifications for sinks in their building plans. Simply made and usually freestanding, the first sinks had a wood exterior with an opening covered with tin or sheet iron. There may or may not have been a drain to dispose of waste water. When cities improved water systems, sinks became more desirable, which led manufacturers to design a more durable product. Cast iron, soapstone, granite, or crockery sinks replaced old wooden ones.

In 1884, *Polk's Oregon, Washington and Idaho Gazetteer and Business Directory* featured an ad for a sink, stating that "property owners contemplating conducting spring water in pipes to house for convenience" are advised to consult with Mr. Sutherland, practical plumber, gas and steam fitter. A picture accompanies the ad and shows a sink not unlike those of today.[36]

Domestic advisors favored sinks and believed that every well-run kitchen should have one. They dutifully advised homeowners where they should be placed, what they should look for when purchasing a sink, and how to keep them clean. "A well-appointed sink is a necessity in every kitchen, and should be near both window and range....It should be provided with a 'grooved' and movable dish drainer, set so as to drain into sink," instructed Estelle Woods Wilcox in *Practical Housekeeping*.[37] A proper sink should have "two pumps, for well and for rain-water," and the dish drain should have "grooves cut to let the water drain into the sink....Under the sink should be kept a slop-pail; and, on a shelf by it, a soap-dish and two water pails," counseled Catharine Beecher.[38] Both advisors favored cleaning with carbolic acid and water when the sink or drain became "sour or impure." And they would certainly have approved the "wooden sink fitted at one end with cleverly contrived, wooden cross bars to serve as a drain board" in the John R. Jackson home at Jackson Prairie.[39]

Because pure water systems are a twentieth century phenomenon, nineteenth-century cookery writers offered advice for purifying water. Estelle Woods Wilcox, editor of *Practical Housekeeping*, recommended filtering well water. She gave directions for making a homemade filter similar to commercial ones:

> Take a large flower pot, and insert a sponge in the hole in the bottom, fill the pot with alternate layers of sand, charcoal, and small pebbles. The flower pot thus filled up may then be placed on a jar or other convenient vessel, into which the water can be received as it filters through.[40]

"Ice in Quantities to Suit"

Pioneer riparian households reaped still another advantage. When temperatures dropped below freezing, water in streams and creeks turned into ice. Being able to chop off a chunk of ice for use in storing foods, keeping cream sweet until market day, or making ice cream contributed greatly to homes without refrigeration. Though Eliza Leslie, a popular cookbook author, wrote in the 1840s that "no family should be without [an icebox]," they did not take up space in pioneer homes.[41] Until the "iceman came" to the Northwest in the late 1860s, pioneers had no reliable way to acquire the ice which made refrigerators work.

However, by the time Euro-Americans began settling in the Northwest, a well-developed industry for harvesting and shipping ice around the country flourished on the East Coast. Frederick Tudor, a Bostonian, receives credit for starting the first ice shipping company in 1806. But Tudor's company did not begin growing until 1825 when Nathaniel Wyeth, from neighboring Cambridge, Massachusetts, invented a method of quickly and cheaply cutting uniform blocks of ice, and joined up with Tudor. Wyeth's horse-drawn ice cutter and other improved implements for cutting, meant that in a short time thousands of tons of ice could be stacked in compact, regular piles and stored, without too much melting, until needed. Mechanical improvements in elevators moved the large blocks of ice from pond to storage to ships, railroads, or the iceman's horse and buggy. Preserving fresh meat, hardening butter, or cooling beer was only as far away as the nearest ice cubes.[42]

The harvested natural ice business began in the 1860s in Oregon and Washington Territory. One of the earliest seems to be the business managed by Philip Hornung. This snippet of information comes from an advertisement in the 1865 Polk's *Portland City Directory* where the proprietor's advertisement promised that he was "prepared to supply Hotels, Saloons, Steamboats and Private Families with CLEAR COLUMBIA RIVER ICE. A good Ice Wagon will be in attendance to supply customers regularly everyday of the season."[43]

Whether Mr. Hornung made good on his promise is difficult to determine. The advertisement did not appear the next year. Between 1866 and 1869 no ice houses make the list of business establishments in the Portland city directory. Was that because the supply melted, demand disappeared, or Mr. Hornung did not want to pay the price of an ad? One would like to know.

Transporting ice from frozen lakes to cities became an important industry in the mid-nineteenth century. *Harper's Weekly, May 7, 1870.*

Washington and Oregon did not have to rely on the Columbia River for ice. According to an article that appeared in 1869 in *The Commercial Age*, Olympia, Washington Territory, "Portland finds relief in cargoes of the precious mineral [ice] in more favored northern points."[44]

The correspondent who wrote to *The Commercial Age* felt that "a dearth of ice is a sad calamity to bar-rooms and butter plates," then went on to describe an account of ice harvested and "packed" on mules and horses from ice caves near Dalles City:

> The method of mining is very simple, and the packing is both rude and wasteful. The ice is quarried in slabs at 200 lbs; and two of these wrapped in gunny bags are loaded upon each animal. The distance to the steamboat landing on the Columbia is about 35 miles, and the loss in transportation is nearly 50 per cent, which might be greatly reduced by more careful packing.[45]

Ice caves formed by lava have been a source of ice for centuries. In central Oregon, the Arnold Cave (sometimes called Crook County Ice Caves), provided settlers a continuous source of ice.[46]

A few years later, the ice man began delivering in Washington Territory. The Puget Sound Ice Company ran ads throughout most of 1872 in Seattle's *Puget Sound Dispatch* announcing that it was a wholesale and retail dealer "IN ICE," and "ice in quantities to suit will be delivered every morning (Sundays excepted) in any part of Seattle at three cents per pound." On the advertisement is a picture of a horse and buggy, the traditional mode of transportation for the iceman. The company delivered ice until 1888 but the owner, Marshall Blinn, lost money.[47]

On April 5, 1873 Mr. J.W. Page wrote to *The Daily Pacific Tribune*, Olympia, Washington Territory, that "hot weather is coming on when people need something cooler than whiskey," and that he "is again in the ice business, and will deliver to all leaving orders with him." He doesn't say where the ice came from, but in January 1876 *The Washington Standard* noted that a Mr. Burmister "is filling his ice house with large slabs of ice from the clear lake on the Capitol grounds [Olympia]. If the cold weather continues much longer he will have sufficient of the 'cooling element' to supply a larger population than ours a couple of seasons."[48]

Though Mr. Page suggested he could deliver ice in hot weather, in the summer, supplies ran short and caused the ladies of the Methodist Episcopal Church in Olympia to close their ice cream parlor, "the supply of ice being exhausted." "Our citizens are compelled to ship their supplies of ice from Victoria," ran a notice in *The Washington Standard*, July 23, 1873, evidently not in time for the church ice cream social. The supply of ice did improve as *The Washington Standard* reported in 1879 that "They are 'playing' that it is summer in Seattle by serving ice cream as extras at the restaurants of that ambitious little city."[49]

The Northwest experienced colder weather in the nineteenth century; Lake Union, in Seattle, froze several times. Maybe that is what prompted the Ryan family in Sumner to build an icehouse. "George is building...the first icehouse [in Sumner]....We think by putting water in vats we can freeze a little each year," Lucy Ryan wrote to her grandmother in 1876.[50]

Cutting ice from a frozen lake, as the commander at Fort Walla Walla in the 1880s found out, required a great deal of fortitude and very warm clothes to protect the workers in freezing conditions. On one ice cutting expedition weather took a turn for the worse, and "before the ice carriers reached Walla Walla, the thermometer dropped to 11 below zero. This was the coldest March day up until that time ever experienced...two of the drivers and one helper had frozen their hands and feet and had to be hospitalized."[51]

Once workers cut ice, it had to be stored. Traditionally in colder climates people constructed a below-ground ice pit, roofed with boards or thatch. By the time ice harvesting became big business, special above-ground rooms kept the ice from melting and used an insulating material such as sawdust for separating the blocks. The houses came in all sizes, shapes, and materials—wood, stone, and brick. *Dr. Chase's Third, Last and Complete Receipt Book and Household Physician on Practical Knowledge for People (1890)* described one building method that the Doctor admitted he copied from a neighboring farmer:

> [It] was simply a bin made of rough boards, 16 feet square, and roofed over, leaving a large opening in the front and sides...a layer of sawdust, about a foot thick, on the ground, and then stacked the ice snugly in the center, 18 or 20 inches from the walls, and then filled in with sawdust, and up over the top a foot or more thick.[52]

In Washington Territory, pioneers living in the colder climate, east of the Cascade mountains, frequently mentioned ice houses. Ellen Moore, daughter of Harvey and Alcena Nickel, recalled that the family ice house was built in back of their large cabin and used to store "milk, cream, butter and other foodstuffs," as well as "cantaloupes and watermelon buried in the sawdust covering the ice."[53] Pioneers in Summit Valley (Stevens County) relished the days that they sliced venison, packed it into fruit jars, and kept the jars cold by immersing them in icy water. "Kept that way in the cool cellar by the addition as needed of a block of ice from the family icehouse."[54] In the Thorp area an ice storage facility located near the Thorp ice pond operated from 1890 to the 1920s.[55] "W.J. Hamilton and Jas. Ewart are putting up large quantities of ice for next summer's use," reported *The Palouse Gazette*, December 27, 1878.

Harvesting natural ice continued as a business until after World War I, but began to decline in the 1870s when people switched to the more reliable manufactured ice. That industry was also started by a Boston area inventor, Jacob Perkins, who obtained a patent for making artificial ice in 1834. Between that time and 1868 when the first ice-manufacturing plant began operating on a regular basis, several improvements were made. A notice in *The Commercial Age*, October 23, 1869, briefly describes one invention:

Of the various methods of manufacturing ice artificially, the simplest consists in placing a vessel containing water under the receiver of an air pump, and exhausting the air. The water is rapidly evaporated and the free vapor absorbed by strong sulfuric acid, and in about three minutes a decanter of water can be thus frozen.

The ability to produce ice cubes even in warm weather gave artificial ice plants a distinct advantage over those who could only cut the ice when the temperature dropped. The rising importance of sanitation standards tipped the scales in favor of the new product. By the end of the century, scientists suggested that contaminated natural ice caused typhoid. By 1889, Oregon had four manufactured-ice plants; Washington two. By 1909 each state had twenty-five plants making artificial ice. Artificial ice had definitely usurped its rival, real ice.

Homemakers who wanted to use that which the iceman delivered had to have an appliance to house ice. Those homes that received ice from The Puget Sound Ice Company must have had some type of container that slowed down ice's tendency to melt.

Iceboxes have been around since the early part of the nineteenth century. Thomas Moore received the first American patent in 1793. Ten years later Moore published a pamphlet describing his method for keeping butter cold and firm. He fitted a cedar tub with a tin container that held ice, and insulated the tub with "coarse cloth lined with rabbit skins, the fur side next to the cloth and the pelt next to the wood." Moore's directions became the basis for all the early iceboxes. By the 1850s more astute inventors realized the importance of air circulation and so added this concept to efficient cooling.[56]

The early iceboxes (sometimes erroneously called refrigerators) generally constructed from oak, pine, or ash, came in a variety of sizes and shapes. Lined with zinc, slate, porcelain, galvanized metal, or wood, they used charcoal, cork, flax straw, or mineral wool for insulating materials. A pan set in the bottom held melting ice water and had to be emptied frequently. D. Eddy & Sons (1840) was the first company to set up a business for manufacturing iceboxes. Like most aspects of the early ice business, this too had a Massachusetts connection. The Eddy family lived in Boston.

Distrustful of new machines and not wanting to waste money on an unproven appliance, people no doubt followed Catharine Beecher's instructions for building their own icebox

Take a barrel and bore holes in the bottom....Lay some small sticks crossing, and set a half barrel within, with holes bored in the bottom.

BARTLETT'S IMPROVED REFRIGERATOR.

Early refrigerators were really fancy ice boxes. This one has a faucet which made it easier to drain water from melting ice. *Scientific American, March 19, 1859.*

> Nail list [supports] along the edge of each, and make a cover to lay on each, so that the cover resting on the list will make it very close. Then put ice into the inner one, and the water will filter through the holes in the bottom, and while ice is preserved, it will make the inner half barrel a perfect refrigerator.[57]

True refrigerators started competing in 1882, and by 1913 an electric refrigerator entered the market. However, not until 1917 did inventors truly understand the principal upon which refrigeration worked.[58]

But what type of refrigeration were the Northwest homeowners using? A scrutiny of business inventories and newspaper advertisements for Washington Territory in the 1870s and 1880s, years when the ice man promised deliveries, finds no mention of iceboxes or refrigerators. This absence cannot be explained by the idea that before East Coast railroads chugged into the Northwest, refrigerators were too heavy to ship. After all, stoves are heavy, yet just about every merchant stocked them and advertised that fact in the local newspapers.

Several explanations come to mind. Was the ice business so haphazard that homemakers did not know from season to season whether ice would be available, thus making an icebox uneconomical? Were people so used to preserving their food by pickling or drying that they did not consider iceboxes or refrigerators necessities? Did the wealthy homeowners bypass Washington merchants and order their iceboxes and refrigerators directly from manufacturers in the East? Or did the homeowners build their own, not wanting to waste money on an appliance that might or might not have worked?

We know that the last explanation describes the Blackwell family of Tacoma. Ruby Chapin Blackwell recalled that in 1884, when Tacoma built an ice factory, her family did not have a regular refrigerator. "Instead, my aunt had built an ice box. This was set inside a larger wooden box, and the space between was packed with sawdust. She got the idea from *The American Agriculturist*. It held, as I remember, only butter and milk."[59]

Not until 1888 in Seattle, 1889 in Tacoma, and 1890 in Spokane does one find evidence that Washington residents had an opportunity to purchase iceboxes or refrigerators locally. Seemingly, before adding refrigerators to their inventories, the merchants had been waiting for the supply of ice to become dependable and clients to trust the "new" products. Even then, the new appliances did not become best sellers. A Tacoma merchant who advertised that his sale would last only one week ran his sale ad for almost two months. Most of the Spokane merchants announced reduced prices shortly after they first advertised. The following announcements indicate what Northwesterners purchased:

> "A RUN ON REFRIGERATORS! For one week only, commencing Monday Morning July 29, We will offer our entire stock of Refrigerators at ONE FOURTH OFF. $12 Refrigerator for $9; $20 Refrigerator for $15. Housekeepers cannot afford to have their butter, milk, meats, etc. spoil when they can be preserved at such a trifling expense. A Refrigerator will pay for Itself Four times over in one season."—F.S. Harmon and Co., *Tacoma News,* July 29, 1889.

> "Just received a Car load of each: ICE CHESTS, ICE BOXES, Refrigerators, Ice Cream Freezer."—E. Lobe, proprietor, The Golden Rule Bazaar, *Seattle Post-Intelligencer,* May 17, 1888.

"Perfection Refrigerators...Pure Dry Cold Air. Antique Finish Elegantly carved, solid bronze linings, patent charcoal sheathing, circulation perfect. Call and see the latter demonstrated by means of the glass door and pin wheel."—Boyd & Goss Hardware Company, *Spokane Falls Review,* May 4, 1890.

Neither iceboxes nor refrigerators achieved the status of the cook stove until well into the twentieth century. Many people in rural areas did not purchase a refrigerator until after World War ll. They, like their ancestors, used a creek or well to keep food cool. That old system did work. But at least by then, homemakers in most of the Pacific Northwest did not have to "go up the hill to fetch a pail of water."

Chapter Three
We Have a Cook Stove

WHETHER FOOD CAME FROM the barnyard, garden, or nearest commercial outlet, there had to be ways to prepare and preserve it. Baking, broiling, stewing, and simmering require heat. Until cook stoves worked their way West, which they soon did, pioneers relied on the old hearth method of heating foods.

Few cook stoves survived the long journey over the Oregon Trail. When emigrants realized that light wagons traveled best, they discarded all heavy items. Instead of cooking over a stove, overlanders contrived a makeshift oven out of a dirt hole, piled on wood or buffalo chips, started a fire, and set out the frying pans and camp kettles.

They continued the practice in their new homes, but instead of lighting a fire in a hastily dug ditch, the settlers used a permanently built fireplace. And even though hearth cooking still required gathering fuel and making a fire, the cook did not have to worry about wind blowing in her face or rain putting out the fire.

Progress, however, does not always continue in a straight line. Emigrants did not build fireplaces or purchase and install stoves on the first day they arrived in their new land. Until then the reliable outdoor oven fire provided heat for cooking. "There was not a cook stove in the town [Steilacoom, 1853] that could be purchased, so the cooking had to be done over an outdoor fire beside a big stump," recalled Mrs. M.E. Shorey.[1] William Harris's tale of baking grouse over an open fire describes the method:

> A fire of vine maple leaves a fine body of coals. A hole dug in the ground big enough to receive a dutch oven, and twice as deep with room about the sides over the top, the hole partly filled with those coals and ashes; two grouse picked and drawn but left whole less head and feet to first joint, salted and a chunk of fat bacon inside each bird

and placed in that oven and set in the hole on those coals; the oven covered several inches over the top and sides with coals and ashes and left over night; the kettle removed and uncovered.[2]

Wherever they heated the cooking kettle, homemakers worried about starting a fire and keeping it going. Before the era of cheap matches, people routinely preserved some hot coals from each day's fire by covering them during the night, hoping that in the morning adding an additional log would be sufficient to stir up the flames.

If that ploy did not work and fire had to be restarted the settlers "borrowed" the fire from neighbors or turned to the old practice of using flint with a box of tinder. "We ran out of matches and father put some powder in an old flintlock gun, then put in a rag and fired. This set the rag afire, then he ran like a madman and grabbed the rag and blew only to make a blaze which he dropped onto the kindling."[3] That is also the method the James family used when they first settled in Grand Mound in the 1850s. Soon, however, the Jameses purchased matches and felt fortunate to have them. The "matches cost twenty-five cents per dozen, and when I see how they are wasted now, I think of those times," lamented Mary Ann James.[4]

Mary Ann James had a reason to complain. When one could buy a sugar bowl for fifty cents, an eight-quart tin pan for eighty-eight cents, and a pair of cashmere gloves for fifty cents, twenty-five cents for a dozen matches must have seemed a lot of money.[5] "Settlers were very saving with them," observed J.H. Horner.[6]

The first matches, aptly named Lucifers, had a tendency to explode when jostled, and would not strike when damp. "Matches would not go," complained Michael Luark.[7] The trip west did nothing to improve their longevity. Safety matches that ignited only on the box they came in appeared after the Civil War, but years passed before manufacturers designed and made available the cheap, easily carried, throw-away match that we know.

Pioneers found that matches came in a "block of wood split length-wise into about 100 sticks, not separated entirely, but each still attached at one end to the block, ready to be broken off when needed. The separated ends were coated for a half inch by dipping them into melted sulphur, and were then tipped with a fulminating compound that would ignite by friction."[8] They also spoke of China matches which came "1,200 in a bunch, sold for 25¢, and there was 12¢ revenue tax on them.[9] Decorated match holders or match safes (holders with lids), added a touch of color to pioneer kitchens. Wilson and Dunlap charged twenty-five cents for a match safe in

1859. Because matches had a tendency to ignite when rubbed against one another, "safes" provided a good storage place.

Until the cook stove established its place of importance in Northwest homes, cooking centered around the fireplace. Pioneers constructed fireplaces with available materials, such as sticks plastered with hay or clay. The Sidney S. Ford family who settled near present-day Centralia "used...rocks to construct the mammoth fireplace, so large it burned four-foot logs, dragged into the large living room by horses and then rolled on the fire." Keeping that room clean must have been quite a chore.[10]

Phoebe Judson provided innovative, detailed plans for making a fireplace when there were no stores for purchasing bricks, cut stones, or tiles:

> The fireplace was built of blue clay that was hauled from some distance, mixed with sand, and then pounded into a frame mode. When it became dry, he [her husband] burned the frame, which left the walls standing solid. An old gun barrel, the ends embedded in either jamb, answered for a crane to attach the hooks to hang the pots and kettles. The chimney, built of sticks and mortar, ran up on the outside of the house.[11]

Making a place for hanging pots and pans from a gun barrel surely is an excellent idea, but most settlers did not follow this innovative design and just hung a plain, stout iron bar across the fireplace opening. Whatever the construction, the bar had to be strong enough to hold the big black iron pots that pioneers used for baking bread and simmering savories, soups, and stews.

Attaching a crane to the bar or fireplace wall helped the cook move the pans sideways; notched vertical rods (trammels) let her hoist the cookware up and down. With these tools she did not have to constantly watch to see if the water boiled over or the beans burned on the bottom. And though Judson called her gun barrel a crane bar, the correct name is chimney bar.

When supplies of brick became available, pioneers choose them for building a fireplace. Learning the art of brick-making while "building a brick chimney for myself which is the first brick ever I layed," pleased Patterson Luark, especially when the chimney drew well. The bricklaying job took Luark four days.[12]

A Variety of Cookware

Though by the middle of the nineteenth century a variety of cookware began appearing in household stores, most emigrants baked and fried in their reliable cast iron implements. These strong unbreakable pots and pans could stand intense heat. They had been invaluable on the trek west when most cooking had to be done over an open fire.[13]

The cast iron Dutch ovens, sometimes called bake-pans, and spiders—or frying pans—came with curved lids to hold hot coals. The better ones stood on short legs enabling cooks to set them directly over the heat source. Susanna Ede remembered the cookware "had an abundance of hot coals to put on top and under skillets and for such salt-rising bread as we could bake."[14] A recipe for fried potatoes, printed in *The Washington Standard*, November 11, 1874 gives a vivid description of using a spider. The author of the recipe must have had secret thoughts of becoming a poet!

> *Fried Potatoes*—Fried potatoes can be made in perfection in any kitchen by the use of very simple apparatus, consisting of a sharp blade set slanting into a wooden trough with a narrow slit in the bottom, two wire screens or sieves, and a common spider. Select eight large potatoes, pare them, and slice very thin with the cutting machine, soak them in cold water for two hours....Pour them upon the screen to drain and put on a spider, with a pound of clear lard, over a brisk fire. Wipe the sliced potatoes dry on a towel, wait until the lard is smoking hot, and pour a large plateful into the spider. The result is like a small sea in a white squall; and now the cook shows the artistic soul....Patient and calm, with steady and incessant motion of the skimmer, she prevents adhesion of any two affectionate slices, and watches carefully for the tender blush of brownness to appear....Haste then takes the place of caution, lest any martyrs burn for the protection of others, and they must be quickly spread upon another sieve to drain and dry and greaseless enough for the fairest fingers; then served hot to melt away like a kiss on sweet lips, with a drying crackle like the fallen leaves in autumn.

Dutch ovens are superior cooking utensils, good for baking bread and cakes or stewing beans and fruit. When pioneers talked and wrote about early cooking, they frequently commented about baking bread and stewing meat in a Dutch oven.

The reflector oven (tin kitchen) brought forth plaudits as praiseworthy as those for the Dutch oven. This handy gadget came in different shapes and sizes, but the most common configuration consisted of a tin cylinder either completely open in the back or with a door that opened. The little door made it easier for cooks to test food without moving the oven. More complex ones came with a dripping pan for catching grease, a shelf for baking biscuits and cakes, and either a spit or hooks for roasting meat. The Ede family used one that measured two and one-half feet long, one and one-half feet deep, and eighteen inches wide. "[It] rested on the hearth in front and on sheet iron legs eight to ten inches high in back. It had a lengthwise shelf on which to set vessels to cook, bake, or roast....We baked pies, bread, cake and roasted meat to perfection in it." When in use the open side faced the fire.[15]

Stoves! Stoves!

In spite of the fact that just about every dish could be cooked to perfection in a Dutch or reflector oven over hot coals, pioneer women wanted a cook stove. The trend started with Narcissa Whitman, who six years after arriving at Waiilatpu Mission (near Walla Walla) wrote to her family, "...we have a cooking stove...which is a great comfort to us this winter, and enables me to do my work with comparative ease, now I have no domestic help."[16] Whitman, a missionary wife who came to Oregon country in 1836, used a "Hudson's Bay cook stove of a very small and primitive make; the oven was directly over the firebox and two kettles which were of an oblong shape sat in on the side, something like the drum on the sides of a stove."[17]

With the same burst of enthusiasm, other pioneer wives happily wrote home that the kitchen now had a cook stove. Just as their contemporaries in the States, hardworking housewives in the Northwest wilderness wanted the newest labor-saving, modern convenience.

Lucky newlyweds, Rachel Malick Biles and Louisa Boren Denny had a short wait. Soon after her wedding in 1852, Rachel Biles wrote to her sister in Illinois that "We have a very nice new cooking stove and...a nice new cupboard and very nice glass wear and queens wear [pottery] of every kind."[18] David Denny, Louisa Boren's husband, obtained a ship's cook stove with a railing around it and installed it in the one-room cabin before their wedding, also in 1852.[19]

Others sometimes had to wait years. The Firth family, who came in 1864, did not get a stove until 1875. Short of funds, they could not afford a stove until Lila Hannah Firth's mother "raised a large drove of turkies that year and with that turkey money she bought her first stove, with a 10 gallon reservoir on the back of it to provide water for kitchen use."[20]

In the latter half of the nineteenth century a large industry developed around the manufacture of cook stoves. During the 1850s just two New York cities, Troy and Albany, had gross sales of stoves annually exceeding $2 million—a large number of appliances given that a stove sold for around $25.

STOVES! STOVES!! TIN, SHEET-IRON &c.

O. B. TWOGOOD,

[Late Backus & Twogood.]

WOULD inform the public that he has now on hand a superior lot of *COOKING* and *PARLOR* stoves, together with a good assortment of Tin, Japaned, Sheet-iron and Hollow ware which is offered at rates that will not fail to suit the purchaser.

The public are invited to call and be convinced, at the old stand, Main St.

Oregon City, Feb. 11, 1854—52tf

Every cook wanted a stove. In the 1850s cook stoves usually sold for around $25. *Oregon Spectator, Oregon City, February 11, 1854.*

Encouraged by increased sales, astute businessmen in Oregon and Washington territories arranged to have stoves sent west. Before transcontinental railroads connected Portland and Seattle with the rest of the country, that meant a long ocean journey. All seaworthy vessels headed west had to travel a circuitous route south around the Horn of South America, north to California, then up the coast to Oregon Territory. Once there merchants still had to transport the heavy, bulky stoves to their business establishments, and pioneers had to arrange transportation and installation in their homes.

In urban areas well-packed roads made travel relatively easy. A sturdy wagon pulled by horses or mules could move the stove from the boat dock or business establishment to the home. In rural areas transporting 200 pounds or more of metal across muddy roads and streams with no bridges required planning. Wanting to please their wives, or perhaps "keep them on the farm," several pioneer husbands developed ingenious methods for carrying a new cook stove into the wilderness.

Along the bend of the Nooksack River in Whatcom County, pioneers solved the moving problem by taking doors and all moveable parts off, pushing a long pole through the frame, and letting men carry the stove by holding on to both ends of the pole.[21] William Harris, who also lived in Whatcom County, "placed two strong poles about 10 feet long as thills, one on each side of the horse and...across the poles I nailed strong strips of wood, placing the stove thereon and securely fastening it."[22] The independent men and women who had traveled across the country in covered wagons did not mean to let a few miles of rugged terrain keep them from having a cook stove.

Of course in such a lucrative market, home-town entrepreneurs wanted to take advantage of the cook stove's popularity. In Oregon, in 1871, Oregon Iron Works opted to manufacture stoves and so compete with Eastern establishments. According to Thomas Rogers, who eventually took over that business, the company had not learned "to turn out a reliable article." However, Oregon Iron Works sold the patents to Lake's Emigrant Stove and Tin Store, which invited customers to "see the stoves made in Portland before you buy a stove." Lake's either made a better stove or had more business acumen because the business proved successful.

Thomas Rogers and Stephen Richards bought out Lakes in 1876, and renamed the shop Willamette Stove Works. Evidently they knew something about building a stove, for their cook stove took first prize at the Oregon State Fair of 1876. The "Wide West," "Pacific," and "Right Good" cook stoves became popular through the Northwest and California. With such popularity the company, which now called itself Oregon Stove Foundry, increased its inventory of better-designed cook stoves and added "a great source of supply to the trade of the great Northwest and Southwest country." Finally pioneers had opportunities to furnish their kitchens with a local product.[23]

As early as March 13, 1850, an advertisement in the *Oregon Spectator*, a newspaper in Oregon City, indicated that businesses carried cook stoves and all accessories at reasonable prices:

> Stoves! Stoves! Pipe
> Just received a well selected invoice of cookstoves of most improved variety patterns with pipe and extra sets of cooking utensils.

In 1859 C. Crosby and Company, Tumwater, charged $25 for a #7 cooking stove and $1.25 for two extra stove pipes. In 1861, in Whatcom County, cook stoves sold for $32.[24] Unfortunately, records do not indicate the model or quantities available. Michael Luark had no trouble purchasing a stove but had problems finding stove pipes. "There is a good warming stove, in the house but we can't put up a cook stove for want of an elbow for the stove pipe, so it goes." Luark spent four days searching for someone or someplace that stocked the proper size elbow.[25]

From both pictures in early ads and pioneer descriptions we know that early stoves resembled the one that Narcissa Whitman had used, and the ones the emigrants packed but then abandoned as they traveled along the Oregon Trail. These simple step stoves had several boiling holes (lids) "arranged in steps," but no broiler.[26] Residents like the John and Amanda Sherling family in Molson started out with a "little 4-lid cooking stove, connected to a single pipe."[27] The number before lid—as in "4-lid cooking stove"—specified the number of surface openings available for cooking. Generally higher numbers indicated larger stoves.

Cast-iron cook stoves that pioneers used benefited from technological advancements. When in 1842 the first patents for "new and original" designs entered the marketplace, the race commenced for better, more elaborate cook stoves. Stove companies spent thousands of dollars to promote their products and issued trade catalogues advertising their stoves as "richly and tastefully ornamented with tiles, nickel, and handsome carving...nothing is wanting in the matter of convenience and perfect operation."[28]

The new innovations included water reservoirs that allowed the cook
to keep a supply of hot water in the kitchen, warming ovens that doubled
as places for drying fruit and keeping foods warm, and built-in reflector
ovens with a rotisserie spit for roasting meat. Laura House recalled that her
mother purchased a "wonderful cook stove [that] stood on legs with a door
and hearth in front. On the hearth in raised letters was the manufacturer's
name 'Bridge Beach And Company, St. Louis.'"[29]

Better designed flues and dampers produced more fuel-efficient fires
while newly manufactured stove furnishings, such as shovels and buckets,
made the job of removing ashes easier. Surely numerous homemakers ech-
oed Mary Borst and boasted that they now had a very fashionable stove:

> My cookstove was the envy of all my women visitors. It had been
> brought around the Horn. All the years of cooking over the fireplace
> with heavy iron kettles and the Dutch oven I brought with me to my
> marriage were put behind me. I could fry meat and cook the rest of
> our meal on the high back part of the stove while the water for dishes
> was also heating. I only had to lift up the iron lid of the reservoir on
> the front portion and dip out pans full of scalding water.[30]

Eddy's advertisement in *The Washington Standard* for a kerosene cooking stove that would "Bake, Boil, Stew, Fry and Roast with the greatest
Economy and facility," illustrates that the Northwest followed the trend to
search for alternate fuels. According to the advertisement, Eddy's stove was
the only kerosene stove "that burns with out smoke or odor." Kerosene-
heated stoves supposedly gave off less heat than wood-burning ones and so
kept the house cooler in summer, when preserving kettles heated up the
kitchen.[31]

Recognizing the diminishing supply of wood on the East Coast, and
housewives' clamor for easier methods of cooking, manufacturers came
out with alternatives to stoves. Inventors touted fireless cookers and assorted cooking crocks as ways to save fuel, labor, and money. The cookers,
boxes with wells or kettles that held heated stones, or specially designed
soapstone discs that kept food hot, came in a variety of sizes and shapes.
An advertisement in *The Oregonian*, June 22, 1888, for a cooking crock is
an example of another type of appliance that stressed saving fuel.

COOKING CROCK

Saves Labor, Saves Time, Saves Worry, Saves Money, Saves Scorching
food, Saves Scalding. Nothing can burn in it, No Acid Affects it, No
heat Affects it. Cheap and Durable.

Housekeepers--Attention!

A GREAT DISCOVERY

THE PATENT FIRE-PROOF

Cooking Crock!

Saves Labor,
  Saves Time,
    Saves Worry,
      Saves Money,
        Saves Scorching Food,
          Saves Scalding.

Nothing Can Burn in It,
  No Acid Affects It,
    No Heat Affects It.

CHEAP AND DURABLE.

☞Ask Your Grocer For It.

CHAS. HEGELE & CO.,

Sole Agents for Oregon, Washington and Idaho.

17Je:m:t:t:s:$1m

Manufacturers were quick to advertise their latest products in area newspapers. *The Oregonian, Portland, June 22, 1888.*

Actually this crock sounds similar to the one Elof Norman's family made for cooking beans at a high altitude. Norman wrote that they had beans "served in every way," and needed a more efficient way of cooking. Therefore, "Papa built a large box insulated with straw, so a boiling bean kettle could cook a long time with out fire. That helped some."[32]

Finally, to make stoves attractive as well as functional, designers attached fancy glass and enameled oven doors and covered parts of the plain black surface with decorative tiles. Local dealers made certain that the public knew they carried the most advanced designs. Because most letter and journal writers did not leave detailed descriptions of their cook stoves, but only noted, "I have a cook stove" or my "cook stove has a reservoir," it is through these advertisements that we can surmise what kind of stoves might have gained popularity in the Northwest kitchen.

"Goodhugh's air-tight cooking stoves, assorted sizes"— *The Columbian*, Olympia, October 16,1852.

"Advanced cooking stove with ovens, a very desirable pattern with extra castings"—*The Washington Standard*, Olympia, February 1, 1862.

"Charter Oak Cook Stoves with the world renown and only WIRE GAUZE OVEN DOOR"— *The Palouse City News*, January 21,1890, Palouse City, Whitman County.

"Buck's Celebrated COOK STOVE, With or without extension, and for either Wood or Coal"— *The Seattle Post Dispatch*, December 21, 1871.

"Medallion Range and Buck Royal Acorn and Western Empire Cook Stove" — Nelson Waite Company, *The Chehalis Valley Vidette,* July 5, 1883.

"For Sale—the Celebrated Cooking Stove—THE PEERLESS only stove which won Gold Metal at Paris expedition 1867"—*The Weekly Argus*, Port Townsend, March 30, 1871.

Unfortunately, pictures and advertisements only tell us what might have been available, not who bought what or which stove sold the most. Presumably economics, availability, location, and personal choice influenced decisions. Homemakers who had to keep an eye on the budget might well pick the older model. If stoves had to be transported to a rural area, weight would surely enter in the decision. On the other hand, a wealthy city family with servants to do the cooking might choose the newest, most ornate model.

The era of cast-iron cooking stoves lasted until the turn of the century when rolled steel replaced bulky, brittle iron. Illustrated advertisements in twentieth-century Washington state cookbooks indicate that for many years stove companies offered the same model for those who burned wood, combination wood and coal, gas, or electricity.[33] "My mother always cooked on an old fashioned Monarch Range (coal and wood)," Minerva Herrett wrote.[34] As late as 1911 Annie Brune, who settled in Molson, Washington, choose wood:

Mama got a new all black Home Comfort cookstove in 1911. The date was right on the firebox lid. The reservoir was blue and white on the top. Just the covers and top frame under the reservoir covers. One cover opened from the front and one from the back. We never used the one that flipped up from the back, except when the reservoir was cleaned and I hated that job. The salesman demonstrated the strength of the oven door by jumping from the floor onto the oven door. The reservoir was on the left side right by the firebox. There was a little crack in it and you could heat the water—it would boil if you weren't careful—and then you could just boil it away. And you could roll (the reservoir)away from the stove. It was on a track slide with a small wheel with a crank that turned it. And then Mama got two nice kettles and one big kettle of blue and white swirl porcelain.[35]

When homemakers purchased a cook stove, they had to update cooking utensils. Dutch ovens and heavy cast-iron frying pans with short legs would work on a stove, but better to have pots and pans specifically designed for cook stoves. The foundries that manufactured stoves happily turned out new cast-iron pans and hollow ware with recessed bottoms that fit into the stove's lid openings. They were not shy in suggesting that cooks would need special lids to cover the stove openings and lifters to uncover the lids when putting the pot to boil. Northwest businesses regularly advertised that they had cooking stoves with pipes and extra cooking utensils.[36]

But the new cast-iron cookware had competition. Japanned ware, tinware varnished with a hard brilliant coating, graniteware, cast iron with an enameled coating, and new machine-made stoneware, took their place on the kitchen burners. Utensils that were easier to keep clean and did not rust or get surface damage when in contact with acid foods opened up a whole new culinary era. Japanning coated the tin with enamel and turned the cheap, light tinware into a useful, ornamental utensil, commonly colored dark "maroon-y brown." Graniteware, sometimes called "enamelware," combined the advantages of glass with the strength of metal. The familiar gray and blue speckled pans made to resemble granite are still sold. "We used tin and enamelware for cooking and dishes and also had some cast iron pots," recalled Henry Sherling.[37]

By the 1840s tinsmith shops that assembled pots and pans, kettles, and cutters could be found in every town and village. Tin peddlers traveled all over the country selling and repairing tinware which, by 1870, came from factories rather than artisans' shops. "Tinware manufactured at short notice," advertised C.E. Williams, December 23, 1867, in *The Daily Pacific Tribune.* This implied that Williams soldered together parts formed by dies, presses, and lathes. He did not design and cut out sheets of tin.[38]

From the earliest days of settlement area merchants stocked a variety of tinware. An itemized list of merchandise printed in the *Oregon Spectator*, on April 1, 1847 turns up tin pint cups, coffee pots, strainers, scoops, colanders, dippers, and buckets and pans sold according to size. Financial records from Wilson and Dunlap and Henry Roeder record numerous tin implements.

Catalogs from companies such as Dover Stamping Company show that the consumer had multiple choices of pots and pans. Tin canisters that held spices sat on numerous pioneer shelves. Homemakers who bought milk pans had to decide between flaring milk pans or straight milk pans, each of which came in ten sizes. F.A. Walker's illustrated catalog issued in 1871 recommended 429 utensils.[39] American manufacturers excelled in suggesting to the consumer that a perfect home needed a myriad of goods. Territorial businesses tried their best to make that happen.

O.B. TWOGOOD

Would inform the public that he has now on hand a superior lot of COOKING and PARLOR stoves, together with a good assortment of Tin, Japanned, Sheet-iron and Hollow ware which is offered at rates that will not fail to suit the purchaser.[40]

Though the new kitchen ware was easier to clean, housewives did have to use quite a bit of elbow grease to remove dried bits of food. Also both cast iron and tin had to be thoroughly dried or else they rusted and developed holes. Graniteware stained easily and chipped when the dishwasher tried to remove stuck food. In the rush to supply large numbers of implements, factories produced inferior utensils that did not function well. According to statements in the Walker catalog, tinware and Japanned ware imported from Europe "are of much stronger material and finer finish than the American."[41]

Detailed instructions for solving all these problems filled housekeeping manuals. The authors wrote many paragraphs telling cooks how to wash and thoroughly dry pots and pans:

In washing tin ware use soft water and soap, and wash well, rinse with hot water, wipe well, put on the hearth or stove to dry perfectly; once a week wash tin-ware in water in which a little sal-soda has been dissolved....To wash the outside of pots, kettles and all iron ware, place in a tub or large dish-pan, and with soap on cloth, rub them briskly and hard; if necessary scrape with an iron spoon or old knife to get all dirt off, rinse in hot water, wipe, and place on stove to dry.

Enameled ware may be cleaned by filling the vessel with hot water, with soda dissolved in it—one ounce to a gallon; let it boil twenty minutes; then if the stain does not all come off, scour with fine sand or brick dust; rinse well with hot water and wipe dry. If by carelessness...it [food] becomes burned on the porcelain kettle, empty immediately, fill with water, put in about pint of wood-ashes to two gallons of water, let it boil twenty or thirty minutes; clean with sand or brick-dust as above, if it does not all come off....To clean a brown porcelain kettle, boil peeled potatoes in it. The porcelain will be rendered nearly as white as when new.[42]

Repairing tinware kept tinkers busy. "Mrs. Huggins brought out all the dishpans, pails, and tin cooking utensils with holes plugged with a piece of rag or dough and kept the tinker busy for two days," recorded Edward Huggins. He called it a "red letter day" for the Huggins family.[43]

To help American women decide what cookware to purchase, domestic advisors offered extensive lists of implements for a well-run kitchen. This one, from Beecher's *The American Woman's Home* of 1869, is a good example

> Crockery—Brown earthen pans are said to be best for milk and for cooking....Tall earthen jars, with covers, are good to hold butter, salt, lard, etc....Stoneware is better and stronger, and safer every way than any other....
>
> Iron Ware—A nest of iron pots, of different sides...; an iron hook, with a handle, to lift pots from the crane; a Dutch oven...; two skillets, of different sizes, and a spider....
>
> Tin Ware—Bread-pans; large and small patty-pans; cake-pans, with a center tube to insure their baking well; pie-dishes (of block-tin;) a covered butter-kettle; covered kettles to hold berries; two sauce-pans;...an apple-corer; an apple-roaster; an egg-boiler; two sugar-scoops, and flour and meal-scoop;...a milk-strainer; a gravy-strainer; a colander; a dredging-box; a pepper-box; a large and small grater....
>
> Wooden Ware—A nest of tubs; a set of pails and bowls; a large and small sieve; a beetle for mashing potatoes; a spade or stick for stirring butter and sugar; a bread-board for moulding bread and making pie-crust;...an egg-beater; a ladle for working butter; a bread-trough, (for a large family;) flour-buckets with lids, to hold sifted flour and Indian meal.

Dishes, bowls, crocks, and jugs do not go in an oven or on top of a range, but they are necessary for mixing, stirring, and serving meals. In addition to the tinware dishes that the early pioneers relied on, cooks could choose from a wide selection of tableware. Bowls and dishes, plain or decorated, came in earthenware and pottery as well as fine china and glass. Settlers happily exchanged their battered tin cups and plates for sparkling white Queensware pottery, and their dented tin coffee pots for shiny Britannia ware. Wilson and Dunlap listed a crate of white Queensware in their 1856 notebook, noting that they stocked all kinds. "Britannia Tea Pots

THE TRAVELING TINKER.—[Drawn by John Bolles.]

Tinkers traveled throughout towns and cities repairing tin cookware and other household equipment. *Harper's Weekly, November 26, 1870.*

and etc.," advertised a merchant in the *Oregon Spectator* on March 27, 1847.

Queensware, a type of pottery, originated in England as cream-colored. But Americans preferred white and manufacturers accommodated their taste. Britannia ware is a special variety of pewter that contains no lead. If kept polished it is said to resemble silver. Decorative as well as functional,

Britannia cruet stands that held glass bottles for vinegar, ketchup, oil, and bitters occupied a place of honor in Northwest nineteenth-century homes.

In the early years of settlement, pioneers purchased whatever they could get. In 1847, the year the Chambers family left Portland for Puget Sound, Elizabeth Chambers "traded a pair of turkeys for a set of plates...the dishes which was the first earthen ware that we had possessed since we were married [1845]."[44] And Lucy Ryan, a newlywed in 1875, wrote her grandmother that "dishes are second-hand and mixed, many cracked and handles broken off the tops. There are no forks or cover dishes. I paid $10 in gold for them."[45] "Cover" (covered serving bowls) and deep dishes show up frequently in Wilson and Dunlap inventories.[46] Other items listed in newspaper advertisements from the 1850s and 1860s show that home-makers bought cups and saucers, sugar bowls, pickle dishes, gravy dishes, tumblers, small and large bowls, covered butter dishes, water pitchers, punch bowls, and soup tureens.

Special serving dishes for certain fruits and vegetables, as well as fine china, imparted a high status to Victorian dining rooms. Crystal bowls or "boats" curved to hold a bunch of bananas, and silver orange peelers, spoons, and "knives, distinguished by a sawtooth blade on one edge," suggested the family had money to purchase imported foods.[47] By 1884 a merchandise list obtained from the territorial court records of McDonald and Schwabacher, Columbia County, included oyster dishes, platters, gold bead cups and saucers, gold bead plates, sauce dishes, salt cellars and salt dishes, syrup and cream pitchers, and assorted size glass tumblers.[48] Pacific Northwest homemakers could now dine in style.

Lamenting her lack of serving dishes for canned fruit and preserves, Adelaide Gilbert described for her mother the type of china popular in the Pacific Northwest in the 1890s:

> Miss Sampson was over here while I was away yesterday and left for me an elegant celery dish—flat oblong china and gilt Limoges (5 dollars). It is very exquisite but as usual so many other things I would prefer.... I have no dish with my china for canned fruit or preserves & I have a nest of oblong platters only suitable for celery and cold meats.... There is such a fad here for nice china—the most exquisite things in the china stores—One fish set—1 doz. plates—a platter and gravy boat 65 dollars—dainty gilt decorations around the edges and deep sea green coloring all over—shaded out from center on which lies a beautiful fish somebody will buy it.[49]

Like most supplies available in the fluctuating Northwest market, what dishware pioneers set on the table depended on the area economy as well as each family's financial status.

Did cook stoves and new equipment make homemaking easier? Probably, but not immediately. Early stoves still used wood, so chopping wood continued as a time-consuming chore, although presumably stoves used less wood than open fireplaces. Small stoves only two to three feet high meant that the cooks continued to stoop and bend when placing heavy pots and pans on the boilers or in the oven.

Purchasing a stove also required spending money for special equipment, such as stove lifters for uncovering the boiler openings, and shovels and buckets for removing and storing ashes. And owing to the absence of temperature controls and switches that turned on heat with a flick of the wrist, cooks had to learn to regulate ovens by operating a complicated system of dampers and ventilators. As Lucy Deady wrote in 1852, "stoves took getting used to."

> The day we went to housekeeping, Judge Deady installed in our kitchen an iron cookstove, the first one I had ever seen. We had visitors the first day we started housekeeping....I put the roast into the oven and made a big fire and the first thing I knew the smoke was pouring out of the oven at a most alarming rate. I didn't know what to do, so I called my husband. He opened the door and out rushed a cloud of smoke. He patted me on the shoulder and said, "don't mind. There is plenty more meat where that came from."[50]

Additionally, stoves—unlike fireplaces—had to be cleaned and polished to prevent rust, which caused the brittle iron to crack. Cleaning pipes filled the room with black soot. Blackening and rubbing on stove polish stained hands and strained muscles. No one liked that stinky, messy, hazardous job. Kate Polson's sister, Birdie, who lived in Seattle in 1881, felt fortunate to have her husband perform this task:

> The stove in the kitchen had been smoking and he cleaned the pipe also the ashes from under the oven, when I was getting dinner there was a sound like the report of a pistol and in the oven there was a crack across the bottom.[51]

Ever helpful, cookery instructors gave detailed instructions for operating and cleaning cook stoves (although most cooks in the kitchen probably ignored the complicated rules and learned by doing). Directions written by Sarah Rorer in 1886 are representative. She used coal for fuel, but noted that the same directions applied to wood-burning stoves

> Study the draughts of your range....Close the dampers, and this will throw the heat around the oven...."Fix" your fire as soon as breakfast is over. Open the draughts and dust damper, rake the fire well, until free from every particle of ashes; then open the top and brush the soot and the small pieces of coal, if any, from the top of the oven into the fire. See that the corners are free from ashes, and fill the fire-box even full with coal;...If you add more coal than this, you cut off the upper draught, and, of course, lose much heat. Now clean out the ashes; and carry them away. Dust the range of stove and polish it while cool; a paint-brush makes a very nice brush for putting on the polish. Watch the fire carefully, allowing it to burn briskly until the blue flames appear on the surface and then, if you are not going to use it immediately open the top (the damper being out) and thus keep it in good condition until wanted. Always take off the draughts as soon as you have finished a meal, thereby saving labor and fuel. The best ranges are ruined and large quantities of coal are wasted daily by filling the ranges too full and leaving the draughts open to burn like a fiery furnace.[52]

If those cumbersome instructions did not discourage the cook, the directions for temperature control probably did:

> To test the oven put half a sheet of writing paper in the oven; if it catches fire it is too hot; open the dampers and wait ten minutes, then put in another piece of paper; if it blackens it is still too hot. Ten minutes later put in a third piece; if it gets *dark brown* the oven is right for all small pastry, called "Dark brown paper heat." *Light brown paper heat* is suitable for vol-au-vents or fruit pies. *Dark yellow paper heat* for large pieces of pastry or meat pies,...bread, etc. *Light yellow paper heat* for sponge cakes, meringue, etc. To obtain these various degrees of heat try paper every ten minutes till heat required for the purpose is attained. Remember that "light yellow" means paper only tinged; "dark yellow" paper the color of ordinary pine wood; "light brown" is only a shade darker, about the color of nice pie-crust, and dark brown a shade darker, by no means coffee color.[53]

Most pioneers recalled simply testing the heat with one's hand. They learned by experience if an oven temperature got too hot. Recognizing the problems with the paper testing system, Estelle Wilcox added: "All systematic housekeepers will hail the day when some enterprising Yankee or Buckeye girl shall invent a stove or range with a thermometer attached to the oven, so that the heat may be regulated accurately and intelligently."[54] Oven thermometers became standard equipment in the twentieth century, although early ones were not very accurate.

Did food taste better cooked in graniteware on a stove rather than in a Dutch oven over hot coals? Who is to say? All cookery depends on the cook, the ingredients, and the expectations of those served. Hearth cooking, properly done, turns out tasty, appetizing food. Many moaned the demise of the fireplace for baking bread and grilling meat, and complained that bread baked in a stove ended up with a hard, black crust. Laura Schaffer's pronouncement that "It was impossible to bake bread in it [cook stove] without burning the bread but it was better than the camp fire I had been using," recognizes the problems.[55] But whatever their problems and despite the fact that cook stoves did not do all that the advertisements promised, stoves earned a permanent space in the kitchen.

Exterior and interior views of George Steinbach's log cabin home, built in 1876. The home is now part of Old Aurora Colony, a National Historic District. *Photograph by Jacqueline Williams, courtesy Old Aurora Colony Museum.*

Well-dressed men and women enjoy a picnic on the Willamette River in Oregon. *Courtesy Oregon Historical Society, #35251.*

Catharine Blaine became Seattle's first school teacher. The Rev. David Blaine founded Seattle's Methodist Episcopal Church. The Blaines came to Washington Territory in 1853. *Courtesy Museum of History and Industry, Seattle, #5930.*

A barbecue helps to celebrate the arrival of the Northern Pacific Railroad to Seattle on September 14, 1883. *Courtesy Museum of History and Industry, Seattle, #1609.*

An Ellensburg, Washington, home with an attached ice house, built *c.* 1910. *Courtesy Museum of History and Industry, Seattle, #13212.*

Children line up possibly to feast on their favorite foods, or to pose for a group photograph to record this 1890s picnic. *Courtesy Museum of History and Industry, Seattle, #15117.*

The Benson L. Northup family of Seattle in front of their log cabin home, built with an attached lean-to. *Courtesy Museum of History and Industry, Seattle, #14057.*

An old log cabin with a clay fireplace became the kitchen and dining room of Phoebe and Holden Judson's "ideal home" in 1870 in the Nooksack Valley (Lynden, Washington). *Courtesy Lynden Pioneer Museum.*

A woman feeding her chickens. Seemingly they were free-range rather than penned in a chicken coop. *Courtesy Latah County Historical Society, Moscow, Idaho, #25-2-12.*

Above: Families enjoy a leisurely dinner in their well-appointed dining room (#30-19-3). *Below:* Farmers, who had most likely worked long hours in the wheat fields, feast on fresh-baked bread, home-canned fruits and vegetables, and roasted meats (#25-2-12). *Both courtesy Latah County Historical Society, Moscow, Idaho.*

An afternoon picnic outside Moscow, Idaho. *Courtesy Latah County Historical Society, Moscow, Idaho, #30-10-10.*

Women workers had to stand in order to fill cans with salmon in this Northwest cannery. *Courtesy Whatcom Museum of History and Art, Bellingham, Washington, #7289.*

Elizabeth Tosh stands in front of a milk house, an insulated building that kept dairy products cool in the days before refrigeration. *Courtesy Marymoor Museum, Redmond, Washington.*

Lucinda Collins Fares's family homesteaded in Snoqualmie Valley. Her home and butter were well known by all who traveled over Snoqualmie Pass. *Courtesy Snoqualmie Valley Historical Society, North Bend, Washington.*

Chapter Four
Flour: Staple of Subsistence

"FLOUR, FOR YEARS, WAS almost unobtainable. At a barn-raising in the eighteen fifties, of all the men who attended and carried their dinners, only one had bread and that was in the shape of a biscuit," reported Flora Engle, who lived on Whidbey Island.[1] "As it [bread] was not rained down from heaven, some of the emigrants were obliged to go hungry for the 'staff of life,'" lamented Phoebe Judson, that marvelous observer of pioneer life.[2] As late as 1884-85, John Jelinek, a bachelor who lived near Spokane, recalled that "it was a pretty tough time with all of us....I had only half a sack of flour left...Some of my neighbors didn't even have that."[3]

The newcomers wanted bread made from wheat flour to set upon the table at meal times. They agreed with Arthur Denny who observed that though "some substantial life-supporting food can always be obtained on Puget Sound,...it is hard for civilized man to live without bread."[4] Even two weeks without bread proved a hardship for the Masterson family. "We had everything in plenty except bread, and because it was the staff of life, we felt awkward trying to eat without it. The children cried for bread, and mother cried because she had none for them.... I think we were without bread about two weeks."[5]

A number of factors caused the shortages. First, several years are required to produce a good crop of wheat and enough seed for future plantings. "[We] were obliged to plant and re-plant for three years before they dared to use any, and during those three years the five families never saw bread, let alone tasting it," Sarah McAllister Hartman wrote in her story about the early days at Bush Prairie, Oregon Territory.[6] And that was when the weather cooperated. Too much rain in spring caused a late planting and a late harvest, which had a greater chance of being damaged by frost; rain during harvest time made it difficult to dry grain and produced smut, a fungus. Hot and dry summers caused crops to wilt; freezing winters like that in 1862 destroyed the wheat.

Wheat berries contaminated with smut had to be removed from the general pile before grinding or else whole crops spoiled. Michael Luark tried to prevent that disaster by soaking the wheat in Blue Vitriol (copper sulfate). He dissolved "¾ of it [pound of vitriol] in water and soaked my 5½ bushels of spring wheat about 12 hours to destroy smut."[7] When in 1860 Chambers' flour mill acquired a machine, of "the most approved patent" to remove smut, *The North-West*, a Port Townsend newspaper, announced the news on September 27, 1860.

Wet grain that sprouts before it is threshed makes sticky, difficult-to-chew bread. No doubt other pioneers experienced situations similar to the one described by Sarah Hunt Stevens, whose family lived in Marion County, Oregon:

> Father usually stacked his grain, as it was considered a safe method, but that year his stacks were sprouting and showing green before he got his wheat all threshed. Everybody had to eat sticky bread that year. I remember how awful it was. Loaf bread could not be made at all from the flour and the everlasting biscuits would stick to your fingers when you ate them and were a sickly gray in color and very heavy.[8]

As a matter of fact, in 1852 bad harvests had settlers eating the seed put away for the next year's crops. If not for George Bush, a successful farmer who generously supplied seed, scarcely a pioneer family in the Puget Sound area would have had baked bread that year.

Because territorial mills could not keep up with the demand for flour, much had to be imported from other states or foreign ports—an unsatisfactory process as flour holed up in ships for four to six weeks had a tendency to arrive full of weevils and "caked several inches thick all around inside the barrel for the salt water would get in the barrels."[9] Furthermore, imported flour carried a high price tag, the going rate being $20 a barrel (196 pounds) in 1852. And because pioneers purchased such large quantities during their infrequent shopping sprees, and did not have adequate storage areas, flour tended to become rancid. An editorial comment in *The Columbian*, Olympia, Washington Territory, August 13, 1853, expressed the pioneers' concern:

> Our market is almost bare of this indispensable article. Our traders should know that from the present time onward the demand for flour will be very much augmented. If the merchants of San Francisco wish

to know what they should ship to the SOUND we tell them flour and other staples of subsistence, but flour more particularly than anything else.

Grist Mills for Grinding

Since the seventh millennium B.C., communities throughout the world have realized that flour is an irreplaceable staple food. It was no different in the developing Northwest. Shortly after sending out explorers to search for furs, the British planted wheat and constructed a grist mill in 1828 at Fort Vancouver, one of the British Hudson's Bay Company enterprises. Over the next decade others followed their example. In 1836 near Champoeg, Oregon Territory, Rev. Samuel Parker noted in his journal that "hunters recently turned to farmers, cultivate the most commonly useful productions—wheat of the first quality to as great an extent as their wants require."[10] In what became Washington Territory, the Whitman mission at Waiilatpu added a mill in 1838.

As soon as settlers arrived, they too set about building grist mills for grinding flour. In the winter of 1846-47 Michael Simmons, a member of the first group of pioneers to settle north of the Columbia River, located a small flouring mill at Deschutes Falls (Tumwater).[11] Soon after, billows of yellowish-brown flour floated in the air as communities up and down the Northwest set up pairs of stones to grind flour.

Martha Ellis, who came to the Northwest in the 1850s as a child, remembered her first wheat planting, "for we children had to be the scare-crows until the wheat got too high for the crows to pull up."[12] Rebecca Ebey recorded in her diary how grist mills would aid her community:

a grist mill there [Coveland on Whidbey Island] will be a great advantage...and our farmers have some wheat coming on, and will be able before another year to make their own bread in place of having to bring it from California and pay twenty dollars per hundred for it.[13]

To turn wheat berries into grain, early grist mills used various sized grinding stones made of granite. In order for grain to be cut rather than smashed, they cut a grooved pattern into the stones. Simmons used a simple set of stones hewn out of granite blocks found on the beach. He housed the apparatus in a log house.

Describing an old Hudson's Bay mill set up on the Colville River in 1843, W.P. Winans wrote that in 1861 the mill "was a hewn log building, about 30 x 50, two stories, with an attic, covered with cedar bark. It had a single pair of stones, made of the granite of the neighborhood."[14]

The grinding process that turns wheat berries into flour is simple. Two stones, enclosed in a wooden box called a vat, are placed on top of each other with only a minute distance between them. As stones turn and cross each other they crush the berries and send grain to the bottom of the vat. Here a small scoop-like apparatus pushes the flour into a sack or bin. Grain that comes from this first milling is a mixture of the starchy matter (endosperm), the oily germ that contains the vitamins and gluten, and bran.[15]

Most early mills in Oregon and Washington Territory used water power to move the stones. However, steam power was considered more efficient and some mills switched to that energy source. In the Northwest, St. Helen's Flouring Mills favored steam and proudly announced:

> The proprietor of the above mills would inform his friends and the public generally that he has just started his **Steam Flouring Mills,** which are capable of making 80 barrels superfine Flour per day. He also has engaged the services of an experienced miller of San Francisco, and will be able to make as good Flour and as much from a bushel of Wheat as any mill in Oregon.
>
> He will grind Wheat for Farmers for every eighth bushel. He also will grind all kinds of feed, Corn and Buckwheat, at reasonable rates and short notice.
>
> The highest market price paid for Wheat, delivered at the mills. Thirty-eight lbs. S.F. Flour and 10 lbs. of shorts and bran will be given in exchange for 60 lbs. of merchantable Wheat. Buckwheat ground and bolted.
>
> Flour, Shorts and Bran for sale at the mills and at his store in St. Helen's, by the sack or quantity as cheap as can be bought in the Territory.
>
> B.M. DU RELLE
> St. Helen's, O.T. Sept. 15, 1854.[16]

A small ad in *The Sunday Welcome,* October 1875, advertising portable grinding mills, suggests that homeowners might have been grinding their own grains. Doing so guarantees fresh flour and in communities without access to grist mills it became a necessary chore. Advertised as "best French Burr," portable mills came in all sizes, some with a genuine Dutch bolting cloth.

The James family used a portable mill in 1852. "Father got a little steel burr of a grist mill, bigger than a coffee mill, of Mr. George Bush, and had the mill fastened to a post on the porch of the cabin and it was a chore for us younger ones to grind enough meal for breakfast."[17]

The whiteness of the flour ground in grist mills depended on the number of grindings and whether mills had equipment for bolting (removing the bran and germ). It took numerous grindings and passings through sieves to produce a "white" flour, or what merchants called super-fine flour or extra superfine. Putting stones closer together produced a finer meal. To let settlers know about the fine and light flour turned out by Lincoln Mills, located in Tumwater, that mill held a testing. They put out a sample of their flour next to one from the Salem Mills, a mill known for its fine flour, and announced the Tumwater flour as "being the lightest."[18]

In America, millers have used bolts or sieves to remove the coarse bran in wheat for hundreds of years, but until the mid-nineteenth century when rotary mills simplified the process, bolting flour added another time-consuming job to the milling process. Settlers either purchased or made themselves several different types of bolting screens. Bolting cloth sold by the yard in area stores. One early type in use in Washington Territory con-sisted of "2 or 3 silk-covered frames which would vibrate back and forth and sift the flour through the silk meshings." Another at the Gowdy Mill in Stevens County in 1861 utilized a stationary wire screen with a revolv-ing brush inside. Unbolted flour contained large flakes of bran.[19]

The early grist mill at Fort Vancouver had a simple wire bolt; the Simmons mill did not bolt flour. Mrs. Andrew Chambers remembered that settlers living near the Simmons mill were so pleased when they learned her family had a sieve wire, "for they had no bolting for their small grist-mill. They thought it a fine thing to have a sieve wire so they could take the bran out of their flour."[20] Commenting on the difficulty of separating the bran, C.H. Montgomery described a most inefficient method used around 1860 in Colville valley:

> I went one day to get some bran and found the Judge [Yantis] bolting the product as it came from the stones. He was shaking a small box over a larger one; the bottom of the small box was covered with cotton cloth...and the larger box was receiving what went through. He asked me how much bran I wanted. I said half a bushel and he replied, "I can't get that much today." I watched him a short time and began to think so myself, for the cloth was so coarse that all went into the larger box.[21]

But whatever apparatus sifted the coarse grains, small amounts of bran and bits of the oily germ, which causes flour to become rancid,

remained in the flour. It also had a yellowish tinge from the natural caro-
tene found in wheat kernels, and might be damp from an inadequate drying process. Mill owners more concerned with profit than purity added
substances such as glass, whiting, ground stones, or plaster of Paris to make
flour whiter and/or heavier.

A 1909 Washington state cookbook's admonition that "to make good
bread, first of all, you must have good flour and it must be thoroughly
dried out," indicates that methods for keeping flour dry did not disappear
with the pioneer period. To accomplish this, the authors, ladies from the
Church of the Holy Family in Auburn, wrote:

> Let it [flour] set on the back of the range, or some other warm place
> for twenty-four hours, and the difference it will make in bread and
> cake will surprise you. Some cooks keep a lot of dried-out flour on
> hand all the time, and regard it as a great secret.[22]

Pacific Northwest homemakers purchased flour that varied from unbolted coarse ground wheat to superfine. Superfine, the closest to pure
white flour, cost the most. "$6 Per Barrel Extra superfine flour from
Tumwater," B.F. Cooper advertised in 1863.[23] Pioneers tried to limit their
purchases of the cheaper grinds, middlings, bran, and shorts, but when
low bank accounts and/or a scarcity of grain prevailed, cooks mixed and
kneaded these grinds into bread. "We first used our flour, then made bread
of the middlings, then came the shorts and we expected to have to use the
bran for bread," recalled Melvin Hawk.[24] "That first winter in Oregon
[1852] we lived on shorts bread, wild game and little molasses," Lavina
Flora Hamilton pointed out.[25]

Phoebe Judson's story about a neighbor's incessant use of bran illustrates its importance and dislike:

> Our family was subsisting on bran, and were all sick, when my hus-
> band had the good fortune to find employment. I naturally expected
> that with his first day's wages he would bring home some nourishing
> food, but, what was my indignant disappointment, when in the place
> of food, he handed me a cook book. That goes to show the "true in-
> wardness" of some men's judgment; the good deacon (for such he was)
> no doubt expecting his wife from those receipts to manufacture a vari-
> ety of delicacies out of bran.[26]

The cheaper "flours," brans, shorts and middlings, became available
because mills did not have the capacity to adequately separate the bran and
germ from endosperm. The quality of shorts (bran plus germ) and middlings (endosperm plus bran) depended on the mill. To improve the quality

of shorts, cookery writers advised mixing it with an equal part of wheat flour. Improved milling equipment for processing flour began to appear on the market in the 1870s.

Of course, some early pioneer families would have been happy to bake a loaf of bran bread. "Poor families never so much as saw a piece of bread....We had fern-root bread, which amply filled its place," noted Sarah Hartman, a pioneer who came with Simmons's party in 1844.[27] The Hartmans were one of the few families that mention using native foods, although many admitted that had it not been for the Indians' kindness in sharing food they would have starved. The settlers purchased or traded for fish, elk, and berries from Native Americans, but they had little desire to use unfamiliar native plants, such as camas or fern roots. There is also little evidence that emigrants wanted to learn Indian cooking methods, preferring familiar foods and recipes.

Living in an area that lacked a grist mill, pioneers slowly and laboriously ground grain in a coffee mill—many families kept two, one for wheat, one for coffee. Coarse flour settled in the drawer of the old-fashioned coffee grinder, which, like crude grist mills, crushed rather than cracked wheat berries.

The coarse flour from the coffee mill grinders and boltless grist mills made a nourishing hot cereal called mush "made in an iron kettle out of graham flour. Not the graham flour we get at the present time [1932], but the whole wheat ground, nothing taken out," recalled Margaret Chambers."[28] Pioneers also relished cold mush, cut into thick slices and browned in fat, then served with greens and/or salt pork.

Lacking sufficient amounts of wheat to grind into flour, wheat hominy and boiled wheat replaced bread as the dish of the day. Lane County, Oregon, pioneer John Champion Richardson's remarks are typical. "When the flour gave [out]...we had to live on boiled wheat and potatoes for six weeks. It was boiled wheat and potatoes and for a change it was potatoes and boiled wheat."[29] Wheat berries also doubled as a type of chewing gum if they were picked when "the milk in the kernels is in right condition." At least that is what the Chambers children did.[30]

Hominy is traditionally made from corn, but several pioneers stated their "choice was the wheat hominy." When fried in bacon grease or butter they said it made a tasty dish. Mary Waunch, who lived in Centralia, prepared it by "soaking the grains in lye and rubbing the loosened hulls off between her hands and washing the swollen white kernels until the water was clear."[31] Waunch longed for the time when she "could vary their diet with spring greens." A series of recipes from *The Washington Standard* of March 29, 1873 shows several ways of preparing this popular dish. The fried hominy recipe is from *Kentucky Housewife.*

> *Hominy Plain Boiled.*—Soak a quart; boil in the tea-kettle boiler until soft; eat with syrup, milk, sugar or butter. Salt to taste.
>
> *Hominy Gruel.*—Mix the hominy in the milk; boil in the tea-kettle boiler; salt to taste. Good for invalids and children.
>
> *Hominy Bread.*—Beat the eggs well; stir the hominy and meal well together; add the eggs; salt and make a thin batter; bake.
>
> *To Fry Hominy*—Having boiled your hominy very tender, drain it, and put it into a pan with some rich highly seasoned gravy, mash it fine, stirring it till it gets nearly dry, and serve it up warm. It is eaten with any kind of nice meat.[32]

To stretch the "staff of life" pioneers added potatoes to the wheat dough, and in the Denny household they "made biscuits of potatoes alone."[33] In emergencies, the Firth family, who lived on San Juan Island, made the flour go farther by adding meal ground from the seeds saved for next year's planting. One hopes the family had a surplus of seeds; the records do not say. Lila Firth described the process:

> We had a good ratproof Granary made of large hewn logs, plastered well inside where we kept our seed grain through the winter. In these emergencies Mother would go to the granary and get some wheat and we would sit down and look it over carefully and take out all wild seeds, if any, then she would grind the wheat through the coffee mill, it came out a very fine meal. She would put a few cups of that meal in the flour when she made bread.[34]

By the time Euro-Americans settled in the Northwest, improved technology enabled bakeries to produce large amounts of hardtack, or pilot bread, a slow-baked, bread-like mixture of flour and water that lasts for years. Although few spoke kindly about this fresh bread substitute, countless pieces soaked up gravy on pioneer plates. Cooks tried to improve its bland taste. One method combined hardtack and wild berries into a sort of pudding served with cream. Puddings made of hardtack and molasses acquired the name dandy funk. Most every merchant and trader in the fledgling towns had hardtack for sale. A variation of this advertisement in *The Port Townsend Register* of January 1860 appeared in other territorial newspapers:

CRACKER BAKERY and WHOLESALE and Retail Flour Warehouse
J.F. Blumberg, Proprietor

Now prepared to execute orders for any amount or kind of Hard Bread
that may be called for, and believes that he can furnish to his customers, a better and cheaper article than can be delivered here, from San
Francisco.

The wheat grown around Puget Sound in Washington Territory during the 1850s, according to Catharine and David Blaine, "is nearly all
alike...except that the farmers make a difference between winter and spring
wheat."[35] Michael Luark noted that "some have spring wheat but most
[farmers] are going to sow winter wheat."[36]

In order to have a little variety from the "wheat that the Hudson's Bay
Company brought from Chili, and it is called the Chili wheat," Blaine
asked her family to "send a few grains of different kinds of wheat in a letter
or paper...and label them. I would like to see some of our wheat growing
here."[37] Whether or not her family followed through with the request we
don't know, but undulating "amber waves of grain" *(Triticum vulgare)* added
color to the territorial landscape. Growing wheat eventually became an
important industry in eastern Washington.

In the 1860s and 1870s a high-protein strain—hard spring wheat—
replaced the old winter wheat. Bakers welcomed this new wheat because it
contained more gluten than older varieties, but millers found it difficult to
grind and separate the middlings, which contained the protein-rich gluten, from the bran. As a result, millers began experimenting with new
machines and developed middlings purifiers and rollers to replace the stones.
Instead of grinding grain between a single pair of millstones, they put it
through six or seven sets of rollers. These rollers effectively removed the
oily germ and separated the starch and bran. Flour now had more gluten,
which gives it its "rising" power, and less bran, which makes it dark.[38]
Aiming for a pure white flour, millers "improved" rollers until nothing
remained in the flour but the endosperm or starch. Bleaching flour with
chlorine gases (introduced in 1904) removed the last traces of color.

This new processed flour acquired the name "patent flour." Northwest mills like the Goudy Mill and Thorp Mill switched to mechanical
rollers in the late 1870s and 1880s.[39] Others followed and began cam-
paigning to convince buyers to switch to patent flour. "Finest standard
grade of Flour. No more dark colored bread. We know you will be pleased

Loveland's Dough Kneader was one of the many inventions receiving a patent but never finding a manufacturer. It was most probably designed by someone who had never baked bread. *Scientific American, February 17, 1866.*

with our flour. Bring in your wheat and give it a try," advertised the Palouse Flouring Mill in 1890.[40]

Yeast and Yeast Substitutes

Flour, of course, does not magically turn into bread. For that to happen it must be mixed with a liquid and leavening agent, kneaded into a soft pliable dough, set to rise, formed into loaves, and baked in a hot oven. Finding a suitable substance to make dough rise made a big difference in the type of bread baked. Commercial yeast did not become available until 1868. Then several companies entered the market and bread bakers had a choice of cake yeast or the homemade variety.

Recipes for homemade yeast commonly took up pages in popular cookbooks. Instructions called for mixing hops or potatoes and salt with flour, water, and yeast saved from a previous batch. "Mother made her yeast with hops and potatoes and often kept a 'starter' from baking to baking. As the only heat in the house was a fireplace, the sponge was set on the warm bricks at night to ferment until morning," Amy Ryan recalled.[41] If starters had passed their prime and no longer worked, pioneers borrowed from a neighbor—if a neighbor lived close by. On Bainbridge Island in the 1850s, the sawmill's company store supplied liquid yeast to housewives.[42] Recipes from period cookbooks gave precise instructions for preparing a batch of yeast.

> *Hop and Potato Yeast*—Pare and slice five large potatoes, and boil them in one quart of water with a large handful of common hops (or a square inch of pressed hops), tied in a muslin rag. When soft, take out the hops and press the potatoes through a colander, and add a small cup of white sugar, a tea-spoonful of ginger, two tea-spoonfuls of salt, and two tea-cups of common yeast, or half as much distillery. Add the yeast when the rest is only bloodwarm. White sugar keeps better than brown, and the salt and ginger help to preserve the yeast.
>
> Do not boil in iron or use an iron spoon, as it colors the yeast. Keep the yeast in a stone or earthenware jar, with a plate fitting well to the rim. This is better than a jug, as easier to fill and to cleanse. Scald the jar before making new yeast.
>
> The rule for *quantity* is one table-spoonful of brewers' or distillery yeast to every quart of flour; or twice as much home-made yeast.
>
> *Potato Yeast* is made by the above rule, omitting the hops. It can be used in large quantities without giving a bitter taste, and so raises bread sooner. But it has to be renewed much oftener than hop yeast, and the bread loses the flavor of hop yeast.[43]

Homemade yeast and a batch of starter did not always work. Much depended on ingredients, the cook's skill, and the temperature. Yeast needs warmth to work. Cold rooms, the norm in log cabin homes, did not provide a suitable environment for baking bread. "It is near midnight.... I am sitting up to bake my bread. The yeast became chilled so that my bread was slow in rising and this detained me," Catharine Blaine wrote to her family."[44] To keep yeast fresh or restore its potency, cooks in Fourth Plain, a community near Vancouver, Washington, followed this method:

Should the yeast become bitter she could freshen it by adding a piece of charred bread; or she could strain it through bran, or simply wash it in cold water, since the yeast would sink to the bottom and the bitter quality remain in the water, where it could be poured off. Should her supply of yeast give out, she could start more by steeping hops for several hours, then by straining the hops out and making a batter with the remaining liquid. To start it fermenting she would merely get a starter from a less careless neighbor, add it to the batter, and put it away until needed.[45]

Sarah Hale, editor of *Godey's Lady's Book* and numerous cookbooks, advised her followers to first make a sponge so "if the yeast does not rise and ferment in the middle of the flour, it shows that the yeast is not good; the batter can then be removed, without wasting much of the flour, and another sponge set with better yeast." When she knew the yeast and the sponge "was good," the cook could add the remaining flour and thoroughly knead the dough "until not a particle will adhere to your hands."[46]

Domestic advisors considered stone or earthenware jars and bowls the best storage vessels for yeast and for mixing the batter. The writers warned against using empty tin cans for storing yeast because cans might contain verdigris (copper sulfate), a poisonous substance that could contaminate dough. "The yeast was kept in the brown Bennington pottery jar, replenished with a mite of salt and sugar each time bread was baked" recalled Letta May Smith.[47]

Settlers, however, did not always follow the advisors and frequently mixed batter in large tin dish-washing or gold-washing pans. Mary Waunch's grandfather, Grandpa Hagar, set "it to raise in the milk pans."[48] Others might have used wood dough boxes or kneading tables, a place to knead and store dough while it rises. Dough-mixing machines with metal kneading rods are occasionally seen in antique stores and museums, but pioneers did not mention using them. Yet, I suspect at least one husband presented his wife with a "new fangled" machine that was guaranteed to bake better bread. Cast iron and tinware made good baking pans.[49]

When hops and/or potato bins stood empty, those responsible for baking bread mixed warm milk or water with salt and flour, and let the natural yeast in the air work the mixture. They called this salt-rising or milk-rising bread. Beecher considered it inferior bread but settlers seemed satisfied with their results. "I make capital milk rising bread," bragged Catharine Blaine. So did Mattilda Jackson, whose granddaughter saved her recipe:

Salt Rising Bread—Salt rising bread was made for years, there being no yeast available such as that used in these modern times. The batter for this was mixed in a small-iron kettle set in a larger one containing warm water and placed on the hearth in the early morning. This would be carefully tended all day by testing the temperature of the water in the outer kettle by hand and stirring the batter frequently. When this became a light, fluffy leaven it was ready to make into loaves and when baked made a fine grained, pleasingly flavored bread.[50]

The recipe from *Kentucky Housewife* gives clearer directions. Still a novice cook today would have trouble following them:

Salt-Rising, or Yeast—Make a quart of water lukewarm, stir into it a table-spoonful of salt, and make it a tolerably thin batter with flour; mix it well, sprinkle on the top a handful of dry flour, and set it in a warm place to rise, but be sure you do not let it get hot, or it would spoil it. Turn it round occasionally, and in a few hours it will be light, and the top covered with bubbles; then make up your bread.[51]

J.H. Horner, who wrote about early settlers in the Wallowa Valley, Oregon, described another version of salt-rising yeast or what he called sour dough yeast or bachelor's bread. He first tells how to make the yeast.

Sour Dough Yeast—Sour dough yeast is made by stirring up a medium thick batter of flour and water and putting it in a warm place until it sours and begins to raise and foam and run over, when it should be stirred down....

Sour Dough Bread—Partly fill your pan with flour and make a depression in the flour. Pour what sour dough [yeast] you need into this depression and put soda and salt on the sour dough and stir into a thick dough, but not so thick, and don't knead so much, as for light bread dough. Cook in a hot oven.[52]

When mixing up a batch of biscuits or "light bread," cooks used saleratus (baking soda) to make the dough rise. Riley Ticknor, grandson of early pioneers Sidney and Nancy Ford, told his granddaughter, Tove Burhen, that he "preferred 'light bread'(loaf) to biscuits which were the usual fare."[53]

Baking powder (yeast powder) became available in 1854, but because it often contained aluminum or ammonia, consumers did not immediately begin adding it to their baked goods. Fueled by rival company claims that poisonous substances were being added in order to enhance the rising power of cakes and breads baked with baking powder, the controversy over this new product lasted for years. Advertisements on the front page of local newspapers in the 1880s indicate that companies did not mince words in describing their rival's product. Baking powder is occasionally seen in early Northwest grocery inventories, but it did not become a widely used kitchen staple until the late 1880s. Frequently when a novice cook tried to use yeast powder the results were disappointing.

Saleratus, from the Latin sal-aeratus (aerated salt), is potassium or sodium bicarbonate, a chalk-like substance. To work (that is, to activate the leavening process), saleratus has to be mixed with an acid food or chemical, such as cream of tartar. Unlike our present-day baking soda, which must adhere to a standard formula, saleratus's potency depended on which brand a person chose.

Saleratus was first processed by adding carbonic acid to pearlash (derived from the ashes of trees). Fortunately for the trees, by mid-nineteenth century, scientists discovered how to obtain saleratus from the remains of marine plants and sea salt. Manufacturers in that era varied the amount of chemicals added and each thought he had the best mix of ingredients. As a rule saleratus was stronger than today's baking soda. An advertisement from an 1850 *New York Post* describes one manufacturer's product:

> REFINED SALERATUS—This article is much stronger, and in every respect much superior to the kind of Salaeratus, so extensively used....Many consumers may not be aware that the old article of Salaeratus is generally made in Distilleries, the gas used being that which escapes from the whiskey and beer. This article is manufactured by a new and entirely different process;...It is ground fine for greater convenience in use, as it dissolves much sooner than lumps. Three ounces of this will be found equal to four ounces of the ordinary.[54]

Saleratus became available commercially in 1840. Consumers could purchase it packaged in paper envelopes with recipes. In 1857 in Olympia, Washington Territory, saleratus sold for $1.00 a package.[55] Beecher advised that "when Pearlash or Saleratus becomes damp, dissolve it in as much water as will just entirely dissolve it, and no more. A tablespoonful of this equals a teaspoonful of the solid. Keep it corked in a junk bottle." Beecher did not believe in wasting anything and always encouraged women to be frugal.[56]

The graham bread recipe that appeared on January 15, 1863 in *The Oregon Farmer* is a good example of how to use saleratus. We will have to overlook the fact that either the cook or the typesetter left out the amount of flour. In fact, some cookery writers intentionally left out the amount of flour in order to let the cook determine the precise amount. In those years everyone *knew* that bread contained flour and to add just enough to obtain a stiff dough.

> *Recipe for Graham Bread*—Three tea-cups buttermilk, one tables-spoon salt, one and a half tea-spoons saleratus well pulverized. It should be stirred a little thicker than a common cake, put into bread tin, let stand and rise until it has the appearance of being light (which every good housewife can tell,) when it is ready for the oven. When first put in it requires a quick oven; after word a moderate oven. Bake half an hour. The flour should always be sifted.

Graham flour is named for Sylvester Graham, a charismatic food reformer who, in the 1830s, began preaching that unleavened brown bread made from coarsely milled flour led to improved health. If properly milled, graham flour contains the germ and bran. Like most flour in the nineteenth century the quality of graham flour depended on who did the grinding. According to a notice in *The Washington Standard*, December 7, 1878, much of the "graham flour is adulterated with a mixture of cheap flours." That practice continued until federal laws in 1906 established the Food and Drug Administration (FDA) to regulate false claims.

When pioneer cooks had neither yeast, saleratus, or baking powder they turned back to earlier methods of burning wood and used the ash (pearlash) as a leavening agent. In Centralia, Nancy Ford, who settled in 1847, "sifted the fine white ash that formed on the top of the burned logs of hard maple in the fireplace. Then she stored it in cans and used it to raise her biscuit. It raised them just as nice—just as good as soda."[57] Before Americans worried about saving trees, large tracts of Eastern forests were burned in order to supply housewives with pearlash (baking soda).

As soon as sufficient amounts of flour became available, bakeries opened up in the fledging communities. "I get my bread from the baker's," Thornton McElroy wrote his wife from Olympia in 1853.[58] Most likely he purchased his bread from Olympia Bakery and Beef Market. Weed and Hurd, the proprietors, advertised "that they are prepared to furnish Bread, Cakes and Pies of every description on reasonable terms."[59] Account books show that in 1854 in Olympia a loaf of bread cost fifteen cents, mince pies, twenty-five cents, and one dozen cup cakes forty-eight cents or four cents each.[60]

Frequently, early bakeries occupied space in a mill, hotel, or general merchandise store. In Port Townsend in 1860, the Cracker Bakery was part of the flour warehouse. The proprietor offered hard bread, fresh bread, crackers, and cakes along with fresh flour. In Seattle, Eureka Bakery advertised in 1864: "Will always keep a full supply of FLOUR of various brands also a full stock of Confectionery, Cakes, Pies & Bread...also expect to have a Cracker machine and offer various kinds."[61] Ten years later another Seattle bakery boasted that it had "FRESH BREAD EVERYDAY, EXTRA LOAF Bread, (Pan and Bottom), Graham Bread, Boston Brown Bread and Rusk." The HOT BOSTON BROWN BREAD was available Sunday mornings until 8 o'clock A.M.[62]   The town of Colfax in eastern Washington in 1879 had one bakery that supplied candies and nuts along with baked goods; another was part of the Colfax Restaurant. The same was true in Dayton where the Palace Restaurant featured a bakery that offered an assortment of cakes, bread, and pastry.

Recipes for brown bread, which many bakeries featured, show up in local newspapers and community cookbooks. Though the name suggests that this bread might be similar to today's dark, whole wheat bread, it was somewhat different. Brown bread recipes called for rye meal, Indian meal (corn meal), salt, yeast, and molasses. In the middle of the nineteenth century, cooks replaced yeast with baking soda or baking powder and steamed rather than baked the dough. Because brown bread frequently accompanied baked beans, a Boston favorite, it eventually acquired the name Boston Brown Bread.[63] Graham bread recipes are closer to what we think of today as brown bread—a baked bread using more whole wheat than white flour.

Homemakers who still preferred to bake their own bread rather than patronize the local businesses may have followed the brown bread recipe that appeared in *The Washington Standard*, June 1872, or the Boston Brown Bread recipe from *A Feast of Good Things*, written by the ladies of the First Presbyterian Church in Spokane in 1895. Written twenty-three years apart, the recipes are quite similar. Both use baking soda, a mixture of flours, and sour milk. I have included two versions to show that some popular recipes remained the same for long periods of time. Also by this time flour and other grains were no longer scarce items.

> *Brown Bread*—Two cups of corn meal, one cup of flour, two cups sour milk, two teaspoonfuls soda, one-half cup molasses, one teaspoonful salt. Steam two hours, then bake one-half hour. Serve hot.[64]

> *Boston Brown Bread*—One and one-half cups corn meal, one and one-half cups graham or rye flour, one cup New Orleans molasses, one cup sour milk, one cup sweet milk, one teaspoonful salt, two small teaspoonfuls soda dissolved in a little hot water. Steam three hours in a covered pudding mold.[65]

No doubt by the end of the nineteenth century some people looked back nostalgically to the time when every loaf of bread came from a home hearth or oven. But perhaps those who longed for fresh bread did not recall the damp empty flour bins, weak yeast, and too-hot ovens which made baking a chore. What is more, the first pioneers did not have a choice. They either baked bread or went without. Later residents not only had the luxury of shopping at stores that carried full barrels of locally milled flour, they were also able to purchase fresh baked bread from bakeries. Knowing that one had a choice and that all necessary ingredients were on hand surely added to the pleasure associated with baking a loaf of bread.

Chapter Five
Improvising in the Kitchen

Provisions were laid in once a year and were brought from The Dalles, Oregon....Bacon and hams were not always procurable....I ate enough rabbit then to last me the rest of my life.

Mrs. Austin Mires, Kittitas County[1]

SHOPPING IN PIONEER TIMES involved miles of travel along muddy roads that were little more than trails. A trip in 1847 from Ford's Prairie (near Centralia) to Fort Vancouver, 70 miles, meant going "first by oxen to the Hudson's Bay Post at the [Cowlitz] Landing [Toledo], then by canoe down the Cowlitz and up to the Fort."[2] East of the mountains, families living in Pine City, Washington, spent two days on the road when they traveled to Colfax for provisions.[3] Governor Isaac Stevens specifically referred to the urgent need for roads in his first message to the territorial legislature in 1854.

Almost all early pioneers suffered to some extent from shortages of food. In certain localities when settlers shopped they encountered empty shelves or such high prices that they could purchase only limited amounts of supplies. Kitchens often lacked salt and sugar and fresh produce as well as flour. "I suppose your cellar will be stocked with winter apples, but if they were from $5.00 to $12.00 per bushel, perhaps you would think as we do that you could not afford to buy," Catharine Blaine wrote to her family in New York in December 1856.[4] Fortunately for Catharine and David Blaine someone heard of their duress and left "a basket with about three pecks of excellent apples....A Christmas present from someone, I suppose," expressed a joyous wife. And fortunately for the Michael Luarks "Mrs. Borst sent the family a Christmas present of sweetcakes and apples."[5] Others did not have such obliging neighbors and made do with the ever dependable dried apples in their holiday pies.

At one time or another in households throughout the Northwest, the barrels, bags, and boxes that held flour, salt, butter, fresh fruits and vegetables, fresh beef and pork, coffee and sugar stood empty. Diaries and letters are filled with references to hardships experienced during the first years of settlement.

Being miles away from established markets at Fort Vancouver, Oregon City, or The Dalles caused much of the problem. But distance was not the only culprit. Other events contributed to the scarcity of kitchen supplies. From the mid-1840s to the mid-1850s when large numbers of emigrants arrived in the Northwest, and before country stores became common sights in smaller communities, most prepared or processed food had to be imported from the States and foreign ports. Even at Fort Vancouver, where the Hudson's Bay Company's expansive agricultural operations included a wide variety of grains, fruits, and vegetables, vast amounts of staples such as coffee, cocoa, tea, dried fruit, oil, pepper, sugar, and vinegar arrived from London.[6] As late as 1861, *The Morning Oregonian* printed separate lists for domestic produce and foreign groceries in its "Prices Current" column. Salt, sugar, syrup, raisins, tea, and currants came under the foreign list.

When merchants had goods to sell, shelves might be stocked with Boston crushed sugar in barrels, Carolina rice, China sugar, Peruvian sugar, Liverpool salt, Sandwich Island syrup, and Chile peaches. In isolated places steamers conveyed goods from larger ports and established farms to outlying communities. Henry Roeder, one of the first settlers in Whatcom County, built his own schooner-rigged scow to carry goods to wilderness homes. Typical entries in his Record Book, 1856-57 are "Mr. Lysle sends for potatoes, ($5.00) Mrs. Roberts sends for flour wheat ($9.50)." "By 2 gal milk, by vegetebels, by 12 bushel potatoes."[7] "They [Whidbey Island pioneers] bought flour...and corn meal for eight dollars from a vessel that is anchored there [Port Townsend]," Rebecca Ebey noted in her diary.[8]

Consumers and merchants had little control over the source of production. A bad economy in Boston caused factories to produce less, which could decrease or delay the number of ships carrying goods. This in turn might mean that vessels only stopped at ports where they expected to do large amounts of business. In 1852-53, when the census showed that only 170 persons lived in King County, Arthur Denny noted that "few vessels visited the Sound for several months, and as a consequence it was a time of great scarcity, amounting almost to distress."[9] The settlers, anxiously waiting for pork and butter coming from around Cape Horn, flour from Chile, and sugar in mats from China, were not happy.

☞ NOTICE. ☜

PHILIP KEACH begs leave to inform his friends and the public generally, that he has constantly on hand at his NEW STORE in Steilacoom City, the following named articles:

Flour,	Dried Apples,
Pilot Bread,	Honey,
Pork,	Alspice,
Cheese,	Pepper,
Beans,	Ginger,
Butter,	Saleratus,
Sugar,	Candy,
Coffee,	Raisins,
Tea,	Sardines,
Tobacco,	Axes, broad and narrow,
Pipes,	Chisels,
Cigars,	Locks,
Knives and forks,	Hatchets claw,

And a variety of Dry Goods, such as Pants, Vests, Shirts, Boots and shoes, Hats and Caps, Prints, Sheeting, French Muslin, Ribbons, Silks, Window curtains, &c., &c., which he will sell as cheap as any other store North of the Columbia River.

PHILIP KEACH.

Steilacoom City, April 20, 1853.   33tf

EX BARK "SARAH WARREN."

JUST RECEIVED, another lot of New Goods, such as Sugar, Molasses, Vinegar, Hams, Teas, Tobacco, Rice, Pie Fruits, Pickles, Fancy crackers in tins, Pilot Bread, Table Salt, Boots, Shoes, Brogans, Slippers, Garden Seeds, Grind-stones, Nails, Rope, Cook Stoves, Medicines, Stationery, Log and Ox Chains, Liquors, &c., at store of Kendall Co., by

JOS. CUSHMAN.

Olympia, April 9, '53.   31tf

Merchants brought basic food supplies, dishes, and stoves to settlers in the Pacific Northwest. *The Columbian, Olympia, May 21, 1853.*

Though enterprising merchants quickly set up shop to sell goods to eager consumers, businessmen—even in a good economy—never knew for certain if ordered stocks would appear. Much could go wrong when merchandise came in by ships plowing waters from the Eastern states to Puget Sound or up the coast from California. Orders got mixed up or lost, storms blew vessels off course, and poorly crated goods arrived damaged. On the local scene gardens failed to produce, damp weather caused wheat to sprout, and butter and cheese destined for trade turned sour. In the harsh winter of 1862 freezing temperatures killed thousands of cows and pigs causing prices to soar. "When pork was killed in the fall it sold for 4¢ a pound; it is already 25¢ [February] and the prospects are that it may be 50¢," Catharine Blaine wrote her family.[10]

Populations grew so quickly, merchants had difficulty determining the amount of goods to order. Regulating supply and demand in such a quirky, fluctuating economy made opening a store a risky enterprise. Advertisements in territorial newspapers showed a steady turnover in the business community. Merchants closed up shop during a down market, eliminating a source of supplies. "The undersigned were compelled to box up their goods and suspend for a time, but are now pleased to notify their good patrons, that they are now reopening," J.D. & W.C. Holman wrote in a notice to the Oregon City *Oregon Spectator* on June 27, 1850.

Others complained that "the best families in the country are eating their meals and drinking their tea and coffee—when our merchants can offer it to them—from tin plates and cups. Many articles...are not to be purchased in the country."[11] "So many people have come into Oregon during the last six months that provisions are very scarce and very high, in fact there is scarcely anything to eat in the country," lamented Thornton McElroy in 1853.[12]

Trying to help, and wanting to encourage settlement in Oregon Territory, a writer for the *Oregon Spectator* on December 13, 1849 urged merchants to stock a "*good assortment* of dry goods and groceries....We grant there is a large AMT. of merchandise on hand but we also assert *there is not a good assortment* of dry goods and groceries...stoves of all sorts, tin ware...are in great demand. If there is no salt brought in there will soon be none to be had." Checking the current price list of goods for that day shows "salt pr. bush (almost none); salaratus, (none)." Six months later advertisements indicate that ample supplies of coarse Liverpool and fine table salt had finally reached Oregon Territory. Both local and national economics determined the supply and price of salt and other commodities, and businessmen complained that certain companies created a monopoly on goods.

Changing conditions made planning difficult for pioneers. One good year did not indicate that there would be an end of shortages. Nor did a good year for one family mean that everyone in the region had a full larder. Though in 1852 Abigail Malik wrote her daughter that she had baked "green Apl pie And Mince pies and Custard pies And Cakes of difrent kindes...[and] had "plentey of Butter And Milk And...plentey Shougar Laid in For Winter This Year Two, And Salt," other settlers were happy to have a piece of bread.[13] "Improvements are getting along in our town and country, about *as well as could reasonably be expected* [italics added] of as new a place as that of Olympia," reported *The Columbian* on October 23, 1852.

A wet spring caused vegetable prices to soar. An unseasonable freeze, like that in 1861-62, killed cattle. The Blaines found ample food in 1854, but complained of higher prices in 1855. The Boatmans saw 1855 as a year of improvement. Both families came to Washington Territory in 1853.

> It is much cheaper living now than when we came. Indeed, provisions are not so much higher than with you. The last flour we got we paid but $12.00 a barrel, potatoes will hardly bring 50 cents or even 25 cents a bushel, and other vegetables alike cheap. Beef, pork and such things that are imported are still up, but fresh beef sells from 8 to 18 cents per pound. There is no doubt but that by another year there will be nearly as much of everything produced here as will be required for the support of the inhabitants. There has been almost enough wheat this year.
> —Catharine Blaine, October 30, 1854.

> Prices are coming up so as to make living very expensive. Flour is up to $14.00, butter 75 cents...and vegetables will now be scarce and high.
> —Catharine Blaine, February 5, 1855[14]

> Notwithstanding all the hardships and privations of this life, I was becoming satisfied and contented. In the Spring of '55 I managed to get grain and vegetables enough to do us the coming year. We were nearly all living on potatoes straight, with pea or wheat coffee, occasionally a sack of flour for a change. As the summer advanced our little crops matured and when harvest came, we were all surprised at the large yield that we had on our little patches of ground. We got our stuff all harvested and most of [it] thrashed and put away in good shape.
> —Willis Boatman, 1855[15]

Until settlers grew sufficient amounts of fruits and vegetables and butchered their own swine and steers, until they had stores of preserved and pickled foods for use during the dark winter days when gardens lay dormant, and until grist mills had large amounts of local wheat to grind, everyone either relied on whatever provisions merchants delivered to the Northwest, hunted and gathered their own edibles—or did without.

While men plowed the land and waited for a bountiful harvest and vessels laden with goods, women figured out how to stretch available foods and adapt and substitute ingredients. In a land teeming with wild game, rivers overflowing with fish, and forests covered with wild berries, few starved. But in order to have familiar meals that would please their family, cooks had to be resourceful. For some it might be making bread with corn-meal instead of flour; others beat molasses instead of sugar into cake batter, or parched bran rather than coffee beans. But whatever the circumstance, the ability to adapt in an unfamiliar land made daily living easier.

Savory Substitutions

Riley Ticknor, grandson of pioneers Sidney and Nancy Ford, did not taste sugar until he was a grown man.[16] Preston Hamilton and Lavina Flora Hamilton "had no sugar for weeks at a time."[17] When neither fruit and/or sugar could be fetched from the pantry, vinegar masqueraded as lemons, molasses stood in for sugar and fruit, and cooked beans took the place of pumpkin or squash in pies. To make the bean pie, a Yankee invention, "the beans were boiled and the hulls removed in a sieve, [then] the same recipe was followed as for pumpkin pie." The bean pie turned out to be "a delicacy indeed," according to Grace Wall, a Centralia pioneer.[18]

Baked beans did not need sugar to taste good; molasses along with salt pork transformed the humble bean into a favorite Sunday dish:

> The beans were soaked over Friday night and boiled on Saturday morning until when one took some in a spoon and blew on them the shells would split. They were put into the big, black-encrusted bean pot— covered layer for layer with salt pork and then inundated with molasses—and baked the rest of Saturday and until noon Sunday.[19]

Because dried beans kept well they were one of the easiest foods to transport long distances. They were also cheap. Generally white beans seemed to be the variety offered for sale, but occasionally an advertisement stated "Chili and American beans"—presumably the red or brown beans that are native to the Americas and Mexico.[20] The Dements, who lived in

Coos County, Oregon, recalled that the chili beans "were very small...and took a half a day to cook."[21]

Realizing the low cost to supply beans for a fund-raising dinner in Whatcom County in the 1880s, Ella Higginson volunteered to bake a dollar's worth. However, she had not figured the quantity of beans that could be bought for a dollar. "Determined to keep her promise, she scrubbed all her pans and kettles, and put all the beans to soak overnight....The next morning the beans were piled a foot deep everywhere around the table....She baked beans for the library for three days and three nights."[22]

> *Baked Beans*—One quart beans, parboil in clear water, drain, place in bake pan, add two tablespoons molasses, one pound pork, one-half teaspoon mustard, teaspoon sugar, salt to taste. bake in oven all day. Keep covered with water and a tight lid. This dish is all the better for being warmed over.[23]

Growing dried beans requires dry, hot days. It takes several months for tender seeds enclosed in young, green pods to grow plump, and for the pods to wrinkle and wither. Shelling them added another time-consuming chore for overworked settlers living in the drier parts of Oregon Territory. Bill Kindt described a method used by Spencer Butte, Oregon, pioneers:

> We raised all our dry beans. Thrashed them out....We had a big square box that was six or eight feet high and about ten long. We'd hit the beans against the side to knock them out—or beat them with a pitchfork. Then dad had a little fanning mill which he used to clean the grain—various size screens and stuff. We'd run the beans through there to get the chaff out. If you didn't have a fanning mill, then you needed a windy day. You'd spread a tarp or an old blanket outside where there was a good wind blowing. Then you'd take a dishpan or tub full of beans up a stepladder on the windward side of the tarp and slowly pour the beans onto the tarp. The wind would carry the chaff beyond the tarp, while the beans dropped nearly straight down. After a couple of repetitions only the heaviest sections of stem remained to be picked out by the cook, plus any pebbles or clods of dirt which were heavy enough to fall with the beans.[24]

Nineteenth-century families generally considered pies a crucial part of every meal. Homemakers devised countless methods to insure that their families did not miss this American favorite. One creative cook who had neither molasses nor fruit followed old-time recipes and sweetened wild sorrel (greens) with "the syrup called sorghum," and placed it in a pie crust as a filling. She also mixed wild plums with soda, "to take off the worse of the sour taste."[25] Shrewd cooks convinced young and old that a sweet, sticky molasses pie satisfied a sweet tooth as well as a fresh fruit or berry pie sweetened with common sugar. To stretch the little sugar she had, one cook prepared half of her cherry pie with sugar and half without, hoping her guests would mix the two halves and think it all sweet.[26]

Territorial cooks who followed the recipe for molasses pie printed in *The Washington Standard* on July 11, 1874 probably substituted lemon extract or lemon syrup for fresh lemon because citrus fruits were not regularly stocked items. Both molasses and lemon pie developed from the eighteenth-century English "Transparent Pudding" concept, that is a baked pudding using butter, eggs, and sugar.[27] Vinegar pie remained in vogue well into the twentieth century. The one listed here is from a 1910 Spokane cookbook:

> *Molasses Pie*—One and one-half cups of molasses, one half cup vinegar, one egg, two tablespoons of flour, one cup raisins, season with lemon or nut meg; this makes two pies; bake with two crusts.

> *Vinegar Pie*—One cup sugar, four tablespoons good vinegar, one tablespoon lemon extract, one cup hot water, four tablespoonfuls flour. Sift flour and sugar together, add vinegar and egg then the hot water, cook and fill a baked crust and frost with the whites.[28]

Molasses, a by-product of sugar refining, made a cheap sweetener and sugar substitute in the nineteenth century. Its strength and taste depended on the refinery and type of sugar cane. Stored in barrels, molasses added a discernible odor to pioneer kitchens. Pitchers holding smaller amounts often sat on the table or kitchen shelf.

Dried fruit deserves the award for the most pervasive fresh fruit substitute to mingle and mix with sugar and spices. Apples headed the list but pioneers could purchase peaches, pumpkin, currants, cherries, and raisins. The descriptive adjective before a dried apple dish depended on how often it appeared on the menu. Mrs. P.H. Schnebly, a Kittitas County pioneer, remembered them fondly. "The prize dish was mother's apple dumplings. Our guest thought they were made from fresh apples, but at that time no one thought apples could grow here. Mother made those delicious dumplings from dried apples Father brought from The Dalles in the spring."[29] Mrs. Lysle of Bellingham felt differently. Perhaps she had prepared a few too many dried apple pies:

> Accordingly, in two canoes lashed together, they brought all their earthly possessions with household goods. Among these were a keg of candles and a keg of dried apples. Coming around an island a rough sea tipped

the overloaded canoes, and Mr. Lysle, thinking only of the safety of the babies, pitched overboard the keg of candles. Mrs. Lysle grieved for months over their loss, bewailing the chance that it had not been the apples that were cast away.[30]

Dried fruit had to be soaked in water and stewed before using. Cookery writers advised adding sugar when stewing and then seasoning with lemon. Recipes in *The Washington Standard* added dried apples to dried peaches to improve the peaches, and warned to use only first-class dried apples for pies. The recipe writer considered the "not so good ones" tolerable for jelly.

> *Dried Apples*—Take nice apples, soak them over night in rather more than enough water to cover them; In the morning boil them till soft, then add about as much sugar in bulk as there was of the apples before soaking, and cook until they look clear; season with lemon, or add a few raisins when you do the sugar.
>
> *For Pies*—Strain through a colander, sweeten, season with lemon and bake with two crusts.[31]

David Beatty tells how free wild honey substituted for sugar: "As sugar was scarce and very expensive—we used wild honey as the preservative. Honey bee trees were frequently located and it was one of the sports of the time to cut one down and secure the sweets stored in the hollow trunk."[32] To assist the bees to locate near their homes, pioneers fashioned "bee trees," crude beehives, by digging debris from hollow trees and covering the stumps with a rain-tight roof. This made a compact home for a swarm of wild bees.

In eastern Oregon around Klamath Falls and Sisters, the Pruitt Family still carries on the tradition. "Bee hunting is a great part of our family outings," Bob Pruitt, a descendent of pioneers, told me.

The family preferred juniper trees because they "afforded the opportunity to climb the tree or work from the ground, slab out the wood carefully—then after robbing it—place the wood back and wire it up, to use in the future." The honey "is in big slabs of comb," which the Pruitts stored in "five gallon kerosene cans, with the top cut out. . . . At home the family would then cut the top of the comb off—heat the honey and strain it thru flour sacks, tied to a broom handle and each end on a chair, under it a pan to catch the honey. The smell of all this was heavenly. Us kids were forbidden to get close to it for fear of stirring up dust or a stray hair getting in the honey."

The Pruitt family marks the trees in the spring with their cattle brand, a turkey track, and robs them in the fall. They use a bee-box, a wooden contraption about one foot long with three compartments, to catch and hold the bees. By following the route of the bees from the box to the tree, they are able to identify the bee tree. "I'll bet there weren't many covered wagons that didn't have a bee box in its belongings," Mr. Pruitt speculated.[33]

According to *The Oregon Statesman* of August 1, 1854, John Davenport tried to bring the first domestic honey bees into the territory. He "returned from a visit to the States and has brought with him a hive of honey bees, an enterprise hitherto supposed impracticable....The hive in which they were confined is of the ordinary size, three sides being made of wire gauze and the fourth of boards." A notice in *The Morning Oregonian*, March 18, 1861 announces that A.J. Biglow of Sacramento, California, has a "few PURE ITALIAN QUEEN BEES to dispose of...and any person fueling an interest in propagating the honey bee...will have a circular sent." The records do not indicate if Mr. Davenport's bees survived the winter or if anyone introduced them to the Italian queens.

Bees that did endure arrived at Steilacoom's dock in 1856, addressed to Ezra Meeker, Washington pioneer, and to a Mr. Knowles in Cowlitz County. Meeker said "that if the bees had landed at his door from mid-air he could scarcely have been more surprised."[34] Later he learned that the shipment came from his old time partner, "Billy" Buck. The two had crossed the plains together in 1852. The Pacific Northwest bee industry sprang from these swarms.[35]

When chickens did not lay eggs and egg baskets stood empty, eggless cakes rose in the oven and eggless puddings puffed up over the fire. Shortages were particularly bad during winter because hens do not lay eggs in dark, cold, unheated places. Until electricity heated hen houses and provided both heat and light, cooks made do with preserved eggs or went without in winter time.

Catharine "makes very good cake without eggs or milk," boasted David Blaine. I like to think that Catharine Blaine's eggless, milkless cake equaled the one found in the *First Methodist Episcopal Church Cookbook*. The Reverend David Blaine was the first minister of that Seattle church. The church published the cookbook years after Blaine mixed her eggless batter, but well into the twentieth century, Washington and Oregon cookbooks included recipes for eggless cakes. Note that there are no oven temperatures or specific instructions for these recipes, both of which appeared in the early 1900s:

Fruit Cake Without Eggs—1 pound fat pork chopped fine; pour over it 1 pint boiling water or coffee, 2 cups molasses, 1 cup sugar, 2 pounds

raisins, 1 pound currants, 2 tablespoons cinnamon, 1 tablespoon nutmeg, 1 tablespoon allspice, 1 teaspoon soda, 8 cups flour.[36]

Eggless Tea Cake—1 cup of sugar creamed with 3 tablespoons butter,
1½ cups flour, 1½ teaspoons baking powder, ½ cup cold English breakfast tea, 1 teaspoonful vanilla; bake and eat while warm.[37]

Even in the summertime, eggs were not too plentiful during the first
years of settlement. Acquiring a sizable chicken population took time. Cooks
did not waste eggs. Smart cooks added them to the batter, "after all the
other ingredients were thoroughly mixed, two would go as far as three."[38]
Other cookery writers suggested that a "a spoonful of yeast will serve instead of 2 eggs...and two large spoonfuls of snow will supply the place of 1
egg."[39]

Hoping, no doubt, to be helpful to harassed housewives trying to
make puddings without eggs, *The Territorial Republican* on June 7, 1869
printed a recipe that "is not generally known, and will not perhaps be
credited, that boiled carrots, when properly prepared, form an admirable
succedaneum [substitute] in the making of puddings."

> *Carrots A Substitute For Eggs In Puddings*—They [carrots] must, for
> this purpose, be well boiled and mashed, and afterwards passed through
> a coarse cloth, or horsehair sieve. A pudding composed partly of the
> above material will be found to be considerable lighter than if the
> same had been made with eggs, and will impart a far more grateful
> and agreeable flavor.

Actually the recipe was generally known. Some type of carrot pudding
recipe appears in just about every nineteenth- and early twentieth-century
cookbook. Some of the recipes, however, called for eggs.

Before the John Jackson family acquired a stove, Jackson considered a
boiled English pudding the dessert of choice. "The raw mixture was tied in
a muslin cloth and boiled in an iron kettle."[40] It would be nice to know if
the Jacksons followed the traditional English plum pudding recipe that
contains eggs or used substitutes. And did Mrs. Jackson abandon her
husband's favorite dessert when he installed a cook stove? In 1904, the
North Seattle Churches printed a recipe for plum pudding without eggs.
Plum puddings usually had raisins or currants, not plums; the word plum
once meant dried fruit as well as fresh prunes.

> *Plum Pudding*—One cup molasses, one cup suet, chopped fine, one
> cup sweet milk, one cup currants and raisins, three cups flour, one
> teaspoon soda, one teaspoon salt, two-thirds teaspoon each of nutmeg,

cloves and cinnamon. Steam, or boil, in pudding boiler three hours. Eat with pudding sauce.[41]

A great many recipes exist for boiled and baked puddings; they have been popular for centuries. The name derives from the old French *boudin,* or sausage, which the earliest ones resembled. By the nineteenth century puddings most likely contained bread, fruit, vegetables, eggs, milk, and seasonings encased in dough or a crust and appeared at the end of the meal as dessert. Previously, puddings accompanied the main course. Baked puddings resembled pies and the names became interchangeable. Sarah Hale wrote that "many of the directions for making pastry apply also to the preparation of puddings."[42] Other writers said puddings tasted cake-like.

Some pioneers mention making a "duff," a slang name for puddings. That name comes from northern England, where sailors considered it a special Sunday treat. Historians believe they were the ones to change the original word "dough," pronounced to rhyme with "enough," into duff. Traditional recipes called for a mixture of flour, shortening, saleratus, dried fruit, and water placed in a cloth bag and steamed for several hours.

No doubt savoring the taste of her dinner, Rebecca Ebey confided to her diary, "I made a duff for our dinner the first I ever made right and it was good."[43] Ebey unfortunately left no clues to the ingredients she used. Was it a sweet plum duff made with raisins or a savory one that contained vegetables? Josephine County, Oregon, pioneers do recall making duffs with leftover potatoes, stale bread, onions, fat, and seasoning. Ingredients and directions in the following recipes hint at how to make a pudding. Both are made without eggs. Poverty pudding, sometimes called beggars' pudding, has been popular since colonial times. Frugal housewives found this recipe ideal for using up stale bread and cake.

> *Poverty Pudding*—Soak your bread in milk the night before using; when ready, butter your pudding dish, and place in a layer of the bread. Have a dozen apples pared and sliced, and place a layer of apples on the bread, another layer of bread, then of apples, and so on, till your dish is filled; let the last layer be bread, and bake it an hour. To be eaten with sauce.[44]

> *Huckleberry Pudding*—One pint of best Orleans molasses; a pinch of salt; one teaspoonful cloves, and one of cinnamon; one of soda dissolved in a teacupful of sweet milk; flour enough to make it the consistency of pound-cake; one quart of berries; boil two and a half hours in a pudding-mould. Eat with cream and sugar, or pudding-sauce.[45]

When hot summers ripened tomatoes, creative homemakers used the tasty fruit as a flavoring for a variety of dishes. In Kittitas County,

homemakers preserved yellow pear tomatoes in sugar, dried them and believed "they were almost as good as figs."[46] Receiving a "dish of [the] luscious yellow grape tomatoes," *The North-West* of Port Townsend on October
4, 1860 shared the recipe with its readers:

> *Tomato Figs*—Growing like grapes and about the same size, they may
> be readily hung up in some dry place until they wilt, when by packing
> in sugar, an article fully equal to the best fig is produced and is deemed
> a luxury even by those who cannot bear them subjected to any other
> curative process.

Other newspaper editors, no doubt encouraged by their wives' culinary skills, liked the idea of turning tomatoes into figs. This recipe from
The Washington Standard, October 29, 1870, is more detailed than the one
printed in *The North-West*, but readers still have to figure out how much
sugar to add:

> *Tomato Figs*—Collect a lot of ripe tomatoes about one inch in diam-
> eter, skin and stew them in the usual manner; when done lay them on
> dishes, flatten them slightly, and spread over them light layer pulver-
> ized white or best brown sugar; expose them to a summer's sun, or
> place them in a drying house; when as dry as fresh figs, pack in old fig
> or small boxes, with sugar between each layer. If properly managed the
> difference cannot be detected from the veritable article.

Actually, settlers brought this idea with them across the plains. Tomato figs had been used as an emergency food and diet supplement in the
Middle Atlantic states since the 1840s. A Mrs. Steiger of Washington, D.C.,
tried unsuccessfully to obtain a patent for her recipe, but had to be satisfied with seeing it published in the *House-Keeper's Almanac* for 1846. Cookery writers copied and adapted Mrs. Steiger's original recipe without shame.[47]
    The Fourth Plain epicures also boiled ripe tomatoes with sugar, fla-
vored them with honey, and served the sauce as a topping for hot cakes.
The clever women made a seasoning mixture for stews out of green tomatoes, salt, pepper, and cloves, and fooled their husbands into thinking that
green tomato mincemeat pie actually contained real meat.[48] The tomato
seasoning mixture is an adaptation of an old recipe called "Tomata Marmalade," first published in Mary Randolph's *Virginia House-wife*, 1824.

> *Tomata Marmalade*—Gather full grown tomatas while quite green,
> take out the stems and stew them till soft, rub them through a siev,
> put the pulp on the fire seasoned highly with pepper, salt, and pounded
> cloves; add some garlic, and stew together till thick; it keeps well, and
> is excellent for seasoning gravies, &c.&c.[49]

Everyone loved mincemeat. Receiving a box of mincemeat as a Christmas present, Rebecca Ebey happily made "mince meat pies for dinner and they were excellent."[50] When housewives procured the proper ingredients they filled the mincemeat jar with cooked, chopped meat, suet, apples, raisins, currants, citron (citrus fruit similar to lemon), cinnamon, nutmeg, sugar, wine and/or brandy, and let the mixture sit for several months while flavors developed. It has been said that some folks added so much brandy to the mincemeat jar that they "didn't know whether the meat was spoiled or not!"[51] Mincemeat can be made from diverse combinations of meat, fruit, and sweetenings and has been popular since medieval times.

> *Family Mince Pies*—Boil 3 lbs. of lean beef till tender, and when cold, chop it fine. Chop 2 lbs. of clear beef suet and mix with meat, sprinkling in a table-spoonful of salt. Pare, core, and chop fine, 6 lbs. of good apples; stone 4 lbs. of raisins and chop them; wash and dry 2 lbs. of currants; and mix them all well with the meat. Season with powdered cinnamon, 1 spoonful, a powdered nutmeg, a little mace, and a few cloves pounded, and 1 lb. of brown sugar. Add a quart of Madeira wine, and 8 oz. of citron, cut into small bits. This mixture, put down in a stone jar and closely covered will keep several weeks. It makes a rich pie for Thanksgiving and Christmas.[52]

Besides green tomatoes masking as beef, other substituted ingredients ended up in the mincemeat jar. George Anderson remembered that as a boy his family could not find beef so he "chopped deer meat to fill the twenty-four gallon mincemeat jar."[53] Those opposed to alcohol used sweet cider in place of brandy. *Washington Women's Cookbook* included a recipe for summer mincemeat made with green tomatoes. Note that the ingredient list calls for lemons, but the directions mention vinegar. Most probably that is what pioneer women used.

> *Summer Mince Meat*
> 1 peck green tomatoes
> 2 tablespoons cinnamon
> 2 pounds raisins
> 2 tablespoons allspice
> 4 lbs. brown sugar
> Juice of 4 lemons
> 2 cups suet
> Chopped rind 2 lemons
> 1 tablespoon salt
>
> Chop tomatoes and let them drain. Put them in kettle with cold water enough to cover. Let come to a boil. Drain again. Then add suet and

raisins. Cook thoroughly. Add one half cup vinegar and the spices. Cook a little. Can while hot. Makes six quarts.[54]

Other schemes used to enhance the dwindling food supply and transform the humble fare indicate how pioneer cooks adapted and substituted. In Klickitat County, Nelia Binford Fleming's mother added flavor to the flat taste of service (sarvis) berries by cooking them with vinegar and sugar, and the Craigs made sweetening "from the centers of watermelons, crushed and strained and added to the juice from boiled corn cobs."[55]

Unable to purchase oranges, Fourth Plain housewives made marmalade by boiling carrots in a sugar syrup flavored with ginger. In place of citron they used a dried vegetable mixture made from cooked carrots, molasses, spices, and lemons. A note in the *Daily Pacific Tribune* of April 3, 1869 suggested that dried pie plant (rhubarb) could be used in place of peaches or other dried fruit. And on June 4, 1870 *The Washington Standard* published a recipe that used rice as a substitute for macaroni since "true Italian macaroni cannot often be got in country places, and it is expensive everywhere."

> *Rice A La Maccarona*—Boil rice in water, with salt, twenty minutes, when the rice will be soft and the water boiled away. Then empty into a pudding dish, scattering among it grated cheese, or bits of cheese, and a layer of the same on top; brown it in the oven, and serve warm. The cheese should have a good flavor. It is a most savory relishing dish, and one does not tire of it readily.

Catharine Blaine used samphire, a sea weed, for pickles: "[I]t is excellent, so that without cucumbers we can have very good pickles."[56] She followed a custom initiated by other Northwest visitors. As early as 1792, Joseph Ingraham, captain of the American brigantine *Hope*, a vessel sailing in Puget Sound waters, pickled samphire. Ingraham felt that this would be a cure for scurvy. He said the plant lasted until the ship reached China.[57]

In the spring, just about every family picked wild greens, such as young nettles and lamb's quarters. Before kale, chard, and lettuce poked their leafy skirts up through the garden soil, that's all that cooks had on hand. Describing this spring ritual, Elsie Sutton wrote, "In the spring of the year...wild lettuce would come up and we gathered it to eat. It was a slender-stemmed plant with a dish-like top that was cupped [probably miner's lettuce]....We always got this plant when it was young and my mother would fix shortening, sugar, vinegar and thick cream dressing, heated and then poured over the lettuce...then let it stand to wilt." Lacking sugar and shortening, housewives probably cooked greens in bacon grease or plain water.[58]

Growing tired of plain bacon which appeared on the menu twice a day, Guy Waring, who lived in the Okanogan Valley in the 1880s, created what he thought must be an innovative recipe. It sounds like plain gravy but maybe the fancy name imparted a better flavor to the creation:

> *Heifer's Delight*—I consulted Al Thorp's squaw, who was an excellent hand at preparing food, and learned from her to make what was called in the section "heifer's delight." It was a kind of gravy made by adding a small quantity of flour to bacon grease and cooking it until well browned. Water, or still better milk, was then stirred into the mixture until the gravy was smooth. Then the dish was boiled for two or three minutes and served. It took me some time to learn how to do full justice to "heifer's delight" but in the end most of us found it an agreeable dish.[59]

It Tasted Much Like Coffee

Coffee beans, coffee mills, and coffee pots appear in account books of territorial businesses from the earliest days but pioneers constantly complained about coffee shortages. Often, when they wanted a cup of coffee, parched peas, rye, barley, or bran had to do. "[My] husband came home in great glee, giving me a recipe for fixing bran in such a manner that when cooked it would taste very much like coffee," recalled Mrs. Hunter.[60] Other wives told similar tales. Since colonial times, more often than not, a cup of hot coffee contained a coffee substitute:

> *Bran Coffee*—1 gallon of bran, 2 tablespoons molasses, scalded and parched in the oven until it is somewhat brown and charred. Bran treated this way and cooked the same as coffee provided a very tasty drink for a number of months.[61]

All rejoiced when, instead of parched peas or burnt bran, real mocha or Java coffee beans sizzled on the stove. Lillian Christiansen's mother "would fill a bread pan half full of coffee, slip it into the oven and sit by the stove. She would run her fingers through the coffee to feel if it were the right temperature. When it began to heat through, she stirred it with a spoon. When it was a beautiful shiny brown, she took the pan out of doors and blew the chaff out of it. It was ready to use."[62] Albert Polson's mother carried freshly roasted beans "through the different rooms of the house to deodorize and clarify the air."[63] Whether or not coffee tasted "good to the

RECEIVED PER PACIFIC.

KONA COFFEE!

SAN FRANCISCO GOLDEN SYRUP,
—In kegs and bbls;
E. B. SYRUP, in 5 galls ;
BABBITT'S CREAM TARTAR,
—1 ℔ papers (Warranted Pure);
  "   CARB. SODA,
—1 ℔ papers (Warranted Pure);
  "   SALERATUS,
—1 ℔ papers (Warranted Pure);
SAL SODA, for Washing;

KEROSENE, in 5 galls and bbls.

Crushed Sugar and Teas.
TABLE WINE, VINEGAR AND SPICES'
For sale by   **JOHN WILSON,**
127, *Front street.*
Portland, February 13, 1863.   dtf

Coffee has always been welcome in the Pacific Northwest. *Daily Oregonian, February 12, 1863.*

last drop," everyone savored the aroma of freshly roasted beans. "I can smell it yet," is a common refrain in the pioneer reminiscences. The hand-held coffee grinder with a drawer to catch freshly ground coffee, or the larger grinder attached to a wall, decorated and enhanced Pacific Northwest pioneer homes.

Coffee merchants experimented with ground coffee and tried to persuade coffee drinkers that its taste equaled a cup brewed from fresh beans. "Purchasers should always inquire for the Fresh Ground Java...put up at the Steam, Coffee and Spice Mills....We manufacture the following articles [Chartres, Java and Rio Coffee], in accordance with the most recent scientific process known," a Portland merchant announced in 1866.[64] "Pure, Unadulterated AND FRESH GROUND COFFEE without peas and things into it," proclaimed a grocery advertisement in *The Puget Sound Dispatch* on October 10, 1872.

Yet everyone who wrote about brewing coffee emphasized that they used the green coffee beans which came in large forty to fifty pound sacks. The names of the beans such as Rio or Java indicated the place of origin. People preferred to roast and then grind their own beans because manufacturers had not figured out how to properly seal the flavor into roasted beans.

The credit for good pre-roasted beans goes to Arbuckle Brothers, whose offices were in Pittsburgh, Pennsylvania. In 1869 the company patented a method of sealing in the flavor by coating coffee beans with a mixture of egg white and sugar. By continually improving the preserving method and developing unique marketing techniques, Arbuckle's coffee occupied an honored place in pioneer kitchens.[65] An experiment by Elof Norman, who lived in Monte Cristo, Washington, tells why:

> I was curious to see the whole coffee beans, which were new to me. Papa had bought two one-pound bags. One bag was Arbuckle's brand and the other was Lion's Head. Lion's Head beans were cheaper, but the bag had some shriveled up and half green beans in it, so after that we only bought the Arbuckle brand.[66]

In 1878 Caleb Chase and James Sanborn (Chase and Sanborn) produced the first ground coffee put up in a tin can instead of a bag, and in 1898 vacuum cans were introduced. To enhance the coffee and reduce the amount of sediment, cookery writers suggested adding the "white and crushed shell of an egg [after it brewed]. Let stand ten minutes, and it [coffee] will be bright and clear as water.[67]

*   *   *

Discerning if every pioneer followed these suggestions for adapting and substituting ingredients and for how long is impossible. Telling the tales of early foodways from evidence based on scattered sources from different years does not give the complete picture. Daily diaries for every household do not exist and the ones on record do not say if shortages lasted for one month or a year.

What we can say is that decisions about what to cook depended on what foods sat on the shelf or grew in the garden, as well as the cook's culinary experience. A goodly number of hints and suggestions, such as making pies with dried fruit and cakes without eggs, turn up again and again, so these almost certainly were popular ways to cook. The "Tomato into Fig" recipe is repeated in several newspaper "Farm and Home" columns, and just about everyone recalls making bran or barley coffee. Determined to provide suitable meals, Northwest homemakers adapted and substituted in the same ways that homemakers did in other frontier communities.

Chapter Six
Dried, Preserved, and Pickled

TODAY WE DRY APPLES, pickle green beans, and preserve fruit because we want to try out a new dehydrator, use up strawberries left over from family outings to a U-pick farm, or think "made-at-home" tastes better than store-bought. Before the proliferation of canned goods, electric refrigerators, and efficient transportation systems, women pickled and preserved food so that it did not spoil, and because it provided nourishing meals for their families during winter. Prudent homemakers knew the importance of spending hot summer days washing fruit, chopping and grating mounds of cabbages for sauerkraut, and pickling cucumbers and green beans.

The Fourth Plain women who seasoned tomatoes so they tasted like figs did not want to create a new cuisine: they were just being practical. Catharine Blaine dried, preserved, and pickled peaches so that the surplus would not be wasted and to spice up meals when fresh foods disappeared from the market.[1] The Northwest pioneer homemaker, like legions of women before her, spent numerous hours preparing food for future meals. She knew she had been successful if, by late fall, the buttery or cooling room burgeoned with crocks of pickled foods, dried ears of corn, and cans and/or jars of relishes and preserves. One suspects that homemakers viewed the first pink blush on the peaches or the deepening green of a slender cucumber with mixed emotions.

To supply much of the food to be stored, pioneers, even those who did not plan on becoming farmers, plowed, planted, cultivated, and harvested gardens. "Our garden is doing as well as we expect....We shall get a few cucumbers for pickles, a little green corn, and if the vines bear well a great many tomatoes, besides potatoes, beets, onions, and cabbages," Blaine, a minister's wife, wrote on August 5, 1854.[2] "I have 75 apple trees, 12 pears, 10 cherries, 16 plums and a large amount of currants—several varieties raspberries and strawberries. We get from our little orchard all the apples we can use this winter," bragged urban dweller Sarah McElroy in 1861.[3]

Tales of three- to four-pound potatoes and a climate so mild that vegetables could remain in the ground throughout the winter, persuaded families to settle and farm in the western portion of the Pacific Northwest. Travel guides and newspaper editors, hoping to convince emigrants to settle in a particular area, frequently printed such stories: "C.P. Stone, Esq. brought up with him from Port Madison...a stalk on which were blossoms and also pods containing peas....Can we offer a better proof of the mildness of our winters than the above? Green peas grown in the open air in the month of January."[4]

Indeed, many families planted two gardens: a spring garden for early peas, lettuce, and radishes, and a later and larger one for potatoes, squash, dry beans, parsnips, and cabbages, food that would be stored for winter use. At Fourth Plain people called the smaller garden "Maw's garden." In other localities, people referred to it as the spring or kitchen garden.[5]

On the whole, the fertile soil on the west side of the Cascade mountains, particularly in the Willamette Valley and the coastal areas of Puget Sound where the emigrants first settled, yielded sizable crops. But settlers did have to spend hours clearing land covered with cedars and firs, numerous varieties of viburnum, and masses of wild flowers. In other places plows overturned "stone patches, which, it was sometimes said with grim humor that the stones hatched, and under favorable climatic conditions many would grow where one appeared before."[6]

"Grubbing out stumps" frequently appeared as an entry in emigrant diaries. Naturally, settlers tried to choose land that had the least amount of tall timber or required the least labor to make it usable. But that became increasingly difficult as more people moved into the Northwest. In describing land around Grand Mound in Thurston County in 1860, Samuel James noted:

> Some of the country is very sandy, and some is very gravelly, but the greater part, I believe, is like that which I have just described, with a good depth of mould over the top of it. The natural growth of timber and bushes is very large and dense, and there is not a great extent of prairie or natural grassland; there are, however, a great many large tracts where the big timber was formerly destroyed by fire, which are now partly clear and partly covered with a young growth of fir, cypress, alder, willow, and bushes of diverse kind...where a man could cut down a quarter of an acre in a day, and where the soil is very rich.[7]

To get rid of the trees quickly, settlers burned them down by boring holes near the base of the trunk and inserting hot coals. The stumps usually burned out underground, except for cedar, which had to be dug out. Dr. Thomas White observed in 1852 that "you may burn down the largest of them in a short time, & in the same way burn them entirely up without moving any part of them."[8]

Though fires caused by flying sparks commonly occurred, no one in that era seemed to worry about the environment. They did, however, complain about hard work:

> Making gardens here is a different thing from what it is with you where the ground is all cleared off nicely. Here are stumps, roots, bushes, and plenty of such things to be cleared away. We have had his fires burning for two weeks in the yard to burn up the stuff.
> —Catharine Blaine, March 7, 1854[9]

> My husband would rise early and get the breakfast, make a big fire and go out to his clearing for a crop, for on that depended our success. It was raining much of the time and it was hard work to get the fire started on the wet ground to burn green brush and it was nearly noon before one could make much progress...every moonlight evening he would work until midnight and then the fires would hold until morning.
> —Mary Hayden, 1850[10]

> Nearly all of the meadowland (along the Okanogan River) was covered with brush and it was a Herculean task to clear it. There were no bulldozers then. It was all handwork with an axe, a pick and shovel and brushhook and fire. The men would work on the brush in the winter time and burn it in the spring. For years every spring the valley would be filled with smoke from the burning brush.
> —Margaret Bottomly, early 1900s[11]

Besides fighting back encroaching forests, gardeners had to constantly be on alert for gophers, rabbits, squirrels, cougars, deer, bears, and pesky birds. On both sides of the mountains, these critters created a nuisance. "After the gophers and squirrels had feasted upon them [nuts and seeds], and our garden bid fair to produce a crop of sorrel, in the place of vegetables, I began to fear this spot was not the 'ideal home,'" lamented Judson.[12] "In the fall of 1883, I set out thirteen fruit trees. The next spring they were all eaten up by the gophers....I also planted some beans and peas, and everything did well except the ground squirrels ate them up," related Mrs. Theresa Beiler, who lived near Spokane.[13]

Pioneers added valuable organic matter to the soil by turning under unwanted vegetation that grew on the land. "Mr. Judson plowed the garden, turning the wild grass under and the gravel on top, without fertilizing, for we had nothing to fertilize with," noted Phoebe Judson.[14] Early attempts at farming in Klickitat County in 1860, however, were disastrous because "the first settlers did not as yet understand the soil and climate.... It was only after some years of experimenting that they learned the lands best suited to the different crops, and for the first years even the vegetables they used were brought to the valley on pack horses."[15]

Planning gardens began early. A warm winter day reminded farmers and homemakers to check seed supplies and begin planting early crops. Two sets of diary notations, written thirty years apart, illustrate the continued importance of home gardens. Rebecca Ebey's diary entries are from 1853 when there were few settlers and few supplies on Whidbey Island; Sarah McElroy lived in a large home in Olympia, an urban area with established businesses, and penned her entries in the 1880s:

Rebecca Ebey: Whidbey Island, Washington Territory

January 17, 1853: Another beautiful day has dawned upon us. It is so warm and clear that I begin to feel like gardening though it is too soon for some vegetables.

January 20: I have Sam [hired help], digging onion beds.

January 26: The children finished setting out Some fine raspberry bushes and went with Sam to get gooseberry bushes to transplant in the yard procured some very fine ones.

February 22: Mr. Ebey is setting out his fruit trees today in the yard. They consist of grafted apples, pears, peaches, and cherry, and grape, and plum. In the course of three years, if we live, and the trees do well, we will have plenty of choice fruit; which will be a great luxury indeed.

February 25: ...We have sown some cabbage, lettuce and tomato seeds.

March 5: Mr. Ebey is finishing harrowing in his wheat. The crows are very troublesome on it.

March 31: They are just from Fort Nesqually and brought us a handsome present of Grape Slips from Dr. Tolmie which is very acceptable and will give us a good commencement of grape vines if they do well.[16]

Sarah McElroy: Olympia, Washington Territory

March 22, 1880: Commenced garden work. Cut down maple tree and commenced spading, [Mr.] Cook doing the work.

April 6:...set out the sage and thyme
May 12: The spring has been cold and wet. Planted peas, corn, waxy beans, celery, parsnips.
March 22, 1881: Planted garlic tops seed. & 1 small root of garlic cloves for seed garlics. Planted 1 small bed parsley
March 30: Employed Mr. Cook to spade....Have some nice greens from cabbages set out last year too late to head. Also some turnip top greens from last year's turnips. Planted four rows Early rose potatoes.[17]

Potatoes, peas, beans, carrots, cucumbers, cabbages, onions, lettuce, squashes, tomatoes, turnips, herbs, and a variety of fruit trees grew in just about every garden. Then as now cooks boiled, steamed, stewed, fried, and baked vegetables. To add flavor they cooked them with butter, bacon grease, or salt pork, and sprinkled on salt, pepper, herbs, and spices. A recipe popular with Ritzville, Washington, pioneers cooks potatoes with bacon, bread, and sour cream. Norma Jones, who sent me the recipe, said her family, Germans from Russia, came to the area in the 1880s. Sour cream is cream that has soured, not the commercial variety.

Kartofle and Glace—3 cups flour, 4 eggs plus water, 3 potatoes diced, ½ lb. bacon, 5 slices bread, cubed, 2 cups sour cream.
Fill an 8 qt. kettle about half full of water. Add a little salt. Cook until potatoes are done. While they are cooking, cut the bacon into small pieces and fry until crisp. Remove bacon from drippings with slotted spoon and set aside to drain. Cube bread, crusts and all, and fry in the bacon grease until crisp.
Put flour in mixing bowl and make a hole in the center of the flour. Add 4 eggs and ½ egg shell of water per egg. With your hand mix flour and eggs, working from the inside of the bowl to the outside. It is best not to get the dough too stiff so you might not want to work all the flour into it.
When potatoes are done you drop the glace (dough) into the boiling kettle about a ½ walnut size piece at a time. The glace cooks fast and by the time you have cut all the glace it just needs to cook a few more minutes. The glace puffs up like little dumplings.
Now add the sour cream, bacon and bread cubes. When the cream is hot it is ready to ladle into soup bowls for supper. When you had a "good do" it meant you could easily cut the glace with your spoon and it didn't feel like a ton in your stomach all night.[18]

Resourceful women saved the broth (liquor) from cooking vegetables and meat and used it as a base for soup. That strategy added flavor as well as saving water. Most every cookbook devoted a section to preparing soups.

Fruit and Ornamental Trees, Vines, &c.

NURSERY AT THE COWLITZ LANDING!

THE subscriber offers for sale this fall a large stock of superior Trees selected from General McCarver's Nursery, Oregon Territory, in part as follows :

50,000 Trees two years growth from the bud, of large size; 20,000 one year's growth, composing the following different kinds :

APPLES

Early Harvest,
Red Astrican,
Coles Quince,
Williams Apple,
Junking or Early Straw-
berry,
Golden Sweet,
Porter Apple,
Tolpehocking,
Maiden's Blush,
Rambo,
Fall Pippen,
Yellow Bellflower,
Belmont or Gate Apple,
Rhode Island Greening,

Swarn,
Westfield Seek-no-further
Baldwin,
Esopns Spitzenburg,
Ladies' Sweeting,
New Town Pippen,
Northern Spy,
Roxbury Russett,
Ralls Jenating,
Michael Henry Pippen,
McCarver Premium,
McCarver Winter Seedling,
Sweet June,
Dutch Mignon.

PEARS

Butlett,
White Dojenne,
Dearborn Seedling,
Madelene,
Nadoleon,
Fondan,
Dr Awtum.

Marich Louisa,
Juliene,
Jargonelle,
Pound, Monts Large,
Bize Blanca,
Seckel.

CHERRIES

Roal Ann,
Red Camation,
May Duke,
Late Duke,

Dawnton,
Black Monella,
Kehtish Bigedrow.

Also Plums, Nectarines, Apricots and Almonds of suitable size for transplanting, all healthy and well grown. Grape, Currants, Goosberry, Strawberry, &c.

Persons desirous of purchasing trees are requested to send in their orders during the months of August, September, November and December.

All orders for the Sound will be packed in boxes in the best manner, for which reasonable charges will be made.

Catalogue with prices annexed will be sent to all applicants gratis, and postage paid.

E. D. WARBASS.

Eden Farm, Cowlitz Landing, Aug. 22, 1854. –1tf

Advertisements depicted the variety of fruit trees available to the pioneers. *Pioneer and Democrat, Olympia, December 16, 1854.*

Carrot Soup—Four quarts of liquor in which a leg of mutton or beef has been boiled, a few beef bones, six large carrots, two large onions, one turnip; seasoning of salt and pepper to taste, cayenne. Put the liquor, bones, onions, turnips, pepper and salt into a stew-pan and simmer three hours. Scrape and cut the carrots thin, strain the soup on them and stew them till soft enough to pulp through a hair sieve or coarse cloth; then boil and pulp with the soup which should be of the consistency of pea soup; add cayenne.[19]

Settlers either brought seed with them, saved some from previous harvests, purchased seeds from commercial companies, or requested them from family and friends. Even when they could purchase them locally, families preferred planting seeds from home as a way of connecting with those who stayed behind. Louise Swift requested red pepper seeds but wrote "P.S. all seeds are acceptable."[20] Abigail Malick asked for "cantelope seades, musk-mellone, greap, cabage, parcely, and Lettus, and shougar peas, and...enney sort of seades you have." A few months earlier Malick had opened a letter and happily "found some greape seades in it and some sea shell squash seades in It." The Malicks lived close to Fort Vancouver where well-stocked stores sold seeds.[21]

In some localities a scarcity of seeds led to unusual methods of keeping the ones on hand:

She had just a half cupful of seed corn which she had brought with her. This was very precious as nowhere could any be obtained out here. While she was digging the ground her old rooster sneaked up behind her and gobbled up the corn. When she saw what had happened, without any hesitation, she killed the rooster, recovered the corn from his crop and planted her garden.[22]

Some early pioneers entering the Oregon country without seeds or too broke to buy received them free from John McLoughlin, chief factor at Fort Vancouver from 1824 to 1846. Once businesses became established in the territory, seeds sold along with other merchandise. "GARDEN SEEDS, A Complete assortment, superior quality," Kilbor and Lawton advertised in the *Oregon Spectator* on April 20, 1847. "We can buy any kind of veg seed which do not come very well—seeds we bought put up by Quakers are of best quality, Roselle Putnam wrote from Yoncalla, Oregon in 1852."[23]

The early country stores in America displayed and sold seeds from barrels, but in the late 1840s seed companies like the Shakers in New Lebanon, New York, began selling them from packets or "papers," small envelopes bearing the name of the seeds, the community that produced them, and a brief description for planting.[24] In the Northwest, Wilson and Dunlap's account books listed "6 Papers" in 1857 for $1.50.[25] A check of seed catalogs from 1857 indicates that many varieties of vegetables planted today were available to pioneers.[26] Blue kidney potatoes, now considered a gourmet food, took root in John Campbell's 1870 garden.[27] An entry in Michael Luark's diary, January 5, 1865, shows the Department of Agriculture's interest in seeds:

> Receive in mail a package of seeds containing nearly a hundred papers from Department of Agriculture to be distributed in Chehalis County also some blank reports for May of the amount and kind of crops sown this year and its appearance as compared with last year. The prospects of the fruit crop, combined with an ordinary crop and the weather each week. So much for being Agriculture Correspondent to the Department of Agriculture from Chehalis County.[28]

Cellars and Pantries

Basements or root cellars made the best places to store vegetables such as potatoes, carrots, turnips, onions, and cabbages. Cool, dark, and dry spaces keep vegetables from sprouting and slow down the decaying process. "There we stored our food and it kept just like a refrigerator," recalled eastern Washington pioneer Minerva W. Herrett.[29] "We always raised...anything else that would keep in a root cellar," remembered Delia Crofoot.[30] "Root crops of all kinds should be properly taken up and stored away for winter use in the vegetable cellar," commented a writer for the *Puget Sound Herald* on July 9, 1858.

Cellars, cave-like structures propped up with timber or stones, were dug into the earth. Well-designed ones had a good drainage system (so water would not accumulate), adequate ventilation, well-built walls and ceilings to keep the earth from caving in. Some even had shelves lining the walls. In the colder climates of eastern Washington cellars had to be insulated to keep crops from freezing. Not everyone heeded the desired recommendations: vegetables did spoil. Some people just dug a hole in the ground, lined it with straw, and called the structure a root cellar.

Built under the house or as a free-standing structure away from the house, root cellars took advantage of the earth's naturally cool air. Typically, steps led down to the cellar, but those built into a hillside might have a level entrance. Luark dug his cellar "under the east end of the house going under at the end of the porch on a level grade almost as low as the cellar."[31]

Many people complained about the stairwells that led to underground cellars. No one enjoyed leaving a warm house to go outside on a dank, rainy day, lifting a heavy wooden trap door that covered the entrance, and descending slippery steps. What is more, the passage had no lights so one either had to carry a lantern, which may have limited the amount carried on the return trip, or grope down the steps in the dark.

Not everyone agreed that cellars were necessary. Miles Hatch, who lived near Tacoma, gave his wife several reasons for not constructing one in the temperate Northwest:

> You need make but little calculations for a cellar for I think few houses have one in this country. It does not get cold enough in winter or hot enough in summer to make them necessary. A store room in the house is lighter, dryer, cheaper and more convenient. It avoids the necessity of much running up and down stairs and the liability to fall through trap doors into the cellar.[32]

John Campbell, who had trouble with drains getting "choked up and quite a lot of water in cellar," most likely would have agreed with Hatch.[33]

Whether or not one built a cellar depended on where one lived, what products required storing, and the family's needs. In Spokane, Adelaide Gilbert found that a heated back porch was adequate in the winter but only a cellar would do in the hot summertime. "I have been at work down in the cellar this morning getting it ready for keeping food....The little store room off of back porch is too warm and too accessible to flies. I think our cellar will be cool a long time because it is on the north side."[34]

In places where large stumps remained, pioneers had a ready-built storage area. Lucky homesteaders like the Beatty family found "the roots of which had been burned into, leaving hollows, and thus forming excellent places for storing [potatoes]."[35] Plain stumps required a bit of work to turn them into storage areas. Susanna McFarland Ede, who homesteaded with her husband in Grays Harbor, described one method:

> There was a large spruce stump in front of our house that we tried to burn out but could only burn the wood inside the bark and down into the huge roots. We cleaned it all out and stored our winter supplies, such as apples, potatoes, beans, lard, etc. in there, covering it with cedar shakes, straw, and two coats of bear oil. Everything kept nicely until we returned to the beach in the spring.[36]

Other folks dug in the earth and made a storage pit in the field. The vegetables would be dug up with their roots, placed in a ditch, then covered with straw or canvas and dirt. Eula Fisher, who lived in the Dayton area, recalled that there was a "little opening for ventilation and that carrots, potatoes, squash, turnips, and cabbage kept very well; onions did not keep."[37] John Nelson "dug a long trench, lined it with wheat straw, put the potatoes and cabbage in, covered them with dirt and straw...a portion of them [cabbages] sticking through the ground, so it was not difficult to extricate them."[38] Mrs. Hugh Fraser, who spent seven years near Winthrop, observed that in that cold, freezing area the pits were dug five feet deep and the vegetables stayed there until the first days of March, two months before the ground thawed:

> Then the most acceptable gift, more welcome than the hothouse flowers that people in other countries are sending one another as Easter gifts, is a big head of cabbage, smelling of the good brown earth—a green globe, ragged outside, like a beggar saint, but white and juicy to its untouched core, its rank aroma [sweet] to our nostrils.[39]

As homes grew larger, builders incorporated pantries and/or cooling rooms (butteries) as an integral part. Different styles showed up in the Pacific Northwest. In the Borst house, built in the 1860s in the Greek Revival architectural style, the cooling room lay behind the kitchen, completely enclosed, and connected to the kitchen by a door. Vent holes, approximately one-foot square and covered with screen wire, were set in the floor and ceiling. The room had the cool feel of a basement and was lined with shelves.[40]

The Jackson family, who lived in Chehalis, stored their extra supplies in a separate room they called a "buttery." It "had rows of shelves around the wall and work tables near the center....Here were stored the precious food supplies, bags of flour, wooden barrels of brown sugar, sauerkraut, corned beef and butter barrels." The buttery was connected to the kitchen by an "entry," which acted as a covering for the well.[41]

Recognizing the importance of a proper storage area, domestic reformer Catharine Beecher advised building the room with "a small window over the door, and another opening out doors, give[ing] a great advantage, by securing coolness and circulation of fresh air." These cool spaces were an essential part of every home until the refrigerator took its place.[42]

Farmers did not have to rely on the sun to dry apples, peaches, and berries. This large drier used heat from a built-in furnace to dry the fruit. *Scientific American, August 3, 1867.*

Drying

In spite of the fact that emigrants complained of the dispiriting sameness of dried foods, fruit especially remained a mainstay in the pioneer larder. Drying is one of the easiest and most economical methods of preserving food because it does not require sugar or water, and does not need a special container with a tight-fitting lid. Dried food does not spoil, because water is removed and microbes can't survive. The biggest problem is preventing mold, which tends to form if food becomes damp.

Fortunately for the emigrants, strawberries, raspberries, dew berries, salal berries, salmon berries, cranberries, whortleberries, and wild grapes perfumed the air and tinted the landscape in the Pacific Northwest woods. Back yards yielded large amounts of fruit that pioneers "dried in the sun to store for winter, knowing that when the cold weather came, they would welcome stewed fruit."[43] "Gathering a fine lot of berries to dry for winter....I love to wander in Natives Fruit Garden," a happy Michael Luark recorded in his daily diary.[44]

Pioneers boasted of the large bonanza of berries that greeted them from May until Christmas. "How I wish I could send you some blackberries. We have a cellar full of them put up in bottles. Next summer I will dry a lot and send them to you," Sarah McElroy wrote to her brother. She hoped the promise of ripe blackberries would entice him to visit. Apparently she did not succeed, for twenty years later she still used the luscious berries as an inducement. "The strawberries are white with flowers. The raspberries are full of buds....If you are fond of strawberries and cream make your visit right soon and Oh! What a delightful time we will have, and then you must stay until after blackberries are ripe for we have such nice 'blackberry parties,' here."[45] McElroy could also have mentioned the strawberry parties, for these too were popular events. According to the *Pioneer and Democrat* of June 15, 1860, the "Ladies of Olympia" served strawberries, sugar, and cream free to all who came.

Gathering ripe fruit kept the family busy. One day Catharine Blaine "got 10 or 12 quarts of raspberries" which she dried in sugar, and the next day planned to "get some for jam, jell, and wine." Blaine intended to combine some of the raspberries with dew berries and make wine, which she believed "will answer a better purpose for sacrament purposes than the poison we buy." A year earlier Blaine had made jam from raspberries and noted that "some jell."[46]

Numerous rustic homes displayed "wooden strips nailed to the ceiling from which hung the drying strings of round apple slices; or sagging down in a mosquito netting tacked to the ceiling were halved peaches, plums, berries or other fruits also drying for winter pies and sauces."[47] When hanging space for sagging strings of produce filled the small log cabin homes, some people laid the extra fruit out on the roof and covered it with cheese cloth. Here it stayed until the sun's rays absorbed the moisture and soft, plump berries became hard, shriveled-looking fruit.[48] When the fruit finally dried it might be "stored in white muslin bags on the 'buttery' shelves," or in baskets and boxes.[49]

To prepare apples for drying, families in Centralia gathered together and held "apple peelings." They told fortunes with the peelings. "Many a girl peeled her apple in one long piece, swung it over her head threw it over her left shoulder, and blushed when she was teased about the letter it formed for that was supposed to be the initial of her future husband."[50] In the Denny family, children who strung the apples did not consider it a favorite activity. "After the apples were peeled and quartered, we strung them on twine with a large darning needle. The darning needle pricked our fingers and the apple juice made our hands sticky." They did however enjoy apple pie "sweetened with 'golden C' sugar from the Sandwich Islands." This light brown sugar came in a barrel lined with blue paper. "The pies were spiced with bits of cinnamon sticks and nutmeg grated on an old-fashioned nutmeg grater.[51]

Women could have dried fruit in an oven. *Godey's Lady's Book* suggested this method worked if a stove supplied "gentle warmth" and the drying was "done slowly."[52] Farmers with large amounts of fruit might have purchased one of the new commercial drying machines. An advertisement on October 10, 1875 in the *Sunday Welcome* from Portland stated: "A Sample Machine is in Full Operation at the Factory in East Portland, Oregon." It gives the "Fruit A Better Flavor Than any other Machine ever invented." The machine even dried potatoes.

On the other hand, if one had money or did not want to clutter the kitchen with dangling strings of shriveled fruit, grocery merchants stocked several kinds of dried fruit. "There are all manner of dried and preserved fruits for sale in the stores—which are cheap enough when we consider the price of home productions—for instance I can get five pounds of dried peaches or apples for one pound of butter," Roselle Putnam commented.[53]

By 1879 Seattle had a dried food factory that processed "the most delicious fruits and berries, as well as ordinary products of the farm, garden or orchard."[54] And in 1882, consumers in Vancouver, Washington Territory, had a choice of purchasing sun dried or machine dried apples. The sun dried cost eight cents per pound; the machine, ten cents per pound. Pears, dried in boxes, and dried pitted plums were also available for sale.[55]

No one mentioned what gadget they used for peeling, but there is a good chance that an apple peeler removed the red, yellow, or green peelings. This product had been on the market since 1803 when Moses Coates received a patent for a wood apple parer with a small blade and prong of iron or steel. The drawing for this new invention appeared in Anthony Willich's *Domestic Encyclopedia* (1803-04), and subsequently a large number of people began to copy and improve upon the basic design.[56] An advertisement in the *Morning Oregonian* in August 1861 confirms that one type, Sargent & Foster's improved apple parers, had worked its way to the shelves of the Northwest merchants. Between 1803 and 1890 over a hundred patents were issued as manufacturers guaranteed that their implements, now made from cast iron rather than wood, "not only pares the apple, but also cores and slices it, and leaves it in the very best state for cooking or drying."[57]

ALCOTT'S APPLE CORER.

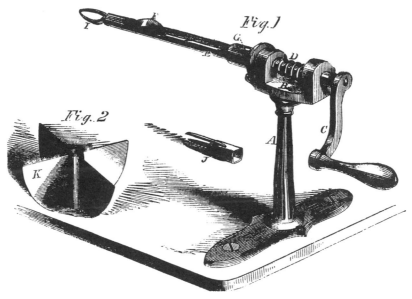

The inventor of this mechanical apple corer proclaimed his invention "cuts out all the core without wasting the juicy flesh." *Scientific American, April 12, 1859.*

The first apple tree planted in the Pacific Northwest allegedly came from English seeds planted at the Hudson's Bay Company's Fort Vancouver in 1826. But the grafted apple trees that pioneers planted in their yards or orchards came from trees that made the journey in 1847 in a covered wagon belonging to the capitalist horticulturist, Henderson Luelling. To insure that his "traveling nursery" survived the arduous journey over the Oregon Trail, he placed 700 grafted young trees, vines, and shrubs into two large boxes packed with a composted mixture of charcoal and rich Iowa soil. They completely filled his lead covered wagon. His daughter Eliza later complained that her father was "almost more solicitous" of the trees than of his family.[58]

The trees, just like the pioneers, endured, and within three years, Luelling had a thriving business in the Willamette Valley. He advertised that his fruit trees had the best "size and flower to exceed any in the United States...many of which we will be able to furnish this fall."[59] Luelling's enthusiasm convinced Elizabeth Chambers: "In the fall of 1853 my husband went to Fort Vancouver on legal business and on returning he stopped at Luelling's nursery...and got 15 apple, 4 pears, 4 plum and 4 cherry trees, all of which he carried home with him on horseback....In the spring of 1854 we planted out our fruit trees and every one grew."[60] "In the course of three years, if we live, and the trees do well, we will have plenty of choice fruit," Rebecca Ebey recorded on February 22, 1853, the day her husband set out grafted apple, pear, peach, cherry, and plum trees.[61]

Preserving—Sweetmeats and Savories

In order to turn buckets of berries into jams and jellies, and pounds of tomatoes into sauces and relishes, homemakers spent hours standing over a hot stove in a hot kitchen. "We are getting everything now in market and all sorts of fruit and vegetables...fruit canning are going to drive me for a while," Adelaide Gilbert complained.[62]

Making certain their families had preserves to slather on fresh baked bread required a variety of tasks. Someone had to gather, peel, core, and/or seed the fruit, measure out and perhaps break up lumps of sugar, haul in water for cooking and cleaning up, make certain there was enough wood for a fire, collect and clean containers, and stir and cook over an open fire or hot cook stove. Lucky homemakers had help from other family members or employed Native Americans to assist with the time-consuming tasks of washing dishes and scrubbing vegetables.

To make jams in the nineteenth century, cooks mixed together fruit and sugar and carefully stirred the mixture so that the fruit thickened rather than burned. When they put up a big batch, wash boilers substituted for pans. Isinglass, a fine kind of gelatin made from the bladder of sturgeon and available commercially, could be used to help the fruit gel, though most pioneers, it seems, relied on the natural pectin in fruit. One of the reasons currant preserves achieved such popularity is that this fruit has large amounts of natural pectin and so gels quickly.

Knox introduced granulated gelatin in 1894 at the urging of Sarah Rorer, a popular cookery writer. Rorer persuaded the company that granulated gelatin "would be easier to measure and would dissolve more quickly." Before that time, commercial gelatin came shredded or in sheets and needed to be soaked before using. Flavored granulated gelatin soon followed the plain variety.[63]

When fruit did not gel, homemakers covered cooked berries with glass, set the mixture outside in a warm place, and hoped heat from the sun would solidify the mixture. After Caroline French tried to make preserves from big, juicy, wild berries, she felt she had been unsuccessful because she did not have a piece of glass to cover the pan. "Next year, when we've put aside more money, we'll get some extra glass so you can make preserves," her husband promised.[64] A strawberry preserve recipe from a 1910 Washington State cookbook used the sun to gel the berries but does not mention covering the plates with glass. Perhaps the recipe writer left out this step.

> *Strawberry Preserves*—Clean and wash the berries, and to 3 pints of berries take 2 pints of sugar. Make the sugar into a thick syrup and drop the berries in and boil long enough to thoroughly skim. Then pour into platters and flat dishes and set in the sun until the syrup around the berries thickens, then put into jars cold, place covers on jars. While the berries are in the jars it is well to cover them with mosquito net. Berries put up in this manner keep well and retain the flavor of the fresh fruit.[65]

Juanita Brown Delaney, great-grandchild of pioneer Samuel James, revealed her family's secret way of making plum preserves. Even her Mama, who didn't think much of Uncle Richard James's method, was surprised that the "flavor was delicious":

> Soon Uncle Richard drove over...with a wooden keg, vinegar, brown sugar and boxes of plums....Uncle Richard filled the keg with plums and left it to sit, behind the cook stove all winter. He came over one April day and asked Mama if she had tried the preserves yet...he got a spoon and saucer and dished up some preserves for the table."[66]

Bemoaning the "good old days," *The Washington Standard* on July 3, 1869 noted: "In these times of canned fruit we seldom hear of preserves, and very rarely do we taste sauce 'put up' as our grandmothers used to prepare it." Was the writer hinting that someone bring him a jar of "the real thing"? He certainly would not have approved the use of canned peaches in the recipe Mrs. Evans gave to Sarah McElroy. But then he did not have to stand over a hot stove "putting up peaches."

> *Peach Pudding (from Mrs. Evans—Tacoma)*
> one can of peaches
> yolks of 3 eggs and whites of 4
> 3 cups of milk
> ½ cup of powdered sugar
> 1 tablespoonful melted butter
> 2 tablespoonful corn starch

Scald the milk thicken with the corn starch—take from the fire beat in the butter then the beaten yolks to which add to sugar whisk to a light cream. Drain the syrup from the peaches. Lay them in the bottom of a pudding dish. Pour the mixture gently over them, bake in a quick oven ten minutes then spread with meringue of whites with a little sugar. Shut in the oven until it is slightly tinged. Eaten hot with sauce or cold with cream.[67]

Jellies required straining juice from either cooked or raw fruit through a special jelly bag made of coarse flannel, muslin, or wool, and cooking the juice with sugar until the mixture gelled. A recipe for apple jelly that appeared in the "Farm and Household" column of *The Washington Standard* on November 15, 1874 gave directions for making and using a jelly bag:

> *Apple Jelly*—Take golden pippins; pare core and quarter them, and boil in water enough to cover them, until quite soft. Then turn into a flannel jelly-bag, and let the juice run out without squeezing at all. The jelly-bag is made like an enormous funnel, with a short nose and sewed up in one seam. Take a square of flannel and double over in 2 points lapping it in the middle, and you will see how it is done. Tie this bag by fastening tapes to each side of it to chairs, and let the juice run into a dish. To one pint of juice put one pound of white sugar, and boil for twenty minutes, then turn into jelly-cups. Add sugar to the jam, and boil for marmalade.

In times of sugar shortages or as a change from sweet preserves, women made "butters"—mashed fruit cooked with a small amount of cider and spices until the mixture thickened. They especially liked apple butter and crab apple butter. The wild crab apples *(Pyrus fusca)* that grow in Washington simmered in countless preserving kettles. The "apples" are small, elongated, yellow to purplish-red when ripe, very tart, hang down from branches in clusters, and make excellent butter or preserves. Phoebe Judson noted they were "about the size of the eastern cranberry....After straining out the seeds and skins they had a very fine flavor."[68] "The apple butter was a rich amber color, and made solid so it could be cut in slices for use."[69] Cooks used a large wooden spoon-like implement with holes in the spoon part to stir the thick apple butter.

In the Kittitas Valley people gathered choke berries, a "prickly job," and made choke cherry butter for their hot biscuits.

> *Choke Cherry Butter*—The cherries are well cooked with a little water, then they are put through a sieve to remove the pits and skins. One

usually starts out using a spoon to push them through; but if one is small, before the kettle is half empty a nimble fist is making short work of separating the pits and pulp. The pulp, well sweetened, is put back on the stove and slowly cooked down until it is nice and thick. Constant stirring is an important part of the process. In the 'seventies, 4X brown sugar was used.[70]

These basic recipes sound simple, but large quantities of jam did not gel and spoilage—due to improperly prepared fruit and dirty, imperfect containers—frequently occurred. Cookbook authors wrote pages about the "correct procedures" for putting up sweetmeats (a nineteenth-century term for fruits preserved as jams, jellies, butters, or leathers). Sarah Hale warned the women to make certain all food and utensils were "delicately clean and dry," never to place a preserving pan flat upon the fire but to always let it rest on a trivet, to stir the preserves gently at first and "more quickly towards the end," to add sugar after fruit in jams and jellies has been reduced so that the flavor and color will be retained, to boil fruit that had begun to ferment, and never to use tin, iron, or pewter spoons for skimmers.[71] Beecher advised packing the finished jars in a box filled with sand if it was difficult to find a cool, dry place, and to use small containers so as "to open only a small quantity at a time."[72]

Most of the women who left tales about *early* cooking procedures recorded that they used brown sugar when putting up preserves. Sold in casks or barrels, brown sugar contained large amounts of molasses and in some instances bits of debris and dirt. In hot weather the syrup might drain and turn storage areas into a sticky mess. Recipes often called for clean sugar. Suggestions for improving the sugar called for "clarifying it [brown sugar] by dissolving it in a little water, stirring into it while cold the beaten whites of eggs, and then boiling and skimming it well."[73] Then of course that wet solution had to be dried. I have yet to read that any pioneer washed the sugar. Just because a recipe appears in a cookbook, even a popular one, does not mean someone followed it.

In the late 1860s a centrifugal machine with revolving cylinders that rapidly separated the syrup (molasses) from the crystallized sugar and produced a pure white (clarified) sugar came on the market. Before then refineries had to boil and drain the sugar several times to remove the molasses. The more boiling and draining, the more expensive the sugar. Elizabeth Chambers Hunsacker observed that "the first white sugar came in cone shape, very hard; about the size of a big dinner plate at the bottom."[74] Wrapped in blue paper, those hard loaves or cones usually weighed about five pounds and varied in color from light to dark brown, depending on how much molasses and how many impurities it contained.[75] To aid the housekeeper, merchants supplied a portable sugar mill which crushed or ground up lumps cut off from the large cones. Federal standards for grading the sugar did not exist so that the terms merchants used for advertising—crushed, powdered, or XXX grind, even "yellow coffee sugar" (brown sugar)—meant different things to different suppliers. Machines designed to accurately figure the grades of sugar appeared in the late 1870s.[76] Granulated sugar, which *The White House Cookbook* in 1909 described as "coarse-grained sugar, generally very clean and sparkling," made its way to the market around the same time.[77]

After fruit thickened and gelled, vigilant homemakers had to find suitable containers and figure out how to seal them properly. No one knew about microorganisms in the mid-nineteenth century, but experience and food authors had taught them the importance of excluding air and keeping cooked food in a clean, dry place.

Women preferred using small glass jars, because they were easiest to clean and one could tell by looking if mold was forming. To cover the jars, *Godey's Lady's Book* recommended brushing egg white on tissue paper "with which cover the jars, lapping over an inch or two. It will require no tying becoming when dry inconceivably tight and strong, and impervious to the air."[78] Though in 1859 McElroy had bottles for putting up blackberries, not everyone in the Pacific Northwest was so fortunate. "There was no glass jars," lamented Laura House, an eastern Washington pioneer. Probably no tissue paper either.[79]

Pioneers used whatever containers they had; the Houses relied on tin cans, which they sealed with sealing wax. Grace Wall's mother "used to fill a five-gallon coal oil can with blackberry preserves. It never molded for she tied a cloth over the top that had been dipped in brandy."[80] Others recycled kerosene cans and used pitch from fir and spruce trees, softened with bear grease to the right consistency, as a sealer. When ready to seal the cans filled with preserved fruit, the pioneers "dipped a cloth big enough to reach well over the hole into the pitch...letting the grease mixture harden before adding the next thickness of cloth." The same can might be used for two or three seasons, or "until the can discolored the fruit: that is, made the juice black and tasting of the tin."[81] One wonders what flavor traces of kerosene imparted to the fruit.

If the town had a tinker's shop, homemakers used new cans, but still had a problem with sealing:

Each can was cut and soldered separately and a loose tin lid was provided. After the can was filled with fruit, the lid would be put in place and wax or rosin poured all over to seal it. Another method of sealing was to take a coarse cotton string or a piece of candle wick and dip it in the melted wax. Then it would be put on the can, under the tin lid, and pressed down until the wax hardened. One end of the string was left loose and when the can was to be opened all that was necessary was to take hold of the loose end of string and pull it out. That would break the seal all around.[82]

Before the introduction of the Mason jar with its self-sealing lid, glass bottles needed special handling to make the lid air-tight. Edith Miller, who grew up in Linn County, Oregon, described a jar "made with a grooved lip to receive a convex disk of tin." At the time of sealing "a waxed string was first coiled carefully in the groove, then the lid would be placed with its *dished* edges fitting in the groove on top of the string. Last of all, wax would be poured into the groove until it [was] quite full. The lid was held down until the wax hardened. When it was desired to open a jar, the string would first be pulled loose and that would break the seal all around."[83] Patented in 1855 by Robert Arthur and referred to as Arthur's Cans, that type of "can" was made out of tin, glass, or stoneware. Unfortunately they were not reusable.

Hunsacker recalled sealing small-necked quart bottles with wooden stoppers when there were no cork ones, and then pouring tallow over the stoppers—a process still used to make jars of preserves look old fashioned. To get the fruit out "we put a double thickness of candle wick around the lower end of the neck of bottle, the candle wick saturated in grease or coal oil. Coal oil was best. We set the wick on fire and when the oil had burned out, the neck of the bottle came off smooth, no chips of glass."[84] Softening the wax around bottles or jars could also be done by pressing hot coals or a warm iron over the top, placing the jar top down on a tin plate set on a hot stove, or by chipping away the wax with a sharp instrument. Homemakers kept a supply of extra wax in a tin container and melted it when needed.[85]

John L. Mason in 1859 invented the container that revolutionized the fruit jar industry. The "Mason" jar, with its self-sealing, reusable lid, made canning cheap and affordable. Though Mason's jar required a few changes before becoming a popular, inexpensive, glass container, from the beginning, canners and housewives appreciated its ease of operation. And as is usual for ever so many inventors, John L. Mason did not profit by its success. The glass factories who picked up Mason's expired patent in 1869 made the money. When pioneers write about using "Mason" jars, they probably purchased jars made by companies that unabashedly adopted the name.

The big disadvantage of John L. Mason's first jars came from the metallic taste and contamination of foods caused by the zinc in the cap, and the difficulty in breaking the vacuum when opening. R. Boyd helped solve the zinc problem by inventing a glass liner made of an opal glass ("porcelain") for the shoulder-seal cap. Other inventors tinkering with the lid and its seal figured out how to get it to open and close easily.[86] Women appreciated the advantages of a clean jar with a self-sealing lid. "I sold 10 dozen eggs at 28 cents a dozen in Tacoma. That paid for two dozen two-quart Mason jars with porcelain-lined tops. I'll fill them with plums," Lucy Ryan enthusiastically wrote to her grandmother in 1876.[87]

Apparently Ryan planned to "can" the plums—that is, put them in a sugar solution, pack the mixture in Mason jars, immerse the jars in water, and boil. Able to obtain glass jars, homemakers added canning to their list of kitchen duties. Unfortunately, early canning instructions were not very precise. One wit noted that instructions "sound as though they were written by a dyspeptic bachelor who was asked to fill space."[88] Indeed, into the early twentieth century, directions in household manuals, cookbooks, and even bulletins from the United States Department of Agriculture were a mixture of contradictions: food was added without precooking, jars were not boiled after sealing, and cold water was added to cooked and uncooked foods. Frequently, a recipe simply says, "can while hot," leaving it up to the cook to know what to do. I wonder how many cooks burned themselves following this recipe printed in *The Washington Standard*, August 28, 1869:

> *Secret to Can Fruit*—The whole secret of success in canning fresh fruit, vegetable or meat, is to cook them well in the can and then to close up hermetically during the escape of the steam. By this means any access of the air afterward is wholly prevented.

Canning operations in America are believed to have started in Boston around 1819 and in New York in 1825. Fishermen looking for ways to keep and transport perishable seafoods, such as lobsters, salmon, and oysters, were the first to use the small, tin cylinder. Farmers with surplus vegetables soon realized the commercial potential from selling out-of-season foods and followed the trend. The can industry boomed during the Civil War when manufacturers supplied cans of condensed milk, patented by Gail Borden in 1856, to the Union army.

Unfortunately, the early tinned fish, meat, vegetables, and fruit suffered from overcooking, loss of flavor, and in some cases spoilage. Alleviating these technical problems proved difficult. Consumers could not be certain that they were purchasing really safe cans with properly cooked foods until the 1920s.[89]

Nevertheless, though some people were leery of this latest product, others did not wait for the perfect can and seized the opportunity to indulge their taste for out-of-season canned tomatoes or pineapples. Northwest merchants stocked canned fruit—although sometimes in very small quantities—as early as the 1850s. By the late 1870s inventories of canned foods may have included asparagus, okra, mushrooms, and tomatoes. In 1884, court records of McDonald & Schwabacher, Washington Territory merchants, list cans of assorted fruits, ground horseradish, Boston baked beans, lobsters, tongue, green corn, ground mustard, sardines, and honey.[90] Clearly, some Northwest residents enjoyed the option of purchasing prepared foods.

Home canning of vegetables is hardly mentioned by the *early* pioneer homemakers. Instead, they write about salting down green beans in brine, slicing cabbage into barrels of sauerkraut, and pickling cucumbers. Brine is a very strong saltwater solution, although sometimes the term is used for the vinegar solution in pickles. Foods put down in brine had to be rinsed several times with fresh water before using. Inexpensive, easy-to-make "Lazy Housewife Pickles" were made from cucumbers cured in brine, freshened in cold water, and mixed with spiced vinegar.[91]

Soaking in salt water prior to adding vinegar draws the water from vegetables. Otherwise the liquid would dilute the vinegar and reduce its effectiveness. Mace, cloves, mustard seed, onions, peppercorns, ginger, turmeric, bay leaves, and pickling spices were known to the pioneer cooks and included in merchants' inventories. As a rule, spices came whole and had to be crushed or ground before use, but as early as 1856 Wilson and Dunlap listed ground ginger, cinnamon, and black pepper.[92] And on September 13, 1866 Portland, Oregon, merchants advertised in *The Morning Oregonian* that they "manufactured...ground alspice, cloves, pepper, cinnamon, ginger and mustard in accordance with the most recent scientific process." Because unscrupulous merchants had no qualms about mixing inferior products or even dirt into the ground spices, many homemakers preferred to buy whole spices and grind them at home.

The large, wooden grater with a square box on top to hold the cabbage as it moved forward and backwards over a sharp blade is a familiar sight in antique malls and museum kitchens because goodly numbers of families made barrels of sauerkraut for winter. The recipe has been popular for centuries. Marine explorers thought it prevented scurvy; unfortunately, however, the fermentation process destroys most of the vitamin C in the cabbage.

The recipe for sauerkraut is easy—grate the cabbage, pack it tightly with salt, then set it aside until fermentation occurs. Grating the cabbage is hard work. Women mention using fifty-gallon barrels and rock salt and mashing the cabbage until it made its own brine. The bacteria that grow in the brine produce lactic acid, which preserves the cabbage. Over the years, the recipe has remained the same.

> *Sauer Kraut*– Spread well cleaned and washed cabbage leaves to cover the bottom of a wine or whiskey barrel. Have 25 heads cabbage cut fine. For 25 heads cabbage take 1 quart salt and mix well. Put cabbage into barrel and press very tightly. Spread on it a clean cloth, then over it some hardwood boards, then a stone to weigh it all down. Let remain 7 or 8 days. Then wash off all the foam that has gathered on the cloth, board and stone. If the washing process is done twice a week the sauer kraut will keep one year.[93]

Sauerkraut usually appeared on the menu as a cold side dish accompanying meat, but cookbooks give recipes for heating it with butter and spices such as juniper. Most every European cuisine had its own special seasonings and fillings. The Sassie family in eastern Washington used a combination of rice and pork sausage, and called the dish Galousties:

> We had these sauerkraut barrels—fifty gallon barrels, and we'd make those full—two a year, and then we'd put a head of cabbage in there, the whole heads down in the bottom, and then we'd stomp our sauerkraut around them, and they would sour the same as sauerkraut, so when you took them out of the Kraut, we made this filling of rice and pork—ground pork sausage and onion and salt and pepper, and we'd cook this rice a little bit, just to get it swelled so it wouldn't swell up after we put it in the cabbage leaves. So we would cook that a little bit all together, and then put salt and pepper to season, and then we'd...peel off the leaves of this head of cabbage, put a spoon a big spoonful in, and fold ends and then roll it and put it in a big kettle. We lined the bottom of the kettle with sauerkraut and then we'd fill

that full, and then just cook it for about three or four hours in that—slow—and, oh that was a good dish.[94]

A Peck of Pickles

Cucumbers are the most popular vegetable to turn into a pickle, but pioneer families also pickled cabbage, peaches, green tomatoes, and green beans. The choice depended on what surplus vegetables were on hand. "Pickle-making time with the smell of the vinegar and spices mingling with the odor of the onions being chopped in the large wooden bowl" whetted the appetites of all who came near the kitchen.[95] A keg of vinegar, the basic ingredient in pickles, merited a prominent place in the pantry. Pioneers bought it from their local merchant or made it at home.

Vinegar is a sour liquid containing 4 to 12 percent acetic acid. Wine and cider make the best vinegar, but any product that will ferment and produce acetic acid is acceptable. The acetic acid discourages the growth of microbes that spoil food. The simplest method for making vinegar is to set out the wine and/or cider in a warm spot and wait until it sours. In large apple-growing areas residents knew they would always have a steady supply of cider vinegar.

When it did not seem prudent to turn cider or wine into vinegar, or only a small amount of these spirited liquids remained in the barrel, home cooks mixed fruit peelings and cores with water, set the mixture aside, and waited for the mass to ferment and turn into vinegar. "My mother even made her own vinegar from apple peelings and a brown gooey stuff she called a 'mother,'" Margaret Keck noted.[96] Tossing in spices, molasses, and/or brown sugar added flavor to the home brew. In the absence of fruit, pioneers produced a usable vinegar by mixing molasses, water, and yeast.

The "mother," a thick, gelatinous product that formed on the top of the vinegar from acetic acid bacteria, helped speed up the fermentation. To get the "mother," pioneers saved a little bit from previous batches or borrowed some from neighbors. A warm spot and a way for bacteria to enter the souring liquid is needed to produce a good bottle of vinegar. In the summertime, sun provided the heat; in winter, barrels sat near the fire. A small bung hole in the barrel top let bacteria in.

Slimy green mold growing on pickled foods indicated that someone brewed vinegar too weak to preserve food. Domestic advisors suggested that covering the jars with paper saturated in alcohol prevented mold. When mold did form, they recommended reboiling the vinegar solution and then putting it back in the jars or crocks. Food advisors also warned the public to stay away from commercial vinegars because these might contain questionable substances that "ruins pickles and is unhealthful."[97]

Before glass jars with good lids became common, pickled foods had to be put down in stoneware crocks or wooden containers. Metal vessels or common earthenware, whose glaze might contain lead, were avoided because the acid in the vinegar corroded the metal and contaminated the pickles. A small amount of alum mixed into pickling solutions kept vegetables firm; whole black pepper, ginger, allspice, mustard seed, onions, and garlic added piquant flavors.

A selection of pickle recipes from Washington state newspapers and cookbooks gives more precise directions. The ingredients in pickles have not changed materially over the years. What has changed is the method. Today pickles are put up in sterilized glass jars and precise instructions are given for processing in a boiling water bath. Vinegar, of course, is rarely made at home any more.

Ripe Cucumber Pickles or Russian Bear—Take large and ripe cucumbers before they become soft; cut in rings, pare, divide in good sized pieces and remove seeds. Cook the pieces very slightly in water salted just enough to flavor well; drain and put in a stone jar. Prepare a vinegar as follows: Two pounds of sugar to two quarts of vinegar (more sugar if desired quite sweet): a few slices of onion; some cayenne pepper; whole allspice, whole cloves, cinnamon according to ones taste, and judgment. Add whole peppers if liked. Much cooking injures the pickle very much. The pieces should be transparent, and firm enough to admit of a silver fork with difficulty when taken from the fire.[98]

Sweet Pickle Peaches—9 lbs. firm, ripe peaches, rub well with a coarse towel, halve them; to 4 lbs. sugar add 1½ pints vinegar with about a dozen whole cloves and about the same quantity of whole mace and cinnamon; boil to a syrup, then drop in fruit a few at a time, so as to keep them whole. When clear lay on a flat dish and drop in more. When cool pack in jars, boil syrup and pour over them.[99]

Sweet Pickles—75 cucumbers from 3 to 5 inches long. Cut up in inch pieces. Put in crock and add 1 cup salt and enough boiling water to cover. Let stand 7 days. Skim every other day if needed. On 8th day drain and add 2 tablespoons powdered alum, and enough boiling water to cover. Let stand 24 hours. On 9th day drain and pour boiling water to cover. 10th day drain and pour over, boiling hot, 5 pints of vinegar, 9 cups sugar, 1 ounce stick cinnamon, ½ ounce celery seed. 11th day, drain off liquid and add 1½ cups sugar. Heat to boiling point and pour over pickles. Again repeat this on 12th, and 13th days, adding 1½ cups of sugar each time. Let stand in open crock or put in jars.[100]

Green Tomato Sweet Pickle—Into a common sized wooden bucket half full of water put a handful of unslacked lime, and fill up with small green tomatoes carefully picked. Let them stand twenty-four hours, then take out the tomatoes, and soak them the same length of time in clear water. Then make a compound of four and a half pounds of sugar, one quart vinegar, one ounce cinnamon and one ounce cloves. This is intended for seven pounds of fruit. Boil the compound together, pour over the fruit, let stand twenty-four hours, then bring all to a boil, and tie closely in a jar.[101]

By the last quarter of the nineteenth century new methods of processing and better transportation brought to the Northwest preserved and pickled foods that the pioneer housewife had so laboriously made in her small kitchen. A perusal of area newspapers and business inventories shows that by the 1870s, residents with discretionary income could purchase preserved tomatoes in syrup, preserved Louisiana figs, Christmas plum pudding, brandy peaches, fruit in cans, canned tomatoes, peas, and corn, a variety of dried fruit and pickles, and bottles of ketchup, mustard, and Worcestershire sauce. Though women still took pride in having a full larder, it was no longer absolutely necessary to spend hours and hours shredding cabbage or slicing cucumbers.

Finally some lucky women now had time to create the delicacies described in *Godey's Lady's Book* and the new women's magazines, such as *Good Housekeeping* and *Ladies' Home Journal.* Whether they had more leisure time or spent less hours in the kitchen is subject to debate.

Chapter Seven
The Barnyard Provides

"WITH OUR COWS, OUR PIGS, our chickens, and garden we shall be able to live almost independently of the help of the people," Catharine Blaine wrote to her family in 1855.[1] Blaine, just like most pioneers, hoped the cows would provide milk with which to make butter and cheese, the pigs would grow fat before turning into meaty hams and bacon, and the chickens would lay eggs.

Soaring prices of these basic commodities put a drain on already meager finances. In 1855 when Blaine paid forty to seventy-five cents per pound for butter, she complained that it "is quite an item...and not using any meat we use a great deal of butter."[2] Twenty-five years later in another part of Washington Territory, Lucy Ryan penned the same refrain. "I must tell you we have a new cow that gives such a lot of splendid rich milk. She is two years old....It's so nice to have cream and milk."[3]

Homemade butter and fresh cured bacon tasted much better than the sort offered by merchants. Comments made in territorial newspapers and by pioneers and cookery writers suggest that the meat and butter for sale may not have offered gustatory pleasure. "A good article of butter is needed in this place....Good butter is exceedingly scarce but a kind not fit for soap grease is not in good demand, there is enough of this sort on hand now," *The Territorial Republican*, an Olympia newspaper, stated on August 2, 1869.

Pickle roll butter, or butter preserved in brine, received the most complaints. As one can imagine, foods sitting in a saltwater bath for perhaps six months tended to have a salty flavor rather than a sweet, fresh taste. Sarah Hale, editor of *Mrs. Hale's New Cook Book*, went so far as to warn her followers "to eat molasses, or honey, or preserves, with bread, and use lard, beef drippings, suet, &c., for gravies and shortening, [rather] than to use bad butter."[4] Gilt edge or fresh farm butter (country made) packed in a wooden firkin or crock received highest ratings. But lofty names did not guarantee purity. On more than one occasion, butter in the bottom of the crock lingered too long to be considered fresh.

Before the days of large dairies, every housewife felt she had to master the art of making good, sweet butter. According to cookery writers, this expertise not only gave the family a necessary cooking ingredient, skillful butter making would also make her husband proud. Many daughters wrote to anxious mothers that they "churned today" or "made some butter." "The coming week I am going to try my hand in the butter," Louise Swift told her mother in July 1863. Evidently she succeeded for in August she bragged "I have made myself about 30 lbs. butter," and soon began making butter every week. The Swifts had three cows and a calf and hoped to soon have more.[5] Even Margaret Stevens, the Washington territorial governor's wife, noted that she had "made some butter."[6]

By selling surplus butter, women helped out with the family's finances and earned a little money for themselves. "Even my little dairy of two cows have for the month past turned me in several dollars. I have sold butter...and have by me 26 lb. for which I should soon have at least 60 or 70 cents per lb. I now milk three cows, we have four," Anna Marie James enthusiastically wrote from Grand Mound, Washington Territory, to her sister in Wisconsin.[7] Hoping that her success in business would lure her family who remained in Illinois, Abigail Malick wrote, "O if you was hear with your Cows you could make A great Deal of money. Butter is now one dollar And A half A pound."[8] Others told similar stories. Only the price changed as butter, like most commodities, heeded the whims of supply and demand.

Butter also became a desirable item for use when bartering, a popular way of exchanging goods when money was tight. Michael Luark gave butter "for goods at 37¢ per lb."[9] Rebecca Ebey felt fortunate when she exchanged three and a half pounds of butter for thirteen pounds of pork.[10] And Roselle Putnam reported that she "can get five pounds of dried peaches or apples for one pound of butter."[11]

Anticipating a bolstering impact on the menu from a tasty topping for fresh bread as well as a chance to acquire pocket money, cooks rejoiced when they acquired a cow and could begin churning. "A good cow at that time was worth one hundred dollars, but that sum appeared small in my eyes in comparison with the luxuries of butter and milk I anticipated she would furnish," Phoebe Judson recalled.[12] "Have I told you that we have a cow," Blaine asked her family. "Mr. Blaine bought one...; costs $40.00;

gives 6 or 8 quarts of milk per day....I sell a dollar's worth of milk at 10¢ [per quart] per week, which will more than pay for her feed."[13]

Pioneers brought the cows with them over the Oregon Trail or acquired them from Dr. John McLoughlin, chief factor for the Hudson's Bay Company at Fort Vancouver. Once herds increased and other sellers entered the market, settlers traded and sold cattle among themselves. "Arrived from Olympia with 3 cows, 1 steer, 1 calf," recorded Henry Roeder, a merchant-trader who bought and sold goods for families in Whatcom County.[14]

Domestic cattle were first seen in the Oregon country at Fort George (Astoria) in 1814, but McLoughlin receives credit for increasing the herd and improving the strain with Durham bulls from England. Others followed suit bringing in cows from California and other parts of the West. By 1860, approximately 182,000 head of cattle roamed the land in Oregon and Washington Territory; by 1870 cattlemen had to accept the fact that too many cattle caused prices to tumble.[15]

First, Milk the Cow

Butter making began with milking the cow—not the most pleasurable task when the job meant "getting up before dawn, herding the cow(s) into a damp and smelly barn, milking them by hand while holding a bulky tin bucket, freezing in winter, bothered by flies in summer." Tethering the cow to a post and then "tie[ing] her hind legs together" stopped the kicking but no one figured out how to eliminate the odor.[16] Relief from milking seemed an important item to write home about. "I have a good deal to do although I do not milk do you or do you content yourself with drinking the milk. I expect you have a very fine cow if she looks anything like the drawing you sent of her," Mary Bozarth wrote from Whidbey Island.[17]

Dodging the cow's tail seemed to be a common problem exacerbated by the cow's natural tendency to kick. At least that is how Phoebe Judson explained her husband's milking failure. As she points out, milking required patience, a trait her husband seemed to lack:

> Neither of us had learned to milk, and it makes me smile now when I think how little practical knowledge we had of farm life. However, I thought it would not take my husband long to learn. It seems so natural for a wife to think her husband smart and wise, but in this case I was doomed to disappointment, for he returned from the corral both morning and evening with less than a quart of milk in the pail.

Sometimes the calf got it all, or he may have spilled it while dodging out of reach of old Bell's horns and tail. One morning, while standing at arm's length trying to milk, she kicked at him, and judging from the irate manifestation on his part, she did not miss him, and when I apologized for the old cow, by saying "the poor thing got too much alkali on the plains," and suggested a little more gentleness and pa-tience, he waxed wroth and told me to "milk her myself"—which I had intended doing all along. As soon as they were both willing, and after a few persuasive efforts, I succeeded in getting six or eight quarts at a milking, and have never regretted my experience, as I often found the art of milking a very convenient acquirement.[18]

Mrs. Cornelius, a cookery writer, warned that cows should be "milked by a person who understands the process, or she will not give it freely, and will soon become dry."[19] Undoubtedly Phoebe Judson qualified. Whether other women acquired the "art of milking" because they "understood the process" is not known, but many cows gave up their milk to wives, not husbands. "Wife is unwell done no work this day except milking the cow," John Campbell, a Mason County farmer, recorded in his diary. Several days later Mrs. Campbell delivered a baby.[20]

In the early years of settlement, cows roamed freely, and on occasion became pests, "breaking up potato fields and eating up potatoes."[21] Rebecca Ebey complained the "cattle are beginning to interrupt our onions . . . before I can get them fenced."[22] Caroline Budlong recalled that in Olym-pia her family and others turned out the cows in the morning and "they roamed around the streets and alleys and in the nearby woods. One cow belonging to a neighbor became so smart she came to the gate, raised it up on her horns and walked in to eat the grass growing inside." At milking time, cows strolled home and "stood bawling" until the gates were opened.[23] All cows were not so wise. Luark's diaries indicate he and his family had often "done nothing but run around hunting cattle."[24]

In 1865, Olympia's town council decided that cows could no longer run through the town but must be kept in barns or fenced lots. But as late as the early 1900s in Colville, "it was nothing to see prominent business-men leading the family cow to a vacant lot on their way to work...and picked up again on the way home in the evening."[25]

Besides destroying crops, roaming cows often ate the wrong foods. Carrots and green corn were fine, but turnips, parsnips, onions, and cab-bage imparted a distinct and unwanted taste to milk. Mrs. Knute Landsworth remembered that when the family first came to Stevens County "there wasn't much clover for the cows to eat and the butter would be quite white. We would color it with carrot juice or purchase a yellow coloring."[26] Others might use egg yolks or the juice from pot marigold flowers (calendulas), adding the colorings to the cream before churning. Cows that ate the proper foods gave the best milk and made the best butter.

After milking the cow, milk had to be strained, put back in pans, and set in a cool place until the cream separated. Milk skimmers, a nearly flat, perforated dish approximately five to six inches in diameter that either fit in the hand or had a long handle, made it easier to remove the cream. *Godey's Lady's Book* suggested a siphon that would "draw off the milk from beneath the surface of the cream."[27] Tin milk pans, skimmers, and strainers were common items in company inventories. The skimmed milk that remained nourished family members as well as farm animals; the cream would be turned into creamy butter.[28]

Keeping Dairy Products Cold

To keep milk and cream cool, and to store other perishables, families constructed a milk house or spring house. "Father has built Anice Milk house," Abigail Malick confided to her daughter on June 24, 1851.[29] Ideally, these cool places were near a source of water (a spring-fed pond, stream, or well) which could be pumped into the room via pipes, thus lowering the room temperature. Lacking that, the structure, which ranged from an ordinary shack to a room built with insulated walls, might be extended into the earth or built on the cool north side of the home. All had shelves to hold the ingredients and implements for making butter and cheese. Several pioneers recalled seeing flowers growing out of the dirt in the milk house walls.

In the large Bigelow home the milk room, which had a sink, was on the north side of the house, connected to the kitchen by an opening called a "pass through." The Chambers family first built one "on the north end of the small porch going out the east kitchen door, [but] moved [it] to a small new building, by itself, not connected with the house."[30] Bessie Craine indicated that their Issaquah milk house, "twenty-five feet square, had double walls filled with sawdust and sawdust overhead."[31] Elof Norman's family did not construct a separate room but his father did build "wooden boxes or cupboards for food with piped-in water from the creek running over them."[32] Kittitas Valley pioneers "Built milkhouses, with double walls filled with earth, and with tight roofs covered with earth....The milk-house rooms were dark and cool, the temperature was fairly even, and the butter kept sweet and fresh on the shelves. The milk was set in wide tin pans, skimmed with a flexible tin skimmer and churned by hand."[33]

Lacking a special milk house, pioneers packed dairy products in a waterproof container and suspended the package in a well or creek. The well acted like a refrigerator because temperatures in the hollow chamber above the water stayed quite cold. Covered lard pails made good water-proof containers, especially for butter.

A letter writer to the *Willamette Farmer* did not think it necessary to have a spring house, but instead suggested keeping butter in a "cold, dry cellar made of brick or stone entirely away from mouldy or decaying wood, vegetable or fruit." He also warned about letting milk sour before skim-ming and "never allow milk in the Spring and Fall to stand for three or four days in a cold, damp room to let the cream rise....Letting the cream stand three or four days, so that it will churn more easily, is about as sen-sible as letting timber lay till it becomes rotten, before using it, because it will work more easily."[34]

No doubt everyone had their own special way of churning; that is usually the way with good cooks. But there were some general rules that had to be followed. First and foremost, everything needed to be absolutely clean. This included the cow, the milker, pots, pans, and milk house. Sec-ond, churning had to be done frequently. Farm wives customarily waited until they had an accumulation of cream before churning, but milk sitting in a pail for several days had a tendency to sour more than was necessary. Beecher and others advised churning every day; Hale thought twice a week would do.

When temperatures rose, churns needed to be set in cold water. Pio-neers did not understand that bacteria spoiled milk, but they did know that in summer milk products soured and became rancid. When tempera-tures dropped, cream had to be warmed before churning, but care had to be taken because butter "hastened by hot water is worse than that which is turnip-flavored."[35] Instructions printed in *The Washington Standard* on July 26, 1873, detail other helpful hints:

> *Butter Churning Made Easy*—Strain the milk shallow, the more sur-face, the more cream, hence large pans are the best. Keep it in a room free from jars [with food]; do not churn in the room; keep it at an even temperature; it must have light and air—it is much like the rest of us, and spoils for want of good, pure air, but it is averse to draughts. Watch it, if you want good, sweet butter, and skim when the milk is thoroughly thick or lopped. If you skim sooner, you will lose some

cream; if later there will be spots on it or mold, and your butter will not keep. After skimming your cream into your cream pail, stir altogether with a case knife or spoon; a knife is best, as it manipulates the particles against the sides of the pail more thoroughly. This process takes but a moment, and if you do it each time that you skim, when you come to churn (if your butter is at proper temperature) your butter will come in less than ten minutes, as the particles are already half churned.

A cylindrical wooden barrel with a wooden dasher (plunger) is the popular image of a butter churn, but by mid-nineteenth century other designs entered the marketplace. Stoneware table-top churns and ones with mechanical cranks gave the old wooden churn competition. A family in the Kittitas Valley used a "water-cooled churn, that is, the tin churn was hung in a wooden frame which could be filled with water, either cold or warm, to make the cream the right temperature for the butter to gather."[36] The Laurie family from Okanogan "had an earthenware crock with a good dasher to make butter."[37] According to those who churned, "if you ever stood for hours pumping the dasher up and down, raising it occasionally to see if there were any flecks of butter on it, you will never forget the old churn."[38]

Despite the fact that so many women churned butter, the terminology associated with this important endeavor occasionally caused confusion. Mrs. Delia Sheffield, whose husband served with Ulysses Grant at Fort Vancouver, admitted that she thought sweet butter meant butter sweetened with sugar:

> Captain Grant asked me if I could make some butter, as he was hungry for some sweet home-made butter. So I saved the cream and churned it, and thinking to please the Captain, I put sugar into it instead of salt, as he wanted some *sweet* butter. At dinner, that evening, I displayed it with great pride. I noticed a smile appearing on their faces, and finally Captain Grant said, "Mrs. Sheffield, is this some of our home-made butter?"
>
> "Yes, Captain, how do you like it?"
>
> "Well, it is the sweetest butter that I ever tasted," he remarked, with a twinkle in his eye.[39]

Some butter recipes called for adding salt to the cream before churning; others mixed the salt in after washing the butter, and some never used it at all. Business inventories showed salt as table salt, fine table salt, coarse table salt, Liverpool salt, coarse Liverpool salt, Syracuse table salt, and just plain salt. In 1865 The Willamette Salt Works advertised that their local salt was "superior to Liverpool or any other Imported article."[40]

Though it sounds as if cooks had many salt choices, in reality people chose between a salt for table use and one for pickling or dairy. Standards for distinguishing between coarse and fine had not been promulgated; distributors assigned names as they desired. Salt came in bags. Users had problems keeping it dry and grainy.

Letter writers to the Washington State Dairy Commission in 1896 complained that inferior salt, and using the wrong amounts, produced storage butter "not equal to eastern butter." Too much salt gave a fishy taste; too little produced a strong flavor and would not mold.[41] Washing rancid butter in chloride of lime mixed with lime water, pure water, and sweet milk supposedly sweetened it. The author of that recipe stated "this preparation of lime contains nothing injurious."[42]

Most people gave butter a final washing to remove all the buttermilk. "That was Mother's job—to work the butter by means of a big triangle tray on legs, with a heavy paddle. She would work it up and down until all the buttermilk was squeezed out, then it was salted and pressed into pound molds and wrapped in butter paper. These were packed into a very heavy wooden firkin."[43] The tray either sat on a flat surface or on legs; a hole at the end allowed water to drain. Those who did not have specially designed butter workers used a large bowl and worked and washed the butter with a wooden paddle. Washing was necessary if butter had to be kept for several weeks or months.

Stoneware crocks made of salt-glazed pottery or special butter mold boxes—square wooden boxes with one removable side—made desirable storage containers. Homemakers also wrapped butter in cheesecloth and packed it "in boxes, each layer well covered with salt."[44] To identify their product and add decoration, butter makers stamped butter with specially designed butter stamps. Many pounds of butter displayed sheaves of wheat, a common design. Specialized dishes and knives for serving butter at the table were available in a variety of shapes and sizes.

Domestic advisors came up with several schemes to have hard butter in the summertime. One suspects the pioneers were not so fastidious as the author of this recipe recommended:

> To have delightful hard butter in summer with out ice—Put a trivet or an open flat thing with legs in a saucer; put on this trivet the plate of butter; fill the saucer with water; turn a common flower pot, so that its edge shall be within the saucer and under the water; plug the flower pot with a cork, then drench the flower pot with water; set it in a cool

place until morning, or if done at breakfast, the butter will be hard by suppertime.[45]

Butter that eventually sold in commercial markets had to be preserved in barrels of strong brine. Then "during winter it was worked over and molded into two-pound bricks....This required lots of hard work, and all hands were kept busy during the packing season." Full barrels held about 300 pounds of butter.[46]

Until the twentieth century, most dairies producing large amounts of butter for resale were family operations. The quality of butter varied with the worker's experience, the milk's freshness, and the atmosphere in the dairy or milk house. If inexperienced employees overworked butter or did not give it a final washing, greasy, sour rolls came to the market. When damp sawdust did not get replaced in milk house walls, germs grew and butter spoiled. And, until public health departments began regulating the industry, inferior butter made from tubercular cows oftentimes ended up in country stores and kitchens. Not until the 1890s, when the legislature authorized the Washington State Public Health Board, did a serious attempt begin in Washington to detect tuberculosis in cattle and regulate the places and methods of making all milk products.

Not wanting to waste any food, cooks turned sour milk into a soft cottage cheese—an easy task since the process only required a warm place, a cheese drainer or mold with pierced holes or slats, and the patience to wait for milk to separate into curds and whey. To add flavor, cooks added salt and/or other seasonings to the drained curds, and may have enriched the cheese with additional cream or butter before serving. Cookery writers suggested sage or spinach if one wanted cheese to have a greenish color. The round or heart-shaped drainers usually were made of wood, tin, or stoneware. Caroline Rohweder Firmin recalled "there is nothing today comparable to its [cottage cheese] flavor and texture."[47] Today, when milk is pasteurized, it spoils instead of turning sour and we cannot duplicate this process. Unfortunately the soft, unripened cheese did not keep; in a few days the cheesebox emitted undesirable odors.

Michael Luark noted that his "wife made a small cheese using Dodges [neighbors] implements."[48] Was it a soft unripened cheese? One wishes Luark and others had recorded more information. Catharine Beecher's recipe for making "Fine Cottage Cheese" makes one want to run out and milk a cow so as to have sour milk.

Fine Cottage Cheese—Let the milk be turned by rennet, or by setting it in a warm place. It must not be heated, as the oily parts will then pass off, and the richness is lost. When fully turned, put in a coarse linen bag, and hang it to drain several hours, till all the whey is out. Then mash it fine, salt it to the taste, and thin it with good cream, or add but little cream, and roll it into balls. When thin, it is very fine with preserves or sugared fruit.[49]

Rennet comes from the stomach of an unweaned calf and is used in cheese making to hasten the coagulation process. Rennet had to be removed from the calf at butchering time. Homemakers washed it well, hung it out to dry, and kept the prepared, dried rennet in a bag until needed. Some cooks pickled the rennet before drying. At cheese-making time, they took a small amount, diluted it with water, and added it to the milk. Most likely, pioneer women made the soft cheese without rennet. Certainly in the early years when few cows roamed the Pacific Northwest, calves were too precious to slaughter for a bit of rennet.

Hard ripened cheeses, such as yellow American, last longer, but the process of making them is more complex. Much depends on the temperature, amount of moisture and salt, length of time for ripening, and the quality of rennet. Such cheeses were usually made in dairies. When properly made and stored, hard cheeses keep and are easy to transport. They appeared in Northwest market price lists as early as 1849, so it seems pioneers had the option of purchasing rather than making this type of cheese. The cheese usually came into markets in large, round wheels that merchants sat on the counter. To protect cheese from the numerous flies that swarmed everywhere, fastidious storekeepers wrapped it in cloth. Stores that had food safes kept cheese in them—a much better protection from flying insects. At purchase time, storekeepers sliced off the amount ordered. Before the days of calibrated equipment to measure moisture and temperature, texture and flavor varied greatly. In 1880, Swiss cheese appeared on the menu of Fountain Beer Hall in Seattle.

Beef

Pioneers preferred fresh beef, pork, and mutton, but fresh meat, particularly beef, turned bad, "which we soon gave up trying to save," admitted Guy Waring.[50] Wells, spring houses, and cellars, the usual places for keeping foods fresh, were not always cold enough. Furthermore, fresh meat attracted flies and rodents and it could not be kept in a milk house near fresh milk and butter.

If the area where they lived had a meat market, families could purchase beef and pork. If not, they shot game for fresh meat and relied on corned beef, smoked hams, salt pork, and sausage for the daily fare. In 1845, Hudson's Bay stores at Fort Vancouver had on hand imported and "country made" meat from domesticated stock and wild game. A check of grocery advertisements in newspapers from 1845-1855 showed beef per pound on foot, and beef per pound butchered. In 1871, The People's Market in Olympia featured a "splendid display of beef, pork, mutton and poultry on Christmas Eve." According to *The Washington Standard* it was as fine an exhibit of choice meats as one could expect to see. Unfortunately there is no way of knowing the quantity or quality of beef sold. Home butchering declined in the 1860s and 1870s when the cattle industry expanded.

Recipes written 150 years ago called for cuts of beef similar to those used today, but there was a difference in quality. Today, meat is tender because it ages for several months before coming to the market. In the absence of refrigerated rooms, that process proved difficult. According to Colville pioneer Senator David E. McMillan, "a good pair of jaws were essential if you were to successfully eat the beef of that day....The housewife had to be an artist in the preparation of tough meat."[51] *Godey's Lady's Book* offered one solution:

> *To Make Tough Beef Tender*—To those who have worn down their teeth in masticating poor old tough cow beef, we will say that carbonate of soda will be found a remedy for the evil. Cut the steaks, the day before using, into slices about two inches thick, rub over them a small quantity of soda, wash off next morning, cut it into suitable thickness, and cook....The same process will answer for fowls, legs of mutton and etc.[52]

Chastising housewives "who feed their families on tough steaks not being willing or able to pay for juicy ones," the "Household" column in *The Vancouver Register* on April 19, 1875 noted that if they "would take a little more pains—that is stew an inferior piece instead of broiling or frying it—they would have more palatable and more nourishing food."

When fresh meat had to be kept for several days, cookery experts advised par-roasting or par-boiling immediately, finishing the cooking just before serving. They warned that fast boiling made meat tough, but slow boiling tenderized it; the success of roasting depended on the fire; and old meats required more cooking than young. Sarah McElroy's recipe for baked steak provides evidence that in the 1880s smart cooks tended to agree with that advice.

> *Baked Steak*—Take a round of beef steak weighing about 3 pounds. It should be thick and juicy but need not be tender. Spread over it a nice dressing of bread crumbs, salt pork chopped fine and flavored with onions, salt and pepper. Roll tightly and tie with a string. Put in a kettle of water and let simmer for three hours. Then put in an oven and brown. Thicken the gravy and pour over removing the string carefully before serving.[53]

Covering fresh meat with a cloth and charcoal or ashes supposedly discouraged flies and other flying insects from finding a meal. And if, in spite of following all these directions, the meat began to spoil, some cookery writers believed that "rubbing with salt will cure it."[54] Recipes frequently carried the warning to "avoid tainted meat" or "do not use meat that is tainted."

Salting Preserves Meat

To preserve large cuts of beef for long periods, farmers "salted it down" or "corned" it, preferably in wooden barrels. Everyone did not do it well. "Dad, 'put down' his own meat. There was a 'meat house' at the end of a passage from the big back porch. He always got it too salty—according to mother who complained each time she must 'freshen' it before frying. I think the abundant salt was necessary because of the damp and not terribly cold climate," recalled Francis Siverson.[55] If they could not find barrels, Spencer Butte pioneers "cut up a big oak tree...dug a trough in it [and] planned to salt meat in that."[56]

For suggestions and recipes about salting beef and pork, men and women could turn to cookbooks. Catharine Beecher described the first recipe written here as *the best* "by a writer, who has resided where they were used." The second she suggested for the "ordinary mode." Beecher gives precise amounts for saltpeter but admits saleratus could be substituted. Those who actually salted meat had more common ways of determining the right amount of saltpeter. Caroline Firmin recalled, "When an egg floated on top of the solution Dad knew that he had enough saltpeter."[57]

> *To Salt down Beef to keep the Year round*—One hundred pounds of beef; four quarts of rock-salt, pounded fine; four ounces of saltpeter, pounded fine; four pounds of brown sugar. Mix well. Put a layer of meat on the bottom of the barrel, with a thin layer of this mixture

under it. Pack the meat in layers, and between each put equal proportions of this mixture, allowing a little more to the top layers. Then pour in brine till the barrel is full.

Brine or Pickle for Corning Hams, Beef, Pork, and Hung Beef—Four gallons of water; two pounds of rock-salt, and a little more of common salt; two ounces of saltpeter; one quart of molasses. Mix, but do not boil. Put the hams in a barrel and pour over them, and keep them covered with it for six weeks. If more brine is needed, make it in the same proportions.[58]

For those in a hurry, a recipe in *The Washington Standard* of November 9, 1872 outlines ways for pickling meat in one day.

Pickling Meat In One Day—Get a tub nearly full of rain or river water and put two pieces of thin wood across it and set the beef on them at about the distance of an inch from the water. Heap as much salt as will stand on the beef, and let it remain 24 hours; then take the meat off and boil it, and you will find it as soft as if it had been in a pickle for weeks—the water having drawn the salt completely through the beef.

To preserve cooked meat, women could either mix it in mincemeat, add it to an aspic, or blend it with flour and shortening and make a pork cake. To prepare an aspic (savory jelly of pressed meat), cooks placed the meat in a mold "in layers well seasoned." Then they filled "the mould with some clear soup nearly cold, which, when let to stand some hours will turn out to be as firm as isinglass [gelatin], especially if shank bones were boiled in the soup." Sliced and served cold, aspic made a tasty summertime accompaniment for potato salad.[59]

Pork cakes, like mincemeat, combined meat with fruit, but instead of letting the mixture ferment, cooks added flour and baked it. Many variations of the recipe appeared and most likely each cook added her own special ingredients "to suit the taste." One printed in *The Washington Standard* on July 2, 1870 is typical.

Pork Cake—One pound of fat pork chopped fine; pour on one pint boiling water; Add three cups sugar, one of molasses, one pound of fruit [dried], eight cups of flour; season to suit the taste.

Fat Hogs

Until the 1860s when beef became a more common commodity in pioneer markets, fat hogs wallowing in the barnyard supplied a large portion of the meat that appeared on pioneer tables. They are easy to raise, don't require special foods, and are not fussy about living quarters. Just about everyone could afford one. A fat one furnished the best pork "but such as we have we use," Luark philosophically recorded after killing "another light pork."[60]

Slaughtered hogs filled the larder with smoked hams, spicy sausages, barrels of salt pork, and tins of lard. On butchering day, everyone in the family worked and neighbors came to help in the "killing, dressing, sausage making and all that went along....A big dinner was provided for all hands."[61] Caroline Firmin recalls that "Almost always we had fresh fried liver for the noonday dinner that day; and for our supper we had spareribs and dressing cooked in one of the big dripping pans."[62]

Accounts by persons who took part in butchering day effusively describe the day's work. The project began at dawn when large amounts of water were poured into big kettles and set to boil over an outside fire. Next an "improvised trough was made large enough to roll the hog about in the boiling water, the hair scraped off with knives. The carcass was then hung by the hind feet to a rack provided in advance and after opened and the entrails disposed of it hung until the second day before it was cut up and salted."[63]

Joe Whaling from Centralia preserved hams, sides, and shoulders by "laying them on boards in the smoke house and rubbing them with salt and putting saltpeter around the joints of the hams. In eight days he'd resalt them and let them lay there about three weeks until they were cured. Then he'd hang them up in three tiers in the smoke house and for a month off and on he'd keep a fire of hard maple going under them. After that he'd rub them over with olive oil to give them a gloss and exclude the aire."[64]

Because Whaling killed twenty or more hogs at a time, he had excess meat for his family. They gave the surplus to the neighbors in exchange for work, and traded the rest for groceries. In Fourth Plain, "curing meat was the job of every man on the Plain, and continued to be so until prepared 'smoke salts' became so common that well cured meat was no longer a matter for personal pride."[65]

The ubiquitous pork ham occupied the smoke house more than other meat, but occasionally it shared space with hams from fresh elk or venison. To prepare the elk hams, Susanna McFarland Ede "cut off the joints and burned the marrow out with a hot iron rod; then I dipped the hams in hot brine and hung them in a chimney. They were smoked with hard wood, mostly alder, and weren't they good! I often prepared the breast of geese the same way."[66]

Spokane Meat Market
SAM. HELLER, Prop'r.

The finest Beef, Pork, Mutton and Veal
constantly on hand. I make a specialty of
Cured Meats such as

HAMS AND BACON.

CALL AND TRY THEM.

Howard street, Spokane Falls.

CITY MEAT MARKET,
Wilson & Dillard, Propr's.

— A full line of —

Fresh and Cured Meats
Constantly on Hand.

Meats Delivered to any part of the City
Free of Charge.

East side of Howard, between Main street,
and Riverside Avenue, Spokane Falls.

Shoulders,　　10 cts. per lb.

Bacon,　　12 cts. per lb.

Choice Hams, 14 cts. per lb.

BEST ASSORTED STOCK OF GROCERIES.

BELL,

THE CORNER GROCER.

Typical advertisements used by Spokane grocery merchants. *Spokane Evening Review,*
December 1, 1865.

Not everyone had access to maple or alder for smoke house fires.
Green willow wood "smoke poured out at every crevice," in the House
yard in eastern Washington.[67] Annie Brune from Molson, Washington,
liked birch because "it wasn't bitter like quaking aspen." She noted that fir
and pine had too much pitch; "it had to be a wood that didn't have that
kind of pitch in it." Brune used a big dish pan to build the fire in. "She'd
put all this green wood on top (of the fire), and it would just make a
horrible smoke in there. And all your hams were hanging in there, and all
the sausages and bacon. The sausages came out before the hams and the
(pork) shoulders because (the hams and pork shoulders) had a coating on
them so the flies wouldn't get at them. We had as many as twelve hams
smoking at one time."[68]

After smoking, settlers had to store the meat so that it would be protected from flies and other pesky critters. Waiting to butcher when the
temperature dropped and the flies flew to warmer climates helped, but if
they needed meat in June, that ploy did not work. In very cold climates,
frozen carcasses hung outside all winter and families cut off chunks as
needed.

In homes where smoked hams and bacons hung from roof rafters or cellar ceilings, meat had to be wrapped in a cloth or spread with ashes or some other substance that flies did not like. Families had to watch it to be sure the meat under the cloth did not become too warm and attract mold, or that rodents were not biting through the covering. Not wanting to decorate their homes with dangling hams, some families stored the meat in grain bins. Surely rodents often discovered it.

Statements from pioneers tell of other solutions. Like generals plotting to protect their troops, each family devised strategies for saving their meat. The Childers "always put ours in a box and in fly time we'd cover them with the leaves of the blue elderberry and the flies would never touch them."[69] Annie Brune made "a flour coating laced with red pepper and daub[ed] it over the ham, and then she would pour pepper into the top of the ham as well. You see, the flies didn't like that." To get rid of the pepper and salt taste, she put sliced meat in a frying pan, covered it with water and "slowly simmered the meat parboiling it five or ten minutes to get the salt out, and then we'd drain the water off and finish by browning the meat on both sides."[70]

A "treatment of hams" printed in *The Washington Standard* on July 26, 1873 guaranteed a method that protected meat for five years.

> *Treatment of Hams*—To preserve hams through the Summer make a number of cotton bags a little larger than your hams. After the hams are well soaked, place them in the bags, and get the best kind of sweet, well-made hay; cut it with a knife, and with your hands press it well around the hams in the bags; tie the bags with strings, put on a card of the year, to show their age, and hang them up in a garret or some dry room, and they will last five years, and will be better for boiling than on the day you hung them up. This method costs but little, and the bags will last forty years. No flies or bugs will trouble the hams if the hay is well pressed around them; the sweating of the hams will be taken up by the hay and it will impart a fine flavor to the hams. The hams should be treated in this way before the hot weather sets in.

While large portions of the pig entered the smoke house, smaller pieces came under the chopping knife and ended up in a sausage mix. Preparing the stuffing and casings took up many hours on butchering day. Pounds of onions and meat had to be chopped, nutmegs grated, salt scooped from large sacks, and entrails (casings) thoroughly washed, cleaned, and dried.

The general sausage recipe called for a mixture of chopped meat, onions, and spices, but every family had its own variation. Some favored sage, others nutmeg; one used scraps and trimmings, another preferred only lean meat. One hopes the housewife had a grinder, grater, or sausage stuffer to help her because twenty-five to fifty pounds of meat were often ground up for the stuffing. These implements were commonly available by the 1850s or easily made at home.[71] Mary Ellen Fogelsong, who lived in Centralia, described how her family made sausage "when we killed our hogs":

> We chopped the meat, seasoned it with sage, salt, and pepper and then stuffed it in casings....The casings of course were the entrails turned inside out in one long strip and thoroughly washed and scraped. We'd tie one end, insert a tin funnel in the other, and push the sausage meat in with a plunger. Then we'd work it back, twisting it every five or six inches to form the links of the yards and yards of sausage in one skin. When completed, we'd loop the strings of sausage around and around the sticks placed between the rafters in the smokehouse. There, looking much like coils of heavy rope, the sausage, along with the hams and bacon, was smoked above an alderwood fire.[72]

In the Brune kitchen, an insufficient supply of natural casings prompted Annie Brune to make her own. "Mama would make (new casings) out of flour sacks. She would sew them and leave the raw edge to the outside and stuff the casing with the raw sausage and then she would cook (the sausage) on top of the stove in boiling water. You see, they had to be cooked or they would spoil." After boiling, sausages followed the hams into the smoke house.[73]

To keep fresh sausage a *Washington Standard* reader in March 1871 sent in this idea: "Cook fresh sausage as for the table, with out flouring it; then put it in thin layers in a sweet earthen or stone pot with gravy from running hot lard over each layer. It will be as good as when first made."

Butcher shops offered sausage, but as this ad in the *Puget Sound Dispatch* suggests, women were fearful of it.

BOLOGNE SAUSAGE, PORK SAUSAGE, BEEF SAUSAGE, GERMAN SAUSAGE, SUMMER SAUSAGE, LIVER PUDDINGS, BLACK PUDDINGS, TRIPE, HEAD CHEESE, ETC.

As there has always existed in the minds of many persons, and more especially the ladies a sort of antipathy in regard to the manufactory of these small goods by butchers, the public, and of course the ladies, are very respectfully invited to visit our sausage department and witness the *modus operandi* of making these goods. Mr. Murphy will be found in this apartment always willing to give any information desired in regard to his trade.

—BOOTH, FOSS & BORST, Seattle Market.[74]

Rendering lard from mounds of fat was the last big chore engaged in at butchering time. "That was such a job. You couldn't have it in the house. You always rendered it outside. Dad would fix a place in the woodshed. We had one of them great big iron kettles. That's what we rendered the lard in. We always liked the cracklings," Irene Albro emphasized.[75] Eula Fisher remembered that the worst part was cutting up the cold fat: "my fingers got numb from doing this."[76] A lard press, an implement with a paddle or crank, squeezed the last bit of grease from the fibrous fat.

The rendered lard went into large tins or earthen or stone jars and was stored in a dry, cold place so it would stay hard. Slow cooking during the rendering process supposedly prevented lard from molding. Opinions differed as to whether salt hindered spoiling. Territorial merchants offered lard in tins or country made.

Lard is an excellent shortening in pies and cakes and a flavorful fat for frying. Youngsters and grownups savored homemade doughnuts and crullers, fried in fresh lard. It also made a protective covering for fresh-cooked meat, a practice called "frying down." To preserve meat under a layer of lard, cooks browned the steaks, chops, and/or sausage, "being careful not to get it too brown or to scorch it," carefully packed the meat into cleaned stone crocks until they were nearly full, and poured hot lard over the meat covering it completely. "Complete coverage was essential, as the slightest air leaks would cause the whole crock full to spoil. The filled crock was then stored in the cool cellar, and the meat would be removed in meal-size amounts, melting the lard from it for use in pie-making or other cooking needs."[77]

Head cheese, pickled pig's feet, and pickled tripe (stomach) headed the list of dishes created from parts of the pig that today are usually discarded. The cheese, which is not a real cheese but meat cooked and molded, comes from the head and tongue of the pig. To make it, the head is salted, washed, and boiled until the bones can be removed and the meat is soft. The cooked meat is seasoned, chopped, and pressed into a mold. When cold, it can be sliced. Brune's daughter's vivid description makes it clear that a strong stomach headed the requirements of making head cheese:

> Mama used to make head cheese, too. She'd get the head and clean it all out—you had to get the eyes out and take the ears off and everything—and then she cooked everything that was meat. But you had to clean the head before you could do that, and she found an easy way to do it. She'd chop it four ways and then it went easier.[78]

Mutton per Pound

Sheep did not receive the acclaim bestowed on the cow and the pig, but mutton was a popular food in nineteenth-century America. Frequent listings of mutton per pound under "Market News" or "Current Market Prices," an item in most territorial newspapers, suggests that pioneers broiled, fried, and roasted mutton. In the John Jackson family "mutton was the meat most often used....The favored ways of cooking the mutton were roasting and broiling. Mr. Jackson was especially fond of a dish he called broiled bones. Also he liked mutton soup."[79]

> *Superior Receipt for Roast Leg of Mutton*—Cover the joint well with cold water, bring it gradually to boil, and let it simmer gently for half an hour; then lift it out, put it immediately on to the spit, and roast it from an hour and a quarter to an hour and a half, according to its weight. This mode of dressing the joint renders it remarkably juicy and tender; but there must be no delay in putting it on the spit after it is lifted from the water.[80]

Mutton is fatter than beef, but cooked in similar fashion. The leg, loin, and neck are the best parts. Smoking and salting supposedly made mutton taste like venison. If the cook could really make mutton taste like venison, as this recipe suggested, she earned her praise.

> *Mutton to Eat Like Venison*—Take a loin of mutton and bone it; lay it on the fat side in a stewpan, with an onion stuck over with cloves, until the meat is slightly brown. Then pour over it one pint of broth, a gill of port wine, half a gill of ketchup; and let all stew together gently for three hours. Serve with a rich brown sauce.[81]

All Rejoiced When Hens Laid Eggs

When clucking chickens laid eggs, all rejoiced. As soon as possible, pioneers purchased hens. "We have two hens and a rooster. The hens have both hatched a brood of chickens a piece, one sat on twelve eggs and the other on thirteen," Blaine wrote in 1855. A year later Blaine's family moved to Oregon City and Blaine had to begin all over with a new brood of chickens.[82]

Fresh eggs brought in extra money, made cakes moist and light, flavored sauces, perked up potato salad, and tasted delicious boiled, fried, or made into an omelet. "I own four chickens, two crowers and two hens.

Won't we have eggs this winter?" Lucy Ryan enthusiastically wrote to her grandmother.[83] In the early years, homemakers valued chickens more for their eggs than their meat. An advertisement in *The Vancouver Register* on March 12, 1875 stated that a dealer in San Francisco could supply eggs for hatching in addition to Brahmas and leghorn chickens.

The Blaines kept chickens "in a yard enclosed with high palings, but the little fellows can fly like quails and they get out some times and do mischief. They have eaten up about seventy five cabbage plants for us." Several families mention that they built a chicken house.[84]

Eggs practically disappeared in the winter. Hens do not lay eggs in cold, dark chicken coops. They need light and warmth. "We didn't buy any eggs. If we were out of eggs, we were just out of eggs. We had chickens, but they didn't lay like chickens do now. They weren't bred up like they are now. So we just had eggs when we had them," Clara Brune recalled.[85]

Until electricity lit up the hen house, preserving eggs for winter use was another challenge for industrious pioneers—that and keeping the fox and other predators away so that there would be eggs to preserve. The most popular preservation method called for "putting eggs down" in a lime water solution. Another recipe suggested greasing eggs with tallow and burying them in bran or charcoal. Extra cooked eggs went into a pickle.

> *How To Put Down Eggs*—Take a good salt, half a pint; of unslacked lime a piece the size of a teacup. Put both in a stone jar. Pour into the jar 2 gallons of boiling water. Let stand till perfectly cool, then put in your eggs. Be sure your eggs are all good. Care must be taken not to crack any of them in putting them in or they will spoil immediately. The eggs must be entirely covered with the brine.[86]

> *To Pickle Eggs*—Boil them hard. Take off the shell place them in pans pouring on good vinegar saturated with ginger, garlic pepper and spice to your taste.[87]

Another more unconventional method of egg preservation turned up in a letter written to the *American Farmer*, a popular farm journal, from a Hood River, Oregon, pioneer. The "gum" he talks about is an old dialect word for items made from hollowed-out logs.

> *How to Keep Eggs a Year*—I think I have struck a plan (or rather the hen struck it,) that will settle the question for all practicable purposes. The discovery was in this wise:—Over a year ago, I had some hens laying in a hollow gum, filled or nearly full of unleached ashes; the gum was upset by accident, and I paid no further attention to it, until I needed some ashes this spring in making mortar. In taking the ashes

off the ground at the end of gum, I dug out four eggs that had been lain there one year ago; they were perfectly sound and good. We used one immediately after finding them, and kept the others four weeks and then used them, and found that they were as good as if they had not been laid a week. There is no doubt that those eggs were laid in the unleached ashes, previous to the gum being upset, over one year ago; the upsetting covered them with ashes, which were leached in course of time by the weather. Let some of your readers try this, and satisfy themselves that eggs can be kept fresh and good one year.[88]

As more and more people made the Pacific Northwest their home, barnyards shrank. Packing houses rather than the farmer and the farmer's wife corned meat and smoked hams and bacon. Creameries churned butter, and ice and refrigeration made it possible to enjoy fresh meat throughout the year, not just on butchering day. In 1881 in urban areas like Port Townsend, farmers were told "do not send any more [eggs] at present as there are a great many in town."[89] But all this took time. Until then, cows, chickens, hogs, and sheep enjoyed a special status as they strutted and scratched around the barnyard.

Chapter Eight
In the Midst of Plenty

Venison, deer, elk, grouse, prairie chickens, geese, ducks, salmon, steelhead, and trout either inhabited the forests, flew over tree tops, or swam in the clear waters of Oregon Territory. Newcomers to the Pacific Northwest filled their plates with wild game and fish. Lucky ones like John Campbell caught a salmon in the morning and "went out in evening and shot a pheasant."[1]

Catharine Blaine supplemented her breakfast "more often consisting of warmed over potatoes, Indian pan cakes and cold water; [and] dinner...a good variety of vegetables, with always pie or pudding for dessert" with "some fresh wild meat if our friends send it in to us, or some of the excellent salmon."[2] The Swift family, who established a homestead on Whidbey Island in 1864, feasted on: "Thursday, a goose pie, Friday venison steak—Saturday, roast venison. Today, cold roast. We have hanging in our store one whole deer and one quarter of another. For this we pay about three cents per pound, at the kitchen door. Fifty cents for a goose, twenty-five cents for a partridge, pay them the Indians in food, goods or money." The rest of the week Louise Swift served stewed chicken and "roasted stuffed kid, one month old."[3] Even as late as 1902, in the new settlements of Okanogan County, settlers repeated the same refrain: "We had little money but wild game, fish and berries were plentiful....Deer, grouse, pheasants and duck furnished much of our food."[4]

As well as providing appetizing meals, a bountiful supply of game and fish made it easier to cope when flour bins stood empty. So much game lived in the woods around Steilacoom, settlers told Charles Prosch "they had but to go to the back doors of their dwellings, any early morning in the year, to shoot a fine doe or fat buck for the family, and in certain localities and in certain season ducks swarmed in such dense masses, covering the surface of the water for miles in extent."[5]

Because of its fine flavor, venison headed the list of game meat pioneers preferred. Hunters rejoiced when they shot a deer and brought it home to their families. Glowing descriptions of venison meals suggest that all those lucky enough to dine on this delectable meat surely would have agreed with Adelaide Gilbert's statement: "Someone has just sent us a fine leg of venison—just think what a present!"[6]

Cooks considered the haunch (leg and loin) the most tender and tastiest part, but they differed as to whether steaks should be cut from the haunch or the neck, the second best joint. Sarah Hale favored the neck; *The Kentucky Housewife* said to use the haunch. They both recommended serving roast venison with currant jelly. A portion of venison haunch added to a pot of broth, potatoes, and vegetables turned a plain stew into a gustatory delight. In order to have some of that good meat when the hunter's gun missed its target, settlers put up what they had in "brine, then cut it in strips and dried it on lines across the kitchen."[7] Contrary to popular opinion, emigrants did not pick up drying techniques from Native Americans living in Oregon Territory. Drying meat is an old way of preserving foods.

> *Venison Steaks*—Cut them from the neck; season them with pepper and salt. Heat the gridiron well over a bed of bright coals, and grease the bars; lay the steaks on it; broil them well, turning them once, and save as much of the gravy as possible. Serve them with some currant jelly laid on each steak.[8]

Large numbers of grouse and partridge nested in the Northwest. There were so many it did not take much skill to bag a brace of grouse at meal time. "When meat was out, and father did not want to butcher, he took the single buggy and drove out...and returned with a half dozen grouse and pheasants," recalled Elizabeth Chambers Hunsacker.[9] Others repeated the same story—though as early as 1870 the seemingly endless supply of game birds may have been shrinking in Mason County. On December 21, 1870 John Campbell noted he hunted "all this day for game to eat on Christmas but only got five pheasants."[10]

Sarah Hale advised cleaning and washing the birds with vinegar and boiling water if "there is danger of birds not keeping....but, as a rule, no game should be washed, for one-half the game...is spoiled by being saturated in water."[11] She advised basting roasting game with butter. Salt pork and/or lard may have been used. With game so plentiful, pioneers probably skipped the vinegar and water bath, and just plucked out feathers, cleaned insides, trussed wings and legs to the body, and hung the birds over a hot fire.

Rebecca Ebey stuffed the pheasants, "which was excellent."[12] Since we know the Ebey family planted many potatoes, perhaps like James Swan she made a mashed potato dressing. Swan, who lived among the Makah Indians in 1859, regularly reported how the white man ate in the backwoods. "We used for stuffing [wild ducks], mashed potatoes with a slice of salt-pork chopped fine, a little pepper and allspice."[13]

In Whitman County, Harry Roberts recalled that prairie chickens were "so numerous my father killed four at a time. We ate only the breasts."[14] Clareta Smith wrote that a "pot roast of prairie chicken or cottontail rabbit was a dish for the gods. They were cut up and put into an iron kettle with several generous slices of bacon and a little water. They simmered gently until they were well cooked, then were allowed to fry down nice and brown in the bacon fat."[15] To cut down on the wild flavor, cooks soaked meat in milk and/or added an onion to the pan.

Beaver and bear meat were not ordinary pioneer cuisine, but even these wild animals occasionally furnished meat at meal times. "The men trapped beaver; and their wives often baked beaver tails after skinning them dipping them in boiling water and then removing the backbones. These unusual bits of delicacy tasted like halibut," recalled Centralia pioneers.[16]

Bear meat did not receive such compliments. The wild taste needed disguising. As Nellie Coupe found out, calling it pork steak made it more palatable:

> While we were enjoying our feast of bear meat, Mr. Coupe remarked that his wife, Nellie was expected home the next day, and that she was of the opinion that bear meat was not fit to eat. In fact she would not even taste it. But when that lady arrived, Aunt Rachel served her some nice "steak" for dinner. Nellie ate heartily and remarked on its goodness; "My, this is lovely steak," she said. "What kind is it?" "Oh, it's just pork," Mr. Coupe answered casually. "Well it's surely the best pork I ever ate," Nellie replied, as she reached for a second helping.[17]

Plenty of Shellfish

Those pioneers living in homes near the coastal waters found an abundance of clams, crabs, and oysters. Acknowledging his good fortune, Thornton McElroy, in 1853, wrote to his wife, Sarah,

> Well I live principally on bread, butter, potatoes, oysters and clams. Don't you think that is very good living?...I get my bread from the baker's, bake my potatoes in the stove and steam the oysters. That is all the cooking I do. I eat some oysters for you nearly every day.[18]

Sarah obviously never lost her love for oysters, for twenty years later she proudly served them to guests: "This week I am expecting a houseful again from Oregon for the Fair...we will give them plenty of clams and oysters which is all I can do for them that they cannot-get-at-home."[19]

Clams, such as the butter (Quahog), littleneck, razor, horseneck, and geoduck, reside in the ocean sand and muddy bays along the West Coast of North America. They thrive in the mild Pacific Northwest climate. Indians have enjoyed their fine taste and ease of preparation for centuries. The Indians tried to "show us how to prepare them. We never succeeded in learning the art of drying them," recalled Sarah Hartman.[20] Actually few tried. There were so many around, most people used them fresh. "Clam chowder, fried clams, clam fritters, in soup and "straight" were among the staples," recalled Mrs. D.T. Denny. One shopped for dinner when the tide rolled out.[21]

Community celebrations and territorial restaurants featured clams on the menu. Clam chowder parties and clambakes provided entertainment for young and old. Butler's Cove north of Olympia "was a famous picnic ground and almost the whole town would turn out to attend clam bakes."[22] At the annual celebration of the Pioneer Association of Port Townsend in 1887, "bushels and bushels of clams literally went down before the mighty onslaught, and eatables from unassuming sandwiches to delicate frosted fruit cake," greeted the guests. "All fell to eating most heartily," reported the newspaper.[23]

Newspapers regularly announced those popular socials:

Chowder Party—On Saturday last a number of ladies and gentlemen, our own happy self included, enjoyed a delightful sail on the Sound, in the sloop "Sarah Stone," Capt. Slater, for whose kindness we are very grateful, and partook of all the luxuries peculiar to an aquatic picnic.—such pleasures on this far north-west coast should be evidence to our friends in the States that we are not by any means without the pale of civilization.[24]

A notice in Olympia's *Territorial Republican* on July 12, 1869 described the clambakes. If they truly followed the "downeast" style, then settlers steamed clams under seaweed in a pit of heated rocks, and served them with corn.

Clam Bakes, Etc.—The principal amusement just now for the happy denizens of this burg is pic-nicing and clam baking—the latter in the genuine 'downeast' style. There are on an average two a week which are patronized by a large part of the community, and an evidence that they are enjoyable amusements is that they are so regularly kept up. The fisheries are also well patronized 'tom cods' being brought to town almost by the bushel. Not a stranger visits our town but he is invited to take a boat ride to the fishing grounds and try his hand, and then pass judgment on the quantity and quality.—As the supply is inexhaustible, this species of amusement will not soon decline.

Forty years later, in 1909, Lynden, Washington, citizens decided to bring back the old-time celebration when "the feature of the meeting [honoring pioneers in Olympia] was a big clam dinner, in which the clams were supplied by a committee of pioneers who had gone out on the flats of the sound there at Olympia and had dug up the bivalves for the occasion." So began the famous Northwest Clam Digger's Club of Whatcom County.[25]

Many historians suggest that New England clambakes originated with Native Americans. But folklorist Kathy Neustadt, in her well-documented book *Clambake*, argues that "it is possible for the clambake to be a part of native American cultural inheritance *and* an invented tradition within white culture."[26] By the mid-nineteenth century, the clambake symbolized American origins and a connection to the Yankee temperament. Most importantly it provided another way to enjoy good food out of doors.

Residents of Spokane could not take a walk on the beach and pick up clams, but they could enjoy the ones sent to them. Adelaide Gilbert cooked them in a stew for her husband who "seem[ed] to get such a craving for them…and said he slept so soundly last night and he knew it was owing to the clam broth." Gilbert also noted that they did get "very nice canned clams."[27]

Besides clams, the key ingredient in clam chowder is salt-pork or bacon. Seasoning, onions, and potatoes add extra flavor; each cook had a favorite combination and technique. Mrs. F.W. Panchot stressed that frying onions "so delicately that they will be missing in the chowder" was the secret to good chowder. Her recipe, printed here, appeared in *The Auburn Cook Book*. Making chowder has been a favorite way of preparing clams since resourceful New Englanders concocted ways of using the many clams found along the Massachusetts shore in the sixteenth century. They did not add tomatoes in New England.

> *Clam Chowder*—Fifty round clams, a large bowl of salt pork cut up fine, the same of onions, finely chopped, and the same, or more if desired, of potatoes cut rather fine. Wash the clams very thoroughly, and put them in a pot with half a pint of water, when the shells are open they are done. Then take them from the shells and chop fine, saving all the clam water for the chowder. Fry out the pork very gently,

and when the scraps are a good brown, take them out and put in the onions to fry—they should be fried in a frying pan and the chowder kettle be made very clean before they are put in, or the chowder will burn. (The chief secret in chowder making is to fry the onions so delicately that they will be missing in the chowder.) Add a quart of hot water to the onions, put in the clams, clamwater and pork scraps. After it boils, add the potatoes, and when they are cooked the chowder is finished. Just before it is taken up, thicken it with a cup of powdered crackers and add a quart of fresh milk. If too rich, add more water. No seasoning is needed but good black pepper. Add sliced tomatoes if preferred.[28]

In Aurora, Oregon, the abundance of crawfish suggested another reason to have a picnic. Henry Finck, who lived there between 1862 and 1872, recalled that they "took the girls along, all were welcome; also, we took a pan and salt and matches. When our tin pails were full we killed and cleaned the crawlers—it took some skill to avoid their claws—and make a fire. In a few minutes they were ready and—well, I cannot say more for them than that they were as delicious as Chinook salmon." Recipes from old Aurora suggest that spicy seasonings and vinegar were added along with the crawfish to the boiling water.[29]

Piles and piles of sun-bleached oyster shells along the shores at Nahcotta, Washington, attested to the quantities of oysters greeting the new arrivals. A nearby Pacific County town grew and developed because of the native oyster, *Ostrea Lurida*, that flourished in Shoalwater (Willapa) Bay. Oysterville, founded by R.H. Espy and I.A. Clark, to supply oysters for the California market, is now on the National Register of Historic Places.

Waverly Root, the noted authority on foods, wrote that "the tiny Olympia oyster...is also considered the tastiest available in its region. Gourmets sometimes pay as much as three times the price of ordinary oysters for the Olympia."[30] The oysters became known as Olympia Oysters after voters chose Olympia as the capital of Washington state.[31]

Succulent oysters were one of the most beloved American foods of the nineteenth century.[32] Rich and poor alike shucked and savored them. Like clams, oysters mingle well in soups, stews, chowders, fritters, and pies. They are good raw and eagerly devoured with beer or champagne. Mrs. Hugh Wiley told her daughter that "oyster soup, made in the wash boilers of that day, was the luxury dish of any important party, but especially the dances" that took place in Washington Territory.[33] A recipe printed in a 1905 Port Townsend cook book gives one way to make oyster soup.

Oysters! Oysters!!
Frank
DEKUM'S
Ladies' Oyster & Coffee Saloon!

JUST RECEIVED DIRECT FROM SHOALWATER
Bay, a Large Lot of

OYSTERS!

And would respectfully inform the citizens of Portland that
he has fitted up an

OYSTER AND COFFEE SALOON

or the coming Season.   No pains or expense have been
spared to make this one of the most Comfortable places of
Resort on the Pacific Coast, and is now ready to serve his
old Patrons and Customers with Oysters in every style, and
all the Delicacies of the season.

The Saloon is open all day and late at night.

N. B.—Families, Hotels, and Parties supplied at
short notice: Orders promptly attended to, and delivered
free of charge to any part of the city.

FRANK DEKUM.
First street, between Washington and Stark.
Portland, Sept. 27, 1862.   d3m

Oregonians, like other Americans, loved to feast on succulent oysters.
Dekum's, a Portland establishment, was happy to make them available.
Morning Oregonian, Portland, October 25, 1862.

Oyster Soup—Two quarts of oysters, one quart of milk, two tablespoons
of butter, one pint of water. Pepper and salt to taste. Strain the liquor
from the oysters, add to it the water and set over the fire to heat slowly.
When it is near boiling, season with pepper and salt; add the oysters
and let them stew until they "ruffle" on the edge. This will be about
five minutes; then put in the butter with the milk which has been
heated in a separate vessel, and stir well for two minutes.[34]

One of the most popular Northwest oyster recipes, "Oyster Pan Roast,"
came from Doane's Oyster House in Olympia, Washington Territory. Considered the "*ne plus ultra* of good eating," the restaurant served sixty gallons of oysters a day. Imagine shucking all those oysters! A plate of Doane's
Pan Roast cost thirty-five cents in the 1880s:

Doane's Oyster Pan Roast—A Pan Roast required a large cupful of oysters, frizzled in four tablespoonfuls of melted butter, a cupful of tomato

catsup, one tablespoonful of Worcestershire sauce, one scant teaspoonful of Tabasco, salt and pepper, poured piping hot over *oven* toast.[35]

In the nineteenth century people preferred to eat oysters during months
spelled with an "R," the colder months. Oysters spoil rapidly at higher
temperatures, and in summertime, without refrigeration, keeping shellfish
fresh proved difficult. Today oysters are harvested year-round; however,
during the spawning season in late spring and summer they are not always
in peak condition. By inserting the "R is in" in his poem, the owner of the
restaurant advertising in *The Puget Sound Dispatch* on October 4, 1880
reminded his patrons that they could safely enjoy oysters:

> Bow down your head, ye haughty clam,
> And oysters, say your prayers,
> The month has come the "R" is in,
> You're on the bill of fare—
> In every style at the
> SADDLE ROCK RESTAURANT.
> 25 Cents Per Plate

The I.A. Clark family, one of the founders of Oysterville, praised
oyster pie and served it often. Lucille Wilson, great granddaughter of Mr.
Clark, sent me her grandmother's recipe from "way back in the days when
she lived in Oysterville." Wilson says she adds celery, pimentos, and mushrooms, but doubts if her grandmother had these ingredients. Actually she
may have, because ships coming from California to pick up the oysters
filled the space with supplies that the settlers needed. Out-of-season fruits
and vegetables from California began coming into the Pacific Northwest
by the mid-1850s. Experiments with preserved milk began in the 1850s.
One recipe described in *Scientific American*, May 29, 1852, calls for heating the fresh milk and egg yolks over a water bath for several hours. The
writer said "this milk will keep good for two years, and if churned would
afford good butter." Gail Borden, who perfected the process, eliminated
three-fourths of the water in fresh milk. Preserved milk, which Borden
called condensed milk, gained popularity during the Civil War. It proved
so popular that manufacturers offered special utensils for holding the cans.

> *Oyster Pie*—2 cups raw oysters, 2 cups water. Cook together, drain
> and cut. Save liquid, then add to it: 1 cup canned milk, bring to a boil,
> thicken with 4 tablespoons flour mixed in ½ cup water, cook until its
> thick stir constantly. Add oysters and butter. Put in baking dish cover
> with biscuits, bake.[36]

Rich Oyster Pie, a variation of the Clark recipe, appeared in *The Washington Standard* on December 9, 1871. Such a gourmet dish using puff pastry offers evidence that oysters made it on the menu in the wealthiest homes.

> *Rich Oyster Pie*—Strain off the liquor from the oysters, and put it on to boil, with some butter, mace, nutmeg, pepper and salt. Just as it boils, stir in a thickening of milk and flour, put in the oysters and stir until they are sufficiently stewed then take them off, and put in the yolks of two eggs, well beaten (do not put this in while it is boiling or it will curdle). Line a dish, not very deep, with puff paste; fill it with white unglazed paper or a napkin, to keep the top paste from falling in; put on top paste and bake. When done, remove the top crust carefully, and take out the paper or napkin, and pour in the oysters. Send it hot to the table.

When in the late 1890s church groups and women's organizations in the Northwest added their recipes to the growing popularity of charity cookbooks, they too included oyster recipes.

> *Oyster Dressing for Turkey or Chicken*—Take 1 loaf of bread (trim off the brown crust) cut into small squares with a sharp knife. Sprinkle with salt, pepper and sage to taste. Dissolve in 1 pt. of the liquor from the fowl 3 tablespoons of butter, pour this over the bread; add 1 can of fresh or cove oysters. Stir with a fork just enough to distribute the oysters evenly through the bread. Add the whites of 5 eggs beaten to a stiff froth; stir this lightly through the mixture and bake 40 minutes.[37]

> *A Quick and Delicious Way to Scallop Oysters*—Put an iron spider on fire and get very hot, add lump of butter size of walnut, then layer of cracker crumbs, then oysters, then crumbs, until dish is full as can be handled. Add cup of milk. Stir quickly. Do not let brown. Add seasoning just before serving.[38]

By the 1880s over-harvesting and waste reduced the supply of the native *Ostrea Lurida,* and non-native species like the Baltimore oyster took its place. In 1870 Shoalwater Bay oyster farmers imported and planted 100,000 large Baltimore oysters.[39] Many families then chose the canned variety over fresh oysters. Merchants proudly announced that they carried "Fresh Canned Eastern Oysters" along with the "line of native...Shoalwater Bay, Samish Bay and Yaquina Bay."[40] At a New Year's dinner given in Ellensburg in 1888, guests had a choice of Puget Sound Oysters or New York Selected Oysters.[41]

A Kettle of Fish

So many fish swam in the rivers, lakes, and inlets in and around Oregon and Washington Territory one did not have to be an experienced fisherman to dine every night on cod, halibut, smelt, steelhead, sturgeon, or salmon. "Smelt...were to be had in such abundance as to be a nuisance to the fastidious, who insisted that the fish be cleaned. Smoked and put away for winter they would be a delight all over again with fresh-baked bread and cold milk."[42] Families filled tubs and barrels with these fish.

Abundant schools of cod swam continuously in the waters bordering the Pacific Northwest, causing *The San Francisco Globe* in 1857 to state: "It appears at last that Cape Cod away down East, is likely to have a rival in that place with a hard name, Steilacoom, Puget Sound ...The fish [codfish] is not so large as the Eastern, but exceeding well cured and sweet. The supply...is said to be inexhaustible."[43] Commenting on that statement from the San Francisco newspaper, *The Washington Republican* answered: "We are not prepared to claim for Steilacoom a successful rivalry with Cape Cod, but we will venture the assertion without fear of contradiction, that take the entire waters of the Sound and Fuca's Straits, and with the same amount of capital invested in the business, Cape Cod would have to yield."[44] Hoping to support cod fishing, newspapers printed recipes for preparing the fish after salting, a time-honored way of preserving that species.

> *How to Cook Codfish*—The codfish should first be soaked in cold water, changing the water every few hours until it is fresh enough. It should not be entirely freshened but left just salt enough to be palatable. It is then put into a kettle, covered with water, and brought up to the boiling point, but not boiled. Let it simmer gently for fifteen to twenty minutes, and it is ready to serve....We have sometimes seen small bits of salt pork fried crisp and served with the pork fat [as an accompaniment]. [45]

Northwest residents knew the importance of having succulent seafood to supplement their meals. Residents and visitors—at one time a president's wife—expressed amazement at such delicacies from the sea. That particular incident happened in 1880 when Mrs. Elisha P. Ferry, wife of the territorial governor of Washington, entertained Mrs. Rutherford Hayes and planned to serve fish and other Puget Sound seafood along with chicken. Near the end of the dinner a maid tiptoed in and quietly reminded the hostess that the chicken had not been served. The *piece de resistance* had been entirely overlooked. Bring it in, Mrs. Ferry whispered. Mrs. Hayes exclaimed, "We have had chicken in many forms and in many places on our way, but this fish service has been a real treat."[46] Mrs. Hayes probably would have been amazed to hear that pioneers complained that they were sick of salmon.

Pioneers broiled, baked, fried, steamed, or stewed the fresh fish. They made a type of chowder by first frying salt-pork until crisp (cracklings), boiling the fish with potatoes, and just before serving sprinkling the mixture with a large amount of the crackling. Seasonings depended on what spices were in the pantry. Sarah McElroy's handwritten personal notebook contains several ways Pacific Northwest cooks prepared fish in the 1880s.

> *Salmon*—First a layer of cold boiled fish. Then bread crumbs—until dish is full, season to taste. Pour a mixture of egg and milk over the whole and bake.
>
> *Boiled Fish*—Sew your fish tightly in a cloth and boil 20 minutes for each pound—Serve with drawn butter and hard boiled eggs. Make drawn butter with the water in which the fish is boiled.
>
> *Baked Cod Dish*—Soak salt fish over night—then boil half an hour. Put fish in a dish with well mashed potatoes on top and all around the fish. Pour on a little milk, bits of butter and put in oven until a nice brown.
>
> *Codfish Fritters*—Make a batter like nice batter cakes, add freshened cod fish [cut?] into shreds and fry in lard.
>
> *Sardines on Toast*—Take sardines—wipe the oil from them, dip in egg and cracker or bread crumbs—fry serve on nice buttered toast. Soak toast before buttering. Oysters very nice the same way.[47]

Nineteenth-century cookery writers told their readers that fresh fish flesh should be firm and thick, the gills bright red, the eyes full and bright, and to prepare it immediately after catching. The same admonitions are given today.

Recipes from period cookbooks include more boiling and frying recipes than ones for broiling or baking fish. Most likely pioneer cooks prepared whole fish, that is with head, tail, and bones intact. Removing all the small bones takes time. Boneless, filleted fish sold in commercial establishments did not appear in markets until the twentieth century.

Bessie Craine's grandfather's fish recipe for salmon seems similar to the way we prepare fish. "He would wrap the fish in wet, butcher's paper. These were put in the oven. When the paper was dry the fish were done. The skin came away with the paper. He would lift out the backbone and there was that beautiful pink fish all ready for salt and butter."[48] Craine doesn't specify the species of salmon, but most everyone considered Chinook, or king salmon the best, followed by coho, sockeye, and chum (dog). In Fourth Plain, women "with an instinct for elegance fighting against pioneer reality," called dog salmon by the Indian name of "calico salmon."[49]

Extra seafood, just like beef and pork, had to be "put down in the salt" when families wanted to keep it for longer than a few days. Salt draws moisture from fish muscle tissue so that when the fish dries, bacterial growth ceases. When Sarah Willoughby found a large quantity of rock cod left by the receding tide in the oyster beds on the beach at Port Townsend she knew her family could not use so much fresh fish. "The result is over half a large salmon barrel of nice salted fish. Jack and the boys cleaned and salted them."[50] Before eating, fish had to be thoroughly washed to remove the salty taste.

> *For Salting Salmon*—For thirty-five pounds four and one-half pounds of salt. Cut head off and cut in pieces about four or five inches in size, take a stone jar and put a layer of salt and then a layer of salmon until the jar is a little over two-thirds full, then weight down, and the brine will raise on it enough to cover it. Place in the cellar, and it will keep good all winter. Before using put in cold water and let stand over night and they will be fresh enough to boil in a little water for one-half hour, then take out and put a little butter and pepper. For frying let stand in the cold water or if necessary change the water and let stand five or six hours longer, then flour and fry to a nice brown.[51]

In many homes, when fish hooks attracted too many fish, the surplus ended up in a pickle solution. A recipe from *The Saint Peter's Cook Book* directed the cook to "boil the salmon in salted water until done, then remove all bones and skin" before layering in an earthen crock with onions, spices, and vinegar.[52] After ten days or two weeks in the pickling solution, a dish of pickled fish might accompany a meal of potatoes and boiled meat. The recipe the Saint Peter's Ladies followed was very similar to those found in early seventeenth- and eighteenth-century cookbooks. English, Dutch, and Scandinavians have served pickled salmon for a long time.

The Northwest Company first introduced the fish salting process to the Oregon territory in order to provide winter food for its employees, a practice later followed by the Hudson's Bay Company. Eventually, salted salmon, particularly spring chinook and sockeye, enjoyed popularity in the Hawaiian Islands, Australia, China, Japan, and the Eastern United States.

By 1866, canning surpassed salting as a better way to preserve and ship the fish. William Hume, who had assisted in starting the first salmon cannery in the United States on the Sacramento River, opened one on the Columbia River at Astoria, and in 1877 Jackson Myers & Co. established the first Puget Sound salmon cannery at Mukilteo. The early cans from the cannery at Mukilteo contained silver, or coho salmon; later ones held humpback, or pink salmon. Knowing that the public might be upset to find pink salmon in their cans, the owners confronted the problem with humor and printed on the label, "Warranted not to turn red in the can." It did not work. Demand for humpback salmon developed very slowly.

Unfortunately, other canneries did not always practice honesty in labeling. Chums and pinks went into cans branded as "Fresh salmon" or "Choice salmon"; "Do-overs" and very poor fish bore the labels of a fictitious company or no company at all. Not until 1906, when the Pure Food and Drug Act began to regulate canneries, did the public have the assurance that the fish on the label resembled the fish in the can.[53]

As burgeoning Northwest towns encroached upon the forests and woods, and thousands of cows roamed the grasslands, herds of deer and flocks of game birds moved further and further away. In the populated areas, venison and game birds more often came from the neighborhood butcher than a homeowner's gun. Increases in the supply of ice and improved refrigeration made it possible to keep fresh meat longer than a few days. A growth in population produced enough profits for merchants to stock grouse and goose as well as beef steaks.

By the 1880s city cooks considered game a gourmet food to be served on special occasions or ordered at fancy restaurants. A check of the menu for the Grand Central Hotel in Tacoma in 1892 shows "Loin of Elk, Sauce Cumberland, Canvasback Duck with Currant Jelly, Blue Grouse with Wheat Cake Dressing."[54] By then, only beginning homesteaders in rural areas considered wild game the main dish for everyday meals.

Chapter Nine
Parties and Special Days

No matter how hard women and men worked during the day, when someone brought out a fiddle and pushed furniture against the walls, neighbors gathered for a dance or party. Feasting and dancing characterized much of the social life of the new Northwest residents. Breaking away from the Puritan/Protestant work ethic prevalent in much of the late eighteenth and early nineteenth century, Northwest residents followed middle class America in the pursuit of leisure time activities. In rural areas where men and women worked hard clearing the land and building homes, an evening dance in a neighbor's house made up for the hardworking day. In urban areas, dances and fancy dress balls gave residents a place to spend their leisure time and a chance to display their wealth.[1]

Judging from statements written in diaries and letters, rich and poor, farmers and politicians, all liked to dance. "Had a very social time of it [and] danced nearly all night until daylight," wrote John Campbell, who spent his days "grubbing out stumps and planting crops."[2] "Tuesday evening attended large party....Danced all the square dances...supper and wine were excellent and abundant," Judge Matthew Deady, a prominent Portland lawyer, recorded in his diary.[3] Even in hard times, dancing parties in the Spokane area continued. Mrs. A.C. Tram recalled going to "dances and parties in paper dresses, floursack dresses—and danced until daylight."[4] In isolated communities, people traveled miles to dance the quadrille. "Twenty or thirty miles was not [a] great distance to go to attend a dance....You went on horseback, sometimes two on one horse."[5] Some even traveled in a sailboat and set up dance floors at logging camps. They would "dance all night then come back by boat next day," recalled Mrs. Hunter, who lived in Thurston county.[6]

"I am learning to dance, many cotillions are held. When I came to Olympia there were but two ladies here, now many more, all generous in providing good things to eat," Thornton McElroy wrote in 1853 to his wife Sarah, no doubt thinking that account might be the incentive Sarah needed to make the long trip west.[7] Whether she finally decided to join her husband because she thought she had better become acquainted with the ladies "providing good things to eat," or because she just wanted to be with her husband and join in the fun, Sarah McElroy soon arrived in Oregon. The parties continued. Several years later she described the activities in a letter to her brother:

> They have private parties here now every two weeks, which are very pleasant....they dance about twice a week....I had our church society here and had a nice little supper in honor of the occasion. It was real pleasant and we had a jolly time lots of music and dancing....I wish I could send you a piece of what we called wedding cake, but I am afraid it would mash all to pieces.[8]

In pioneer times, wedding cakes resembled very rich fruit cakes. Some areas of the country called them bride's cake or plum (English term for dried fruit) cakes. Many cookbooks included both names. The cakes were baked in round tins or hoops and were usually covered with a white frosting if served at wedding receptions. Very large cakes meant to serve sizable crowds might take three to four hours to bake. The traditional tiered wedding cake made its appearance in the mid-nineteenth century.[9]

McElroy's recipe collection included a fruit cake, but none titled "wedding cake." Though she wrote down the fruit cake recipe thirty years after the mention in the letter, it may have been a family favorite for years. In the era when women baked frequently they did not require recipes and so did not bother to write down the recipe until someone asked for it or as a reminder of ingredients. The wedding cake recipe recorded here is from *North Seattle Cook and Recipe Book*. Notice that neither McElroy's recipe nor the one from the north Seattle cookbook gave directions. Experience in the kitchen since childhood taught women how to add and mix ingredients.

> *McElroy's Fruit Cake*—2 cups of brown sugar, 1 cup molasses, 1 cup strong coffee, 4½ cups flour, 6 eggs, 1 teaspoon soda, 2 teaspoons cloves, 2 teaspoons cinnamon, 2 tablespoons vanilla, 2 tablespoons lemon ex., 2 lb. raisins, 3 lb. currants, 1 lb. citron.

> *Wedding Cake*—Fifteen eggs well beaten, one and a half pounds butter, one and a half pounds sugar, one and a half pounds flour, three pounds seeded raisins, three pounds currants, one and a half pounds citron, sliced thin, a half-pint of molasses, one ounce ground mace,

one ounce ground cinnamon, one-half ounce ground cloves. Will keep for years, and if steamed will be fresh and nice.[10]

At least McElroy named the cake served at the dance. Most reports of dances simply said that a variety of cakes and pies turned up at the late-night suppers. Yet, besides baking numerous versions of fruit cakes, cooks creamed butter and sugar and beat eggs for Sally Lunn, Washington Cake, Jenny Lind Cake, jelly cake, election cake, lemon cake, mountain cake, and chocolate cake, as well as rolling out crusts for fruit, custard, and mince-meat pies—all popular sweets that filled the pages of numerous nineteenth-century cookbooks. "The skill of the best confectioners and pastry cooks is being literally exhausted," noted a newspaper writer from Olympia, in 1870.[11] When they had the proper ingredients Northwest families ate as well as those in the States. By the 1870s, women living in urban areas usually had no trouble finding a large assortment of foods.

Cakes like Sally Lunn have been popular since the early nineteenth century. Mountain cake and chocolate cake—lighter, layer-type cakes—achieved popularity when cooks switched to leavening agents such as baking soda rather than depending on yeast or numerous eggs.

Rocky Mountain Cake

The White—Take two eggs; one-half cup butter; one cup sugar; two cups flour; one-half cup of milk; two teaspoonfuls cream tartar; one tablespoonful soda.

The Dark—One cup of molasses; one cup of butter; one-half cup of cold water; one large teaspoonful soda; cloves and nutmeg.[12]

Chocolate Cake

Good Delicate Cake for Chocolate (from Fannie O'Brien)—One cup of butter, 2 cups of sugar, 3 cups of flour—half cup milk, whites of six large eggs, soda and cream of tartar.

Filling for chocolate cake—Soak quarter package of Cox's gelatin in a little water. Heat one pint of milk add also the yolks of three eggs and four squares of chocolate and half cup sugar; flavor with vanilla. Make day before serving.

Frosting for chocolate cake—white of four eggs, one and a quarter pounds of sugar and half cake of grated chocolate.[13]

The recipe for Sally Lunn cakes shows up in McElroy's collection and territorial newspapers. McElroy's recipe followed the traditional way and used yeast as a leavening agent. Rosie's Sally Lunn cake printed in *The Washington Standard* relies on baking soda. Both used sugar, but according to John and Karen Hess in *The Taste of America*, the classic recipe did not use a sweetener. By mid-nineteenth century, Northwest residents, along with the rest of America, had acquired a sweet tooth and would "hoax things up with sugar."[14] Rosie, the name cited in *The Washington Standard* newspaper column, may have been a local homemaker or worker in a bakery, because the editors wrote: "Wc know Rosie's cake is excellent, for we have often been favored with it."[15] By adding whortleberries (*Vaccinium uliginosum*—similar to blueberries), Rosie gave the traditional cake a Northwest flavor.

> *McElroy's Sally Lunn*
>   4 eggs
>   ½ teacup sugar
>   1 Tablespoon butter
>   ¾ teacup yeast
>   1 quart flour
>   1 pint sweet milk
> Make batter about consistency of pound cake and let it rise about 9:30 for tea at 6 o'clock. Sophie finds it better to add a very small handful of flour, when it is stirred down to put into the pans.[16]

> *Rosie's Sally Lunn*—One spoonful of butter, one of sugar, one egg, one pint of milk, one quart of flour with two teaspoonfuls of cream of tartar sifted with the flour, one teaspoonful of soda added the last thing. This is an excellent breakfast cake, as well as tea cake; and is sometimes varied by stirring in a pint of whortleberries.[17]

McElroy's cake collection also includes jelly, lemon, ribbon, and coffee cake. Note that the lemon cake uses baking powder and that the measurements begin to have a degree of specificity. Usually recipes called for impressionistic measurements: a teacup full or butter the size of a walnut. Accurate measuring cups and spoons first appeared in the mid-1880s. Fannie Farmer, a noted cooking instructor and author of numerous cookbooks, received credit for emphasizing exact measurements.[18]

> *Lemon Cake* (splendid [from] Mrs. Ferry)
>   one cup butter
>   two cups sugar
>   ⅔ cup sweet milk
>   2 cups flour
>   white of 8 eggs
>   3 teaspoons baking powder
>   Bake in jelly tins.

Jelly For the Cake (Lemon)
Yolks of 3 eggs—⅔ cup of butter, 1 cup of sugar—juice of three lemons and rind of 2—rub butter and sugar together—Beat yolk and add to beaten sugar and butter and the lemon—Set in kettle of hot water until it thickens stirring all the time—Use when cold between the layers of cake.[19]

To help ladies, particularly a Mrs. G., make a better pie crust, a helpful reader of *The Washington Standard* on June 11, 1870, sent in a suggestion:

> After having gathered together all the ingredients necessary for making a rich pie crust, I rub the shortening into the flour, very slightly, instead of thoroughly as advised; then put in cold water and just barely mix the whole together; and this, I can assure Mrs. G. is the secret of making flaky pie crust.

For those who desired more substantial foods, dance suppers might include chicken, hams, roasts, pickles, relishes, and a variety of seafood. Throughout the area, "it was the custom for the ladies to provide these [dance suppers] and they vied with each other in bringing their best, so the chow was both tempting and plentiful."[20] Since too many cloudy days on the west side of the Cascade mountains often prevented tomatoes from ripening, piccalilli most likely appeared in the relish dishes. The recipe appeared in many period cookbooks.

> *Piccalilli*—Slice green tomatoes; sprinkle a little salt over them and let stand over night, then drain off in the morning till dry. Put them on to boil. Take sugar, Turmeric powder, 1 equal part of mustard and flour, unground cloves and pepper. You can put mixed spices if you have not the cloves. Vinegar to cover. Fix the amount to suit your taste. Boil till you think it is done.[21]

A Grand Ball Will be Given

Public and private balls may have been even more common for the pioneers than dancing at home. Columns of newspaper print announced the latest fancy ball where "the supper was excellent, sumptuous and splendid...the music unsurpassed."[22] "They were always advertised as a 'grand ball,' and none of your common affairs," Charles Prosch recalled.[23]

Besides offering a chance to socialize, balls raised money for the sponsoring organization and provided an opportunity for businesses to create a favorable impression. "Monday night our church has a harvest festival at the Hotel Spokane, music & dancing & supper—all given for 25 cts, so we will take that in too it being so rare a thing for one to get anything for 25 cts. but this is a special courtesy extended to the Church by the Hotel managers," Adelaide Gilbert wrote her mother.[24] Socials seemed to be popular: Gilbert attended one the next week and fortunately for us described the setting and menu. She does not say if the Hotel Spokane subsidized this one.

> The supper room was on same floor [as dancing], large square table filling room—all but space for row of chairs against the wall & room for waiters. In center of table a nice parlor palm—with rows of potted plants extending diagonally from it to back corner of strips of pale green plush—dishes of ices—sherbet and ice cream of various colors—fancy cakes—French candies—delicate sandwiches—coffee—all on lovely china and glass ware—elegant table linen &c.[25]

Since the prevailing custom decreed that newspapers report important social events, there is a substantial record of dining and dancing in the Pacific Northwest.

Christmas Ball, Steilacoom, 1860
The best display in town...had a table spread the whole length of her [Mrs. Coyle's] spacious dining room; and covered with viands of every conceivable description, from the most delicate and fantastic forms of confectionery to the more substantial articles of poultry and fish and flesh; all combining under a very tasteful arrangement.[26]

The Election Ball, November 16, 1868, Olympia, WA. Terr.
Was the event of the evening...a good attendance of ladies and gentleman who enjoyed themselves to the utmost....The supper furnished by the ladies, and under their management and directions was simply magnificent. Epicureans of the first rank must have been highly gratified and indeed both in quantity and quality it was all the heart could wish.[27]

Spokane Resort, 1890s
There was a fine floor in the large room [home of Cashup Davis]...where the guests might dance all night if they wished being served at midnight with a square meal—oyster soup, chicken, cakes, pies and hot biscuits.[28]

Foods listed on an 1872 Olympia luncheon menu show that the women in charge of bringing in the food may have prepared lobster and oyster salad, ham and tongue sandwiches, cold boiled ham, cold boiled leg mutton, and spiced corn beef.[29] In 1870, the Firemen's Ball in Olympia featured roast pigs, turkeys, chicken, geese, hams, beef, and so forth. And for dessert Colfax citizens at the ball to honor the newspaper dined on cake decorated with colored sugar. Pleased with their gift, the editors of the *Palouse Gazette* on January 5, 1878 wrote: "'Words are too weak and worn' to express our gratitude for this handmade present."

Another idea for a luncheon dish appeared in *The Washington Standard*, July 5, 1873:

> *Luncheon Dish*—Take a French roll, and cut thin slices of bread and butter; cut a hard-boiled egg across, lay a slice of egg on each piece of bread and butter, salt and pepper; place an anchovy, or a sardine, nicely skinned, curried round on the egg; garnish with salad.

Salad dressings in that period usually consisted of eggs, vinegar, oil, mustard and mayonnaise. Green leafy lettuce salads, with a simple oil and vinegar dressing, did not begin to become fashionable among the middle class until the last quarter of the nineteenth century.[30] They seem to have had an even slower beginning on the Northwest coast. Few menus from elegant Northwest restaurants that presented several entrees in addition to fish, roasts, game, and desserts even mentioned a separate salad course. When they did, the more popular fish or chicken salads with a mayonnaise dressing predominate. Lettuce seemed to be used as a garnish or a base for the more complex salads. A recipe for salad dressing included in McElroy's collection describes what might have been used:

> *Abbie's Salad Dressing*—Yolks of two eggs. Tablespoonful of butter, even teaspoonful of mustard, half teaspoon of pepper, and some of salt one teaspoonful of flour half pint of weak vinegar. Scald all well together turning all the time.[31]

As more people and supplies entered the Northwest, balls became very elaborate affairs. Dancers in Olympia in 1870 feasted from two long tables

> literally groaning under the weight of the delicacies with which they were laden. A greater variety combined with an equally tasteful display of viands, substantial and ornamental, was never seen in Olympia.... Just beyond the table on the left was what the managers termed a "fishpond," a small square enclosure, enveloped in flags, which contained a toy shop well stocked. For the toys the people fished from the outside.[32]

While at a Fourth of July ball in 1869, partygoers, many in costumes, kept cool by a "fountain in the center of room [which] will throw its cooling jets above the heads of the merry dancers and fall back into a large vase decorated with moss and flowers." "It's equal will not again occur very soon," reported *The Washington Standard.*[33]

Though the women prepared most of the party food in home kitchens, bakeries and caterers were only too happy to help out with the delicacies. If they chose, the women who managed the balls in Olympia could have stepped out of the kitchen and purchased "Jenny Lind Cakes, Ginger Snaps and all kinds of Fancy and Wedding Cakes made to order."[34] Other bakeries made similar claims and in some instances "exhibited beautiful cakes...ornamented with appropriate devices which look almost good enough to eat."[35] In Portland, the proprietor of the New Confectionery and Ice Cream Saloon promised that he could supply balls and parties "at the shortest notice [and] Ice cream, Strawberries, and Fruits of all kinds, furnished during the season."[36]

Women in less populated areas had fewer bakeries to choose from, but even in small towns one could purchase cakes and pastry. Baking in quantities was no problem as long as flour, sugar, butter, and eggs were on hand. A merchant in Dayton, Washington Territory, ran this advertisement in *The Columbian Chronicle* on December 7, 1878: "Ladies Remember, there will be a complete assortment of plain and holiday cakes, fruit, pound, sponge and jelly...on hand at Palace Restaurant and Bakery." In Colfax, several bakeries announced they "regularly had on hand" bread, cakes, and pies.[37]

The New Year's Ball in Tumwater featured food by Mr. Carroll who "had the reputation for being [the] best caterer in these parts," and an announcement of a Christmas Ball in Olympia in 1871 indicated that the supper would be under the "superintendence of Mr. Waldron, whose skill as a caterer is established."[38] Several days later the same paper reported that the Christmas Ball "was a decided success...and the supper served by Mr. Waldron...fully sustained his reputation as a popular caterer."[39]

The many advertisements for the "best selected stock of confectionery" indicated a preference for sweet treats such as stick candies, peppermint drops, dried and preserved fruits, and taffy. "Young Ladies, Old Maids, Old Bachelors, and all other Members of the Human Family can Sweeten their existence by buying some of the Fresh home-manufactured Candies," declared Piper's Confectionery and Bakery. The list included chocolate, caramels, almond, walnuts, fancy creams, bonbons, and fondants.[40] Even small trading posts in rural areas like Bickleton in Yakima County managed to have "thirty pound wooden pails of candy: one horehound, one peppermint and one pink and white sugar candy."[41] Candy merchants let

Young Ladies,

OLD MAIDS, OLD BACHELORS,

AND ALL OTHER

Members of the Human Family

Can Sweeten their existence by
buying some of the Fresh
home-manufactured Can-
dies named here:

Chocolate and other Caramels.

Almond, Walnut, Fruit and Fancy Creams.

Burnt Almonds, Bonbons and Fondants.

Cream Almonds, Taffys of various kinds.

Lozenges, Mottoes, and all other Fancy Candies.

Sticks and Drops, fresh and pure, always on hand.

Cakes of every description.

Wedding Cakes of the Finest Quality made to order on short notice.

Candies at Wholesale, at

PIPER'S

Confectionery and Bakery, Front st.

Merchants relied on fanciful advertisements to entice customers into their stores. *Seattle Post Intelligencer, September 15, 1883.*

their customers know that they were making a superior candy by advertising that "All Candies sold by us are warranted to be manufactured from DOUBLE REFINED SUGAR, that is fine white sugar rather than lumpy brown."

Bessie Craine recalled her mother had brought taffy hooks from Missouri and her family twisted taffy at home. "She would take a big hunk of this taffy, throw it over the hook and pull it out in a long rope, over and over again....This continued until it was a beautiful rich taffy color. Then she would roll it out on a big board and crack it into little chunks."[42] Made mostly from sugar and a small amount of vinegar, taffy is very sweet. The recipe printed here from a Dayton cookbook added paraffin to prevent the finished candy from melting.

> *Chewing Taffy*—Three cups of granulated sugar, ½ cup each water and vinegar, paraffin size of English walnut, butter size of walnut, 1 teaspoon cream tartar; do not stir; boil till it hairs; pour on slab till cool enough to handle, pull till white and cut in strips.[43]

Fresh and dried fruits preserved in a sugar syrup and attractively arranged in a fancy bowl received praise for their visual effects as well as gastronomic appeal. Glassware displaying an assortment of frosted fruit provided a touch of elegance for the midnight supper. Preserved fruits added texture and extra sweetness to fruit cakes and could be counted on to last longer than the fresh fruits. Prudent planners put up preserved fruit when boats brought in supplies of citrus.

> *Orange Chips*—Cut your oranges longways, take out all the pulp, and put the rinds into rather strong salt and water for six days, then boil them in a large quantity of spring water until they are tender; take them out, and lay them on a hair sieve to drain, then make a thin syrup of fine loaf sugar (one pound to one quart of water); put in your peels, and boil them over a slow fire till you see the syrup candy about the pan and peels, then take them out and grate fine sugar over them. Lay them on a hair sieve to drain and set them in a stove, or before the fire to dry. Lemon chips or candied peel may be made in the same way.[44]

To Drink or Not To Drink

Disregarding temperance leaders' advice to refrain from the evils of alcohol, party goers sipped wine and beer along with cider, lemonade, and spruce and ginger beer. Remembrances of dances frequently included the phrase, "Supper and wine were excellent and abundant." Commenting about one such evening, a friend wrote to Eliza Ferry that "although there was every kind of wine in abundance and punch in the evening all went off smoothly and no one was the worse for it (apparently)."[45]

Numerous advertisements attest to the fact that pioneers had no difficulty purchasing wine or whiskey. People living close to Portland could even sip home-brewed wheat whiskey rather than the usual corn-brewed bourbon from Kentucky.

> "Patronize Home Industry" KEEP THE MONEY IN THE STATE! The UNDERSIGNED ARE CONTINUALLY MANUFACTURING and have constantly on hand a superior article of WHISKEY, manufactured entirely from wheat, WHICH THEY CAN WARRANT NOT TO BE SURPASSED BY ANY ARTICLE IMPORTED TO THE STATE.
>
> If the People of Oregon MUST AND WILL HAVE WHISKEY, let them buy STARR'S PURE UNADULTERATED WHITE WHISKEY.[46]

At a New Year's Ball in Colfax in 1877 guests "eagerly devoured" slumgullion (a disgusting food or drink) with a supper of oysters and apples. One would like to know what ingredients the "brew-master" slipped into the drink, for the newspaper account of the ball said: "the latter [those who drank and ate oysters] soon after supper took an athletic fever, and were seen in the back yard rolling over barrels."[47]

A more traditional beverage such as champagne cider or currant wine might have had more appeal for those who preferred to fill their punch bowls with homemade spirits.

> *Champagne Cider*—To 35 gallons good cider put 1 gallon of strained honey, or 6 or 7 pounds of good white sugar. Stir them up well and set aside for a week. Clarify the cider with one quart of skimmed milk or 6 ounces of dissolved gelatin, and 5 quarts of pure spirits. After two or three days bottle the clear cider and it will become sparkling.
>
> *Current Wine*—We here present a recipe for making this wine from a lady, who is successful in making a good article. Three quarts of current juice, three quarts of soft water and three pounds of sugar. This must be put in a keg or jar, and well incorporated together. So soon as it has fermented, close it up, if in a keg—if in a jar, bottle it.[48]

In the Spokane area "etiquette required that invitations to parties should specify whether they were to be eight or ten gallon dances, or possibly even more pretentious affairs." A party "under ten gallons" served Hudson Bay Rum or Kentucky Whiskey and "was an ordinary party, where everyone could go. A ten gallon party was a more pretentious affair and guests would often drive 100 miles or more to attend...[and] would dance through the night and on into the next day."[49] George Fuller, a Spokane pioneer, emphasized that some "deemed it to be their inherent right to get decently drunk."[50] He does not say what type of alcohol the hosts and hostesses served at the ten gallon affairs.

On the other hand, Spokane pioneer C.W. Holiday recalled that "alcohol at a dance was strictly taboo. That was not for ladies and, generally speaking, the men out of respect for them left it alone. Occasionally, a few gentlemen might have a bottle hidden outside to which they would ever now and then betake themselves for refreshment, mistakenly thinking that by chewing a clove, their breath did not smell of whiskey."[51]

Pioneers not only disagreed about whether the list of party foods should include alcohol but, like the rest of the country, they also had dissimilar thoughts about drinking in general. Comments from two women pioneers illustrate the contrasting views.

> The captain of the ship we came from Frisco on has been several times and made me a long visit, brought me the last time, a dozen bottles of porter wine three bottles of champagne and three bottles of clarise. I have not been without wine at all since I left home....They tell me I am a real Californian, for I can take any amount and it does not affect me.[52]

> [Others]...and Julian are at Coupeville at a Temperance meeting a good many of the drinking men have signed the pledge and some of the sober ones and some of the young boys. I hope they may hold out faithful.[53]

People who wanted non-alcoholic beverages could purchase locally made products. The Seattle Soda Works Company manufactured soda, sarsaparilla, root beer, cider, and syrups in 1879.[54] Root beer, invented by Philadelphia pharmacist Charles E. Hires, became the "National Temperance Drink" after Hires convinced reformers that his drink did not contain alcohol.[55]

Spruce beer might be called the Northwest's first micro-brewed beer. George Vancouver made it in 1792 at Nootka Sound off the west coast of Vancouver Island as a drink to prevent scurvy. Vancouver brewed his beer from fresh spruce needles; pioneers drank spruce beer made from essence of spruce (concentrated solution derived from spruce leaves and/or bark). Mid-nineteenth century Americans, including those in the Territories, considered spruce beer a healthy drink.[56]

Spruce Beer—Allow an ounce of hops and a spoonful of ginger to a gallon of water. When well boiled, strain it, and put in a pint of molasses, and half an ounce or less of the essence of spruce; when cool, add a tea-cup of yeast, and put into a clean tight cask and let it ferment for a day or two, then bottle it for use. You can boil the sprigs of spruce-fir in room of the essence.[57]

Holidays

Non-native Pacific Northwest residents, like most Americans, celebrated holidays with special meals. And of all the holidays, the Fourth of July had a special significance as people throughout the territory honored the nation's birth.

Festivities on the glorious Fourth usually began with a flag raising and ended with noise from exploding fireworks or shooting guns. In Spokane "firing the anvil" called attention to the day's activities. "It is said that [the noise from] these explosions could be heard for 15 or 20 miles."[58] In between, party goers feasted on "the fat of the land more than an abundance of the very best," and listened to a rousing burst of patriotism from their elected officials. To honor America's love affair with liberty, many parades throughout the United States featured a Liberty Wagon, with young girls dressed in white waving to the crowd. The one described here, in Washington Territory, copied that custom:

> Upon a platform on the engine appeared the "Goddess of Liberty,"...dressed in white tarletan overskirt, with red and blue sash emblazoned with the word "Columbia" in gilt letters. A liberty-cap and shield...gave character to the *ideal* representations....Next came the thirteen Misses representing the original States, dressed in white, with pink and blue sashes....The next division was a concourse of young ladies representing the thirty-seven States of the Union, with the Territories, dress in white.[59]

At community events the "fat of the land" might mean platters of roasted meat, salads, sandwiches, cakes, pies, puddings, and ice cream. A celebration in 1876 marked the occasion by roasting beef in a large pit. The participants dug a large pit, built a fire, and "then the beef was let down into the pit with chains and the live coals were piled about...until the meat was thoroughly done."[60] In 1865 the Luarks began their preparations on July 2 by purchasing "tea Saleratus and pepper." On July 3 "Borrowed 38 lb flour, bought 15 lbs. sugar and a 10 lb. can of lard and gathering some gooseberries all to be used for picnic tomorrow."[61] From this list of ingredients, Mrs. Luark most likely baked gooseberry pies, light bread, or biscuits. Several other recipes from that period show that puddings and short cake appeared on the picnic table.

> *Fourth of July Pudding*—One-half pint of bread crumbs, one quart of milk, the whites of two and yolks of four eggs, the grated rind of one lemon, and one cup of sugar. Bake, and when done spread the pudding with jelly or preserves, then frost with the whites of two eggs, one cup of sugar, and the juice of one lemon, spread on top of the jelly. Set in the oven and brown. To be eaten cold.[62]

> *Strawberry Shortcake*—Dissolve one teaspoon-ful of soda in one pint of sweet milk. Take nearly flour enough for a thin dough thoroughly mix it with two teaspoons full of cream of tartar, and then rub in one half teacup full of sugar, nearly a teacup-ful of butter, with a little salt. Mix the whole, adding flour enough to make it as thick as tea biscuit. Bake, split into thin slices, and butter the pieces. Have a good lot of strawberries previously well sugared, and put them between the pieces and on top, dipping over the whole a little of the juice of the berries. Let it stand in a warm place until the berries are partially cooked, and eat with sugar sprinkled over, or butter, with sugar and cream if you have it.[63]

When ice could be found or purchased, dishes of ice cream gave the participants added incentive to celebrate the Fourth and other special occasions. In Portland and Seattle by the 1870s, a dish of ice cream could be ordered at some bakeries and restaurants—as long as the supply of ice held. Judge Matthew Deady proudly served it along with cakes, fruit, lemonade, claret punch, and coffee at his daughter's wedding reception in Portland in October 1874. He recorded in his journal that about 250 persons "called, and appeared to enjoy themselves."[64] In 1885 in Lewiston, Idaho Territory, prior to the celebrations, "an announcement was broadcast to every owner of an ice cream freezer in the city to freeze it full and have it ready for the city drayman, who would call for and deliver it free to the picnic grounds. Every housewife...was expected to contribute two or three specimens of her culinary art."[65] By 1890 merchants in Spokane advertised "ice cream in any quantity packed and delivered in any part of the city without charge."[66]

Amy Ryan described the process of making ice cream in her pioneer history of Sumner, Washington:

> Women came in the afternoon bringing cream, eggs, whole milk, sugar, flavoring and cakes. Ice was bought from the butchershop in gunny

sacks. The freezers were packed with alternate layers of mashed ice and rock salt around the can in the center.

When filled, the dasher and the cream mixture were placed in the can and the top put on: the handle was turned round and round until the dasher could no longer be moved. Occasionally the ice had to be pounded down with a broom handle and more ice added, while the water ran off through a hole in the side of the freezer.[67]

Most of the pioneers mention Christmas and New Year's and some note in their diaries and letters that "today is Thanksgiving," but these holidays did not always involve big at-home celebrations with elaborate meals. Thanksgiving, in fact, did not catch on as a national holiday until 1863, when President Lincoln, realizing the nation's anguish over the Civil War, declared Thanksgiving a national holiday to be celebrated in November.

In the very early years of settlement, receiving a fresh orange or a sugar sweet on Christmas marked the special day. "Mrs. Borst sent the family a Christmas present of sweeetcakes and apples....This is one of the quietest holidays yet," Michael Luark wrote on Dec. 25, 1861.[68]

Pioneers often called on friends on New Year's Day. David Blaine wrote his parents that in Oregon City, the "ladies make quite extensive preparations to entertain their friends...[with] several kinds of cake and several varieties of apples; some had chicken, dried beef, bread and butter, nuts and candies, tarts and pies; most had coffee, some lemon syrup and raspberry syrup for drink."[69] Undoubtedly by this time, finding the necessary ingredients specified in cake and pie recipes did not present a problem. Syrups especially required large amounts of sugar. The one printed here uses brandy; people abstaining from alcohol used cider vinegar.

> *Raspberry Syrup*—Squeeze the juice from some fine ripe raspberries; strain it, put it in a preserving kettle with a pound of loaf sugar to each quart of the juice, boil it up, skim it, and cool it. Put it up in small bottles, putting in each a wine glass of brandy, and filling them quite full of the syrup; cork them securely, and keep them in a cool place. It makes delicate ice, and also makes a fine beverage, mixed with iced water.[70]

Instead of dining on turkey purchased at a market, the family hunter went out and "brought down" the holiday bird. "Father [Elisha Ferry] went to Nisqually to hunt...he brought two wild geese for Thanksgiving," one of his sons wrote to Eliza "Lizzie" Ferry.[71] Though turkeys appeared in Fort Vancouver's 1845 inventory, and *The Oregonian* on December 31, 1853 reported "Thirty Dollars a piece was paid for two turkeys," because of the large supply of wild game few farmers or homeowners raised domestic turkeys. According to an article in *The Patriarch* on January 9, 1909, the domestic turkey industry did not begin in Washington Territory until 1866 when Captain Sam Clemens brought a large flock of turkeys to Port Gamble. Here, someone reasoned, the turkeys could grow fat from the refuse at Port Gamble's flour mill. It is not known how long the enterprise lasted. An advertisement placed in the Vancouver area newspaper in 1875 by a San Francisco dealer calls attention to Bronze Turkeys, "the first collection on the Pacific coast."[72]

Out-of-state turkey did not always live up to the promise of the advertisers. The one Russell Higginson ordered from Chicago in 1888 proved to be a disaster. Unfortunately, Ella Higginson did not discover this until she opened the oven door to baste the stuffed turkey. Then an "odd odor" instead of a fresh turkey smell perfumed the air and "every time she opened the oven door the smell was worse." The Higginson family feasted on side dishes, including a plum pudding, that Christmas day.[73]

When families did prepare a special holiday meal, menus followed tradition. Mounds of potatoes, steaming puddings filled with fragrant vegetables, and golden baked fruit pies surrounded platters of roasted poultry. At her first Thanksgiving in Kittitas County, Mrs. P.H. Schnebly recalled "three deliciously stuffed wild prairie chickens, baked a golden brown; mashed potatoes and lots of gravy, dried corn, for we had a very good garden that summer, and winter radishes. But the prize dish was mother's apple dumplings...made from dried apples father brought from The Dalles in the spring. Mother's jelly cake put the finishing touches to a wonderful Thanksgiving meal."[74]

Sarah Willoughby "fattened four young chickens to eat on Thanksgiving...[which] did not have a long enough rest to get rid of the muscle...[and] were very tough."[75] The Denny party, which had arrived just six weeks before Christmas, gave its dinner a Northwest touch and served salmon along with wild goose and dried apple pies. Adelaide Gilbert, disappointed that no one had given her family a turkey, remarked that "big brahma chicks must pay the penalty of size and take the place of the bird associated with that day. Then my cranberry sauce and mince pies are all ready and a Hubbard squash with mashed potatoes will keep the wolf from the door."[76]

Polly McKean Bell recalled that preparing for the Christmas dinner meant time spent in the kitchen:

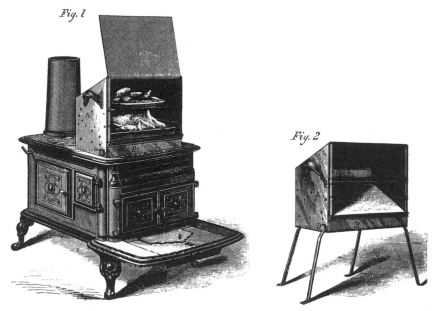

FORMAN'S COMBINED STEAMER AND HEAT REFLECTOR.
Cook stoves with reflector ovens on top made it possible to roast and bake at the same time. *Scientific American, November 16, 1867.*

Big plummy raisins to be seeded—a time-honored unwritten law always observed that every tenth raisin could be eaten by the small industrious worker—citron to be cut, apples to be peeled, currants to be carefully looked over, all these good things destined for the holiday fruit cake and mince pies. The fruit cakes were baked in sizeable tins; the one I remember was a large milk pan. Most of the mothers used old family recipes.[77]

Eventually roast turkey did become a holiday favorite. In announcing a religious service for Thanksgiving, *The Washington Standard*, November 16, 1872, observed that "turkey, geese and chickens will be slain by those of a more practical mind." In Colfax in 1878 "at the home of nearly all our people were enjoyed fat turkeys, chickens and oysters."[78] Certainly by the 1870s, merchants throughout the Northwest stocked all ingredients necessary for a special dinner and hotels featured turkey stuffed with oysters, turkey with cranberry sauce, and turkey with chestnuts on their Thanksgiving and Christmas menus. The editor at the *Palouse Gazette* on December 29, 1877 waxed eloquent about one Christmas dinner he attended:

On Christmas day, about noon, as we bolted into the dinning-room of the Colfax Hotel...we were agreeably surprised by finding our passage barred by a long row of tables covered with all kinds of tempting viands, and decorated as neatly and tastefully as any table for a Christmas dinner. Our surprise took advantage of our dignity, our lower jaw dropped, our eyes protruded, and our stomach was eager for the feast....This opportunity was soon presented....We are not fond of turkey, cake, pudding, etc., but out of respect for the man whose birthday we celebrated we consented to have our plate refilled several times with the above named eatables. In the fullness of our stomach we thank Mrs. James Ewart for that nice Christmas dinner.

Dancing and feasting at midnight suppers indicate that the stereotype of stern-faced pioneers who did not indulge in frivolous activities needs to be altered. The many accounts of dancing all night underscore the fact that men and women in frontier communities knew the importance of social activities. Tables "groaning under the weight of the delicacies" testify that when the pioneers finished work and the music began to play, they preferred sweeter, tastier morsels rather than plain mush or boiled meat.

Elegant dinners and lavish balls, holiday meals served in restaurants, sweet breads, aux champagnes, baked flounder, Madeira sauce, and Charlotte russe bespeak the change from a frontier community to urban living. At the turn of the century, many pioneers still lived and recalled the days of skimpy bags of flour and sugar, but clearly the days of cooking over hot coals had disappeared.

Appendix
Pacific Northwest Population 1849-1890

Compiled from:

Oscar Osburn Winther, *The Great Northwest: A History* (New York: Alfred A. Knopf, 1952).

Winther, *The Old Oregon Country* (Lincoln: University of Nebraska Press, 1950).

Calvin Fisher Schmid, *Growth of Cities and Towns: State of Washington* (Olympia: Washington State Planning and Community Affairs Agency, 1969).

John L. Andriot, *Population Abstract of the U.S.*, Volume 1 (McLean, VA: Andriot Associates, 1983).

Population of Oregon Cities, Counties, and Metropolitan Areas, 1850-1957: A Compilation of Census Counts and Estimates in Oregon (Eugene: Bureau of Municipal Research and Service, University of Oregon, 1958).

Note: Figures from early years are estimates.

1848: Oregon Territory Created
1853: Washington Territory separated from Oregon
1859: Oregon granted statehood
1889: Washington granted statehood

Oregon Territory (Total Population, 1849) 9,083
Oregon (1860) 52,465
Washington Territory (1853) 3,965
Washington Territory (1860) 11,594
Washington Territory (1870) 23,955
Washington Territory (1880) 75,116
Washington (1890) 357,232
Oregon (1890) 317,704

Oregon Territory

1850 Census

Oregon City	697
Benton County	814
Clackamas County	1,859
Clatsop County	462
Linn County	994
Marion County	2,749
Polk County	1,051
Yamhil County	1,512

Oregon State

Oregon Cities	*1860*	*1870*	*1880*
Portland	2,874	8,293	17,577
Oregon City	889	NA	1,263
Salem	625	1,139	2,538
Corvallis	700	NA	1,128
Eugene City	1,183	861	1,117
Roseburg	835	NA	822
Jacksonville	892	NA	839
Ashland	327	NA	824
Dalles City	805	942	2,232

Oregon Counties			
Benton County	3,074	4,458	6,403
Clackamas County	3,466	5,993	9,260
Clatsop County	498	1,255	7,220
Linn County	6,772	8,717	12,676
Marion County	4,150	9,965	14,576
Polk County	3,625	4,701	6,601
Yamhill County	3,245	5,012	7,945
Multnomah County	4,150	11,510	25,203

Washington Territory

Washington Counties

Clark County	2,384	3,081	5,490
Thurston County	1,507	2,246	3,270
Walla Walla County	1,318	5,300	8,716
King County	302	2,120	6,970
Klickitat County	230	329	4,055

Washington Cities	*1870*	*1880*
Walla Walla	1,394	3,588
Olympia	1,203	1,232
Seattle	1,107	3,533
Port Townsend	593	917
Steilacoom	314	250
Tumwater	206	171
Vancouver	1,000	1,722

Endnotes

Endnote Abbreviations

MOHI—Museum of History and Industry, Seattle
SLO—Washington State Library, Olympia
UWL/MUA—University of Washington Libraries/Manuscripts and
    University Archives, Seattle
WSCM—Washington State Capital Museum, Olympia
WSHSL—Washington State Historical Society Library, Tacoma

Notes for Chapter One

1. "Diary of Elizabeth Austin Roeder," October 9, 1854, Box 1, Elizabeth and Henry Roeder Diaries and Letters, UWL/MUA.
2. The Donation Land Law passed by Congress in 1850 granted every resident white or half-breed settler over eighteen years of age, who was either a citizen or who had or would declare an intention of becoming so before December 1, 1851, a grant of 320 acres. If married, the man and wife would each in his or her own right be entitled to 320 acres. The act expired in 1855. The Homestead Act passed in 1862 granted heads of households, or single men or women over twenty-one, who lived on and improved land continuously for five years, 160 acres of land.
3. Hazard Stevens, Correspondence, Notes and Reminiscences, MS 091, SLO.
4. Gary Fuller Reese, ed., *They Came to Puget Sound: Reminiscences of Pioneer Women As Published in the Tacoma Daily and Weekly Ledger, 1892-1893* (Tacoma: Tacoma Public Library, 1984), p. 4.
5. Immigrants to Oregon Territory first settled in the Willamette Valley where the land was fertile and the river falls supplied power for gristmills and sawmills. Later arrivals settled further north around New Market (Olympia), Whidbey Island, Port Townsend, and Elliot Bay on Puget Sound.
6. Fred Lockley, *Conversations with Pioneer Women* (Eugene, Ore.: Rainy Day Press, 1981), p. 140.
7. David James, *From Grand Mound to Scatter Creek* (Olympia, Wash.: State Capitol Historical Association of Washington, 1980), p. 37.
8. Michael Luark Diary, January 14, 1863, Michael Luark Papers, Box 2, Acc. #309, UWL/MUA.

9. *Ibid.*, November 25, 1861.

10. Lois Barton, *Spencer Butte Pioneers: 100 Years on the Sunny Side of the Butte, 1850-1950* (Eugene, Ore.: Spencer Butte Press, 1982), p. xiii.

11. Bruce A. Wilson, *Late Frontier: A History of Okanogan County, Washington, 1800-1941* (Okanogan, Wash.: Okanogan County Historical Society, 1990), p. 161.

12. David Edwards Blaine, *Letters and Papers of Rev. David E. Blaine and his Wife Catharine: Seattle, 1853-1856, Oregon, 1856-1862*, (Seattle: Historical Society of the Pacific Northwest Conference of the Methodist Church, 1963), p. 44.

13. Mrs. Blanch Higbee, Autobiography of a Pioneer Woman, V.F. 590, UWL/MUA.

14. Barbara Zimmerman and Vernon Carstensen, editors, "Pioneer Woman in Southwestern Washington Territory, The Recollections of Susanna Maria Slover McFarland Price Ede," *Pacific Northwest Quarterly* 67:4 (Oct. 1976): 147.

15. Bernice Sapp, Bernice Sapp Notebooks, Book XIII, WSCM, pp. 69.

16. Wilson, *Late Frontier, A History of Okanogan County*, p. 161.

17. For a discussion of architectural styles see, Virginia McAlester, *A Field Guide to American Houses* (New York: Knopf, 1984). For more information about Oregon and Washington log cabins and houses see: Thomas Vaughan, *Space, Style, and Structure: Building in Northwest America* (Portland: Oregon Historical Society, 1974); Leonard Garfield, "At Home in Washington," *Columbia*, 4:1 (Spring 1990): pp. 36-41.

18. Shanna Stevenson, "Daniel R. Bigelow," *Columbia*, 7:4 (Winter, 1993/94): 33.

19. Phoebe Goodell Judson, *A Pioneer's Search for An Ideal Home* (Bellingham, Wash.: Union Printing, Binding and Stationery Company, 1925), p. 87.

20. Lillian Miller Christiansen, Memories of Jefferson County Washington, 1894, Acc. # 1922, MOHI.

21. Financial Records-Invoices, Box 2/11, Wilson and Dunlap Papers, UWL/MUA.

22. Wilson, *Late Frontier, A History of Okanogan County*, p. 162.

23. Kate Polson, June 1895, Box 1, General Correspondence, Perry Polson Family Papers, Acc. 255, UWL/MUA.

24. Clareta Olmstead Smith, *The Trail Leads West* (Philadelphia: Dorrance & Company, 1946), p. 127.

25. *Told by the Pioneers*, 3 Vols. (Olympia, Wash.: Works Projects Administration, 1937), 3: 48.

26. Amy M. Ryan, *The Sumner Story* (Sumner, Wash.: Sumner Historical Society, 1988), p. 47.

27. Leta May Smith, *The End of the Trail* (Hicksville, N. Y.: Exposition Press, 1976), p. 123.

28. Victor J. Farrar, ed., "Diary Kept by Colonel and Mrs. I.N. Ebey," *The Washington Historical Quarterly*, 8 (April 1917): 129.

29. *Pioneer and Democrat*, July 13, 1860, Olympia, Wash. Terr.

30. Edward Huggins, *Reminiscences of Puget Sound* (Tacoma: Tacoma Public Library, 1984), p. 400.

31. Ryan, *The Sumner Story*, pp. 40-41.

32. Nelia Binford Fleming, *Sketches of Early High Prairie* (Portland, Ore.: Binfords & Mort, 1963), p. 48.

33. Herndon Smith, comp., *Centralia, The First Fifty Years 1845-1900* (Centralia, Wash.: The Daily Chronicle and F.H. Cole Printing Company, 1942), pp. 320-321.

34. Blaine, *Letters and Papers of Rev. David E. Blaine and his Wife Catharine*, pp. 140, 153, 195.

35. Susan Williams, *Savory Suppers and Fashionable Feasts* (New York: Pantheon Books, 1985), pp. 59-60.

36. *Ibid.*, p. 60
37. Thomas R. Garth, Jr., "Early Architecture in the Northwest," *Pacific Northwest Quarterly*, 38: 3 (July 1947): 230.
38. Charles M. Dwelley, ed., *Skagit Memories, Stories of the Settlement Years* (Mount Vernon, Wash.: Skagit County Historical Society, 1979), p. 41.
39. Michael Luark Diary, February 2, 1863, UWL/MUA. Luark built his home in 1863 but does not mention if he followed his original plans.
40. Louise Swift to Mother, August 3, 1863, VF #40 Louise Swift Letters 1863-1869, UWL/MUA.
41. *Ibid.*, Hattie Swift to Mother, January 8, 1865.
42. Garfield, "At Home in Washington," p. 36-41.
43. James, *From Grand Mound to Scatter Creek*, p. 29.
44. Jean Bluhm, *The Mary Borst Story* (Olympia: no publisher, 1989), p. 52.
45. See Vaughan, *Space, Style, and Structure*, p. 98 and Garfield, "At Home in Washington," p. 38.
46. Smith, *Centralia, The First Fifty Years*, p. 69.
47. Sarah McElroy to brother, (no date) Box 2-9, Acc. #27,101,169, McElroy Family Papers, UWL/MUA.
48. Correspondence to the author from Dr. Craig G. Gunter, August 29, 1994 and Weldon W. Rau, August 8, 1994. For more information about the Boatman family see Weldon W. Rau, *Pioneering the Washington Territory* (Olympia: Historic Fort Steilacoom Association, 1993). Dr. and Mrs. C.G. Gunter lived in the home at the time of this book's publication and wrote that the early structure is their kitchen and dining room. The home is on the National Register of Historic Places.
49. Blaine, *Letters and Papers of Rev. David E. Blaine and his Wife Catharine*, pp. 57-58, 65.
50. Michael Luark Diary, January 17, 1863, November 5, 6, 1863, January 8, 1864, UWL/MUA.
51. For more information on nineteenth-century pattern books and ideas about these designs, see Gwendolyn Wright, *Moralism and the Model Home* (Chicago: The University of Chicago Press, 1980), pp. 1-45. Also see Dennis A. Andersen and Katheryn H. Draft, "Plan and Pattern Books, Shaping Early Seattle Architecture," *Pacific Northwest Quarterly*, 85:4 (October, 1994).
52. Dorothy Koert, *The Lyric Singer: A Biography of Ella Higginson* (Bellingham, Wash.: Center for Pacific Northwest Studies, 1985), p. 32.
53. Wilson, *Late Frontier, A History of Okanogan County*, p. 166.
54. The Daughters of the Pioneers of Washington, *Incidents in the Life of a Pioneer Woman: True Stories* (State Association of the Daughters of the Pioneers of Washington, 1976), pp. 69.
55. Mrs. George E. Blankenship, *Early History of Thurston County, Washington: Together with Biographies and Reminiscences of Those Identified with Pioneer Days* (Olympia, Wash.: no publisher, 1914), pp. 336.
56. Christiansen, Memories of Jefferson County, MOHI.
57. Stevenson, "Daniel R. Bigelow," p. 33. The Bigelow cabin in Olympia was built in 1853 as a law office for Daniel Bigelow. When he married Ann Elizabeth White the office became their home. It is now a woodshed on the property owned by the Bigelow family.
58. Ryan, *The Sumner Story*, pp. 46-47.
59. Blankenship, *Early History of Thurston County*, p. 127.
60. Christiansen, Memories of Jefferson County, MOHI.

61. Julia Gilliss, *So Far From Home: An Army Bride on the Western Frontier, 1865-1869* (Portland: Oregon Historical Society Press, 1993), p. 50.

62. Michael Luark Diary, January 5, 1865, UWL/MUA.

63. Smith, *The End of the Trail*, p. 125.

64. George Woodward, *Woodward's Victorian Architecture and Rural Art, A facsimile of volume one (1867) and volume two (1868)* (Watkins Glen, N.Y.: American Life Foundations, 1978), p. 71.

65. Jackson, Koontz, Glover Family Papers, MSS 078, Box 2/5, SLO. Note: Whether the sink was installed when the house was built in the 1850s is difficult to know. There was no date given with the typed manuscript of Nettie Beirels.

66. Bessie Wilson Craine, Squak Valley (Issaquah), VF 471, UWL/MUA.

67. Catharine E. Beecher and Harriet Beecher Stowe, *The American Woman's Home or Principles of Domestic Science* (New York: J.B. Ford & Co., 1869), p. 35. These ideas are repeated in Catharine Beecher's *Miss Beecher's Domestic Receipt Book* and *Miss Beecher's Housekeeper and Healthkeeper*. See also Ellen M. Plante, *The American Kitchen 1700 to the Present* (New York: Facts on File, 1995).

68. Kathryn Grover, ed., *Dining in America, 1850-1900* (Amherst: The University of Massachusetts Press, 1987), p. 70.

69. *The Washington Standard* (Olympia), February 11, 1879. In the 1860s and 1870s this newspaper regularly printed advice to farmers and homemakers in a column called Farm and Household. The editor requested that readers send in suggestions and recipes. Material was rarely credited; much appears to have been "lifted" from other sources.

70. Estelle Woods Wilcox, ed., *Practical Housekeeping; A Careful Compilation of Tried and Approved Recipes* (Minneapolis: Buckeye Publishing Co., 1883), p. 459.

71. Ruby Chapin Blackwell, *A Girl in Washington Territory* (Tacoma: Washington State Historical Society, 1972), p. 16.

72. J. Roderick Moore, "Wythe County, Virginia, Punched Tin: Its Influence and Imitators," *The Magazine Antiques* (September 1984): 601.

73. *A. McDonald, L. Schwabacher v. William H. Watson*, District Court at Dayton, Columbia County, Washington Territory, Frontier Justice Case Files-Washington Territorial Court Records in *Frontier Justice 1853-1889: A Guide to Court Records of Washington Territory* (Olympia: State of Washington, Office of Secretary of State, Division of Archives and Records Management, 1987).

74. Sarah Hunt Stevens, *Book of Remembrance of Marion County, Oregon Pioneers 1840-1860* (Portland: The Berncliff Press, 1927), p. 343.

75. Gerald Carson, *The Old Country Store* (New York: Oxford University Press, 1954), p. 209-210.

76. "Special Issue: The Life and Letters of Adelaide Sutton Gilbert, Spokane Pioneer," *The Pacific Northwest Forum*, 5:1 (Winter-Spring 1992): 23.

Notes for Chapter Two

1. Phoebe Goodell Judson, *A Pioneer's Search for An Ideal Home* (Bellingham, Wash.: Union Printing, Binding and Stationary Company, 1925), p. 86.

2. David James, *From Grand Mound to Scatter Creek* (Olympia, Wash.: State Capitol Historical Association of Washington, 1980), p. 26.

3. Leta May Smith, *The End of the Trail* (Hicksville, N. Y.: Exposition Press, 1976), p. 102.

4. *The Washington Standard* (Olympia), August 8, 1874.

5. Jim Attwell, *Early History of Klickitat County* (Skamania, Wash.: Tahlkie Books, 1977), p. 98

6. Conversation with Mary Ann Bigelow, January 13, 1994, Olympia, Wash.

7. Bruce A. Wilson, *Late Frontier, A History of Okanogan County, Washington 1800-1941* (Okanogan, Wash.: Okanogan County Historical Society, 1990), p. 162.

8. Mrs. George E. Blankenship, *Tillicum Tales of Thurston County* (Olympia, Wash.: no publisher, 1914), p. 111.

9. *Told by the Pioneers*, 3 Vols. (Olympia, Wash.: Works Projects Administration, 1937), 3: p. 118.

10. Mrs. Cecil Laramie Deutsch, compiler, *Family Records and Reminiscences of Washington Pioneers*, Vol. V, (typewritten, no publisher, 1935), UWL/Special Collections, p. 176.

11. Wilson, *Late Frontier, A History of Okanogan County*, p. 166.

12. Barbara Zimmerman and Vernon Carstensen, eds., "Pioneer Woman in Southwestern Washington Territory, The Recollections of Susanna Maria Slover McFarland Price Ede," *Pacific Northwest Quarterly* 67:4 (Oct. 1976): 147.

13. Victor J. Farrar, editors, "Diary Kept by Colonel and Mrs. I.N. Ebey," *The Washington Historical Quarterly* 7:4 (October, 1916): 316, 318.

14. Herndon Smith, compiler, *Centralia, The First Fifty Years 1845-1900* (Centralia, Wash.: The Daily Chronicle and F.H. Cole Printing Company, 1942), p. 331.

15. "Letter from Cowlitz, Washington" *Cowlitz County Historical Quarterly* 12:1 (May, 1970): 10.

16. Attwell, *Early History of Klickitat County*, p. 98.

17. Tamar Richardson Hatch Correspondence, March-July 1898, Folder 23, MS/7, WSHSL.

18. Nelia Binford Fleming, *Sketches of Early High Prairie* (Portland: Binfords & Mort, 1963), p. 13.

19. "Special Issue: The Life and Letters of Adelaide Sutton Gilbert, Spokane Pioneer," *The Pacific Northwest Forum* 5:1 (Winter-Spring 1992): 57, 63, 78.

20. Amy M. Ryan, *The Sumner Story* (Sumner, Wash.: Sumner Historical Society, 1988), p. 105.

21. Correspondence from Minerva W. Herrett to the author, September 1994.

22. Granville Owen Haller Reminiscences, Box 3, G.O. Haller papers, Acc. #3437-3, UWL/MUA.

23. Jackson, Koontz, Glover Family Papers, MSS 078, Box 2/5, SLO.

24. Sarah McElroy to Henry B. McElroy, March 19, 1878, Box 2/8, McElroy Family Papers, Acc. #27, 101, 169, UWL/MUA.

25. Mary McWilliams, *Seattle Water Department History 1854: 1954* (Seattle: Dogwood Press, 1955), p. 2.

26. Edmund T. Becher, *Spokane Corona, Eras & Empires* (Spokane: C.W. Hill Printers, 1974), p. 253.

27. McWilliams, *Seattle Water Department History*, pp. 135-37.

28. Linda Deziah Jennings, ed., *Washington Women's Cook Book* (Seattle: The Washington Equal Suffrage Association, 1909), p. 158.

29. Hazel Heckman, *Island in the Sound* (Seattle: University of Washington Press, 1976), p. 96.

30. *The Washington Standard*, Olympia, Wash. Terr., August 10, 1872.

31. Wilson, *Late Frontier, A History of Okanogan County*, p. 161.

32. Laura M. House, "Eastern Washington Territory Pioneer," M-102, WSHSL.

33. Daybook, June 1860, Box 3, Wilson and Dunlap papers, UWL/MUA.

34. Jean Hilts Bluhm, *The Mary Borst Story* (Olympia: no publisher, 1989), p. 54.
35. Ryan, *The Sumner Story*, p. 102.
36. *Oregon, Washington, And Idaho Gazetteer and Business Directory, 1884-85* (Chicago: R.L. Polk and A.C. Danser, 1884), p. 595.
37. Estelle Woods Wilcox, ed., *Practical Housekeeping: A Careful Compilation of Tried and Approved Recipes* (Minneapolis: Buckeye Publishing Co., 1883), pp. 432, 433, 459.
38. Catharine Beecher, *The American Woman's Home* (New York: J.B. Ford and Company, 1869), pp. 371-372.
39. Jackson, Koontz, Glover Family Papers, SLO.
40. Wilcox, *Practical Housekeeping*, p. 472.
41. Waverly Root and Richard de Rochemont, *Eating in America* (New York: Ecko Press, 1975), p. 148.
42. For more information on early ice harvests see Joseph C. Jones, *America's Iceman: An Illustrative History of the United States Natural Ice Industry, 1665-1925* (Humble, Texas: Jobeco Books, 1984), and Oscar Edward Anderson Jr., *Refrigeration in America, A History of a New Technology and its Impact* (Princeton: Princeton University Press, 1953).
43. R.L. Polk & Co., *Polk's Portland City Directory* (Portland: R.L. Polk & Co., 1865), p. 80.
44. *The Commercial Age* (Olympia), October 30, 1869.
45. *Ibid.*
46. Charles Larson, *Central Oregon Caves* (Vancouver, Wash.: ABC Print & Publisher, 1987), p. 8.
47. Clarence Bagley, *History of King County* (Chicago: S.J. Clarke, 1929), p. 371.
48. *The Washington Standard* (Olympia), January 29, 1876.
49. *Ibid.*, May 16, 1879.
50. Ryan, *The Sumner Story*, p. 48
51. Becher, *Spokane Corona, Eras & Empires,* p. 247.
52. Jones, *America's Iceman*, p. 79.
53. Wilson, *Late Frontier: A History of Okanogan County*, p. 162.
54. Kathryn Carlson, *Rich Heritage* (Colville, Wash.: *Statesman-Examiner*, 1979), p. 109.
55. *Thorp Mill Town* (Thorp, Wash.: Historical Preservation Society, Summer 1993).
56. Jones, *America's Iceman*, p. 137.
57. Beecher, *The American Woman's Home*, p. 267.
58. Anderson, *Refrigeration in America*, pp. 113-114.
59. Ruby Chapin Blackwell, *A Girl in Washington Territory* (Tacoma: Wash.: State Historical Society, 1972), pp. 15-16.

Notes for Chapter Three

1. W.P. Bonney, *History of Pierce County* (Chicago: Pioneer Historical Publishing Company, 1927), p. 1231.
2. William H. Harris, *The Harris Journal* (Bellingham, Wash.: Whatcom Museum of History and Art, 1968), pp. 10-11.
3. *Told by the Pioneers*, 3 Vols. (Olympia, Wash.: Works Projects Administration, 1937), 3: 116.
4. David James, *From Grand Mound to Scatter Creek* (Olympia, Wash.: State Capitol Historical Association of Washington, 1980), p. 30.
5. Daybook, 1855-1857, Box 3: Wilson and Dunlap Papers, UWL/MUA.

6. J.H. Horney, "Early Wallowa Valley Settlers," *Oregon Historical Quarterly, 18:3* (Sept. 1942): 223.

7. Michael Luark Diary, Dec. 4, 1863, Box 1/10: Michael Luark Papers, Acc. #309, UWL/MUA.

8. Guy Waring, *My Pioneer Past* (Boston: Bruce Humphries, Inc. 1936), p. 95.

9. *Told by the Pioneers,* 2: 44.

10. Herndon Smith, compiler, *Centralia, The First Fifty Years 1845-1900* (Centralia, Wash.: The Daily Chronicle and F.H. Cole Printing Company, 1942), p. 76.

11. Phoebe Goodell Judson, *A Pioneer's Search for an Ideal Home* (Bellingham, Wash.: Union Printing Binding and Stationery Company, 1925), pp. 86-87.

12. Smith, *Centralia,* p. 164.

13. Cast iron is made by pouring hot metal into a mold; wrought iron is hammered into shape under intense heat at a forge.

14. Barbara Zimmerman and Vernon Carstensen, eds., "Pioneer Woman in Southwestern Washington Territory, The Recollections of Susanna Maria Slover McFarland Price Ede," *Pacific Northwest Quarterly* 67:4 (Oct. 1976): 139.

15. *Ibid.* See also John G. Ragsdale, *Dutch Ovens Chronicled: Their Use in the United States* (Fayetteville: University of Arkansas Press, 1991).

16. Narcissa Whitman, *The Letters of Narcissa Whitman* (Fairfield, Wash.: Ye Galleon Press, 1986), p. 129.

17. Thomas R. Garth, "A Report on the Second Season's Excavations at Waiilatpu," *Pacific Northwest Quarterly,* 40:4, (Oct. 1949): 308.

18. Lillian Schlissel, Byrd Gibbens, and Elizabeth Hampsten, *Far From Home: Families of the Westward Journey* (New York: Schocken Books, 1989), p. 25.

19. Gordon Newell, *Westward to Alki* (Seattle: Superior Publishing Company, 1977), p. 60.

20. Lila Hannah Firth, "Early Life on San Juan Island," VF 310, UWL/MUA.

21. Robert Emmett Hawley, *Skqee Mus or Pioneer Days on the Nooksack* (Bellingham, Wash.: Miller and Sutherlen Printing Co., 1945), p. 34.

22. Harris, *The Harris Journal,* p. 14.

23. See "The Stove Industry in Oregon," Thomas Rogers, Oregon Historical Society, Portland, Oregon for more information about this local company. This typewritten manuscript is in the collections of the Oregon Historical Society. No date.

24. Prices are from financial records found in: Financial Records (Miscellaneous), Box 3/26: Andrew Chambers Jackson Family; and Henry Roeder, Account Book, Box 1: Elizabeth and Henry Roeder Papers, UWL/MUA.

25. Luark Diary, January 13, 14, 16, 1862, Box 1, UWL/MUA.

26. *Told By The Pioneers,* 3: 61.

27. Bruce Wilson, *Late Frontier, A History of Okanogan County, Washington 1800-1941* (Okanogan, Wash.: Okanogan County Historical Society, 1990), p. 161.

28. Tammis Kane Groft, *Cast With Style* (Albany, N. Y.: Albany Institute of History and Art, 1984), p. 85.

29. Laura House, "Eastern Washington Territory Pioneer," p. 75, M-102, Robert Hitchman Collection, WSHSL. In my request for information concerning early northwest kitchens, several correspondents recalled that their mothers "always cooked on an old-fashioned Monarch Range (coal and wood)."

30. Jean Bluhm, *The Mary Borst Story* (Olympia, Wash.: self published, 1989), p. 54. Stove likely acquired in the 1860s, but no date is given.

31. *The Washington Standard* (Olympia), December 23, 1865.

32. Elof Norman, *Coffee Chased Us Up* (Seattle: The Mountaineers, 1977), p. 35.

33. *Citizen Cook Book* (Bothell, Wash.: no date, no publisher), p. 15.

34. Correspondence from Minerva Herrett to author, September 6, 1994.

35. Sue Robinson Dennis, *Growing Up on the Northwest Frontier* (Seattle: Smuggler's Cove Publishing, 1991), p. 62.

36. For a description of the varieties of cast iron implements, see Linda Campbell Franklin, *300 Years of Kitchen Collectibles* (Florence, Alabama: Books Americana, 1991). Dover Stamping Co., R & E Mfg. Co., Wagner, and Griswold are a few of the notable foundries that began in the mid-nineteenth century.

37. Wilson, *Late Frontier, A History of Okanogan County*, p. 161.

38. Gerald Carson, *The Old Country Store* (New York: Oxford University Press, 1954), p. 199.

39. Kathryn Grover, ed., *Dining in America, 1850-1900* (Rochester, N.Y.: The Margaret Woodbury Strong Museum), 1987.

40. *Oregon Spectator*, February 1854, Oregon City, Oregon Terr.

41. See Grover, *Dining in America*, pp. 47-84 for a discussion of technological advances that changed American goods.

42. Estelle Wilcox, ed., *Practical Housekeeping: A Careful Compilation of Tried and Approved Recipes* (Minneapolis: Buckeye Publishing Co., 1883), pp. 463-464.

43. Edward Huggins, *Reminiscences of Puget Sound* (Tacoma: Tacoma Public Library, 1984), p. 394.

44. From Memory's Pages, Incidents in Life of Elizabeth Harrison Chambers, Box 1/1A: Andrew Jackson Chambers Family, Acc. # 939, UWL/MUA.

45. Amy Ryan, *The Sumner Story* (Sumner, Wash.: Sumner Historical Society, 1988), pp. 48-49.

46. Financial records, 1856, Boxes, 2/2, 2/8, 2/11: Wilson and Dunlap Papers, UWL/MUA.

47. Susan Williams, *Savory Suppers & Fashionable Feasts: Dining in Victorian America* (New York: Pantheon Books, 1985), pp. 49-91 describes the immense selection of furniture and dishes between 1850-1900.

48. *McDonald, L. Schwabacher v. William H. Watson,* District Court at Dayton, Columbia County, Washington Territory, Frontier Justice Case Files-Washington Territorial Court Records in *Frontier Justice 1853-1889: A Guide to Court Records of Washington Territory* (Olympia: State of Washington, Office of Secretary of State, Division of Archives and Records Management, 1987).

49. "Special Issue: The Life and Letters of Adelaide Sutton Gilbert, Spokane Pioneer," *The Pacific Northwest Forum* 5:1 (Winter-Spring 1992): 79.

50. Fred Lockley, *Conversations with Pioneer Women* (Eugene, Oregon: Rainy Day Press, 1981), p. 97.

51. Kate H. Polson, General Correspondence, 1878-1895, Perry Polson Family Papers, Acc. #255, UWL/MUA.

52. Sarah Rorer, *Mrs. Rorer's Philadelphia Cook Book, A Manual of Home Economics* (Philadelphia: Arnold and Company, 1886).

53. *The New Practical Housekeeping: To Those American Housekeepers Who Cannot Afford to Employ a French Cook* (No publisher; no date), p. 18.

54. Wilcox, *Practical Housekeeping*, p. 64.

55. The Daughters of the Pioneers of Washington, *Incidents in the Life of a Pioneer Woman: True Stories* (State Association of the Daughters of the Pioneers of Washington, 1976), p. 97.

Notes for Chapter Four

1. *Told by the Pioneers*, 3 Vols. (Olympia, Wash.: Works Projects Administration, 1937), 2: 119.

2. Phoebe Goodell Judson, *A Pioneer's Search for An Ideal Home* (Bellingham, Wash.: Union Printing, Binding and Stationery Company, 1925), p. 90.

3. Edmund T. Becher, *Spokane Corona: Eras and Empires* (Spokane: C.W. Hill Printers, 1974), p. 244.

4. Arthur A. Denny, *Pioneer Days on Puget Sound* (Fairfield, Wash.: Ye Galleon Press, 1979), p. 51.

5. Martha Gay Masterson, *One Woman's West: Recollections of the Oregon Trail and Settling the Northwest Country* (Eugene, Oregon: Spencer Butte Press, 1986), p. xii.

6. Gary Fuller Reese, ed., *They Came to Puget Sound: Reminiscences of Pioneer Women as Published in the Tacoma Daily and Weekly Ledger, 1892-1893* (Tacoma, Wash.: Tacoma Public Library, 1984), p. 3.

7. Michael Luark Diary, April 17, 1862, Box 1, Michael Luark Papers, Acc. #309, UWL/MUA.

8. Sarah Hunt Stevens, *Book of Remembrance of Marion County, Oregon Pioneers 1840-1860* (Portland: The Berncliff Press, 1927), p. 340.

9. Lawrence Denny Lindsley, 1875-1883 (Scrapbook), Box 10, Lawrence Lindsley papers, Acc. #2179-2,3,4,5, UWL/MUA.

10. Howard McKinley Corning, *Willamette Landings* (Portland: Oregon Historical Society, 1973), p. 80.

11. The first mills used by the Whitmans were actually "tub mills" that used iron millstones instead of granite ones. By 1841 the Whitmans used granite.

12. Reese, *They Came to Puget Sound*, p. 122.

13. Victor J. Farrar, ed., "Diary of Colonel and Mrs. I.N. Ebey," *The Washington Historical Quarterly* 8:2 (April, 1917): 133-134.

14. Nelson Durham, *History of the City of Spokane* (Spokane: The S.J. Clarke Publishing Co., 1912), p. 635.

15. See Florence E. Sherfey, *Eastern Washington's Vanished Gristmills and the Men Who Ran Them* (Fairfield: Ye Galleon Press, 1978); Corning, *Willamette Landings*; and Tom Kellecher, "Flour From Mill to Market," in *Food History News*, 6:2 (Fall, 1994), pp. 1, 2, 8 for detailed information about the operations of early mills.

16. *Pioneer and Democrat*, Dec. 16, 1854, Olympia, Wash. Terr.

17. *Told by the Pioneers*, 2: 79.

18. *The Washington Standard*, August 28, 1869, Olympia, Wash. Terr.

19. Sherfey, *Eastern Washington's Vanished Gristmills*, pp. 35, 43.

20. "Recollections By Andrew Jackson Chambers," Box 1/1A, Andrew Jackson Chambers Papers, Acc. #939, UWL/MUA.

21. Durham, *History of the City of Spokane*, p. 636.

22. Ladies of Church of the Holy Family, *The Auburn Cook Book* (Auburn, Wash.: 1909), p. 18.

23. *The Seattle Gazette*, Dec. 10, 1863.

24. *Told by the Pioneers*, 3: 93.

25. Stevens, *Book of Remembrance of Marion County*, p. 245.

26. Judson, *A Pioneer's Search for An Ideal Home*, p. 90.

27. Sarah McAllister Hartman papers, VF 69, UWL/MUA.

28. "Reminiscences by Margaret White Chambers," Box 1/1A, Andrew Jackson Chambers Papers, Acc. #939 UWL/MUA.

29. Lois Barton, *Spencer Butte Pioneers: 100 Years on the Sunny Side of the Butte, 1850-1950* (Eugene: Spencer Butte Press, 1982), p. xiii.

30. "Reminiscence of Elizabeth Chambers Hunsacker," Box 1/1A, Andrew Jackson Chambers Papers, Acc. #939, UWL/MUA.

31. Herndon Smith, compiler, *Centralia, The First Fifty Years 1845-1900* (Centralia, Wash.: *The Daily Chronicle* and F.H. Cole Printing Company, 1942), p. 65.

32. Lettice Bryan, *The Kentucky Housewife* (1839; reprint, Columbia, South Carolina: University of South Carolina Press, 1991), p. 221.

33. *Seattle Post Intelligencer*, Jan. 22, 1905.

34. Lila Hannah Firth, "Early Life on San Juan Island," VF 310, UWL/MUA.

35. David Edwards Blaine, *Letters and Papers of Rev. David E. Blaine and His Wife Catharine: Seattle, 1853-1856, Oregon, 1856-1862* (Seattle: Historical Society of the Pacific Northwest Conference of the Methodist Church, 1963), p. 87.

36. Michael Luark Diary, March 27, 1862, Box 1/10: Michael Luark Papers, Acc. #309, UWL/MUA.

37. Blaine, *Letters and Papers of Rev. David E. Blaine and his Wife Catharine*, p. 87. I checked with Rick Edwards, Park Ranger at Fort Vancouver National Historic Site and there is no record of imported wheat from Chili. Hudson's Bay had been growing their own wheat since the 1830s. On the other hand, by 1852 only 100 acres of land at Fort Vancouver was under cultivation, so maybe other HBC sites did get Chili wheat.

38. Chauncey M. Depew, *One Hundred Years of American Commerce* (New York: no publisher, 1895), pp. 269-270.

39. "Thorp Mill Town" (Thorp, Wash.: The Thorp Mill Town Historical Society). The Thorp mill has been restored. It operated continuously from 1883 to 1946.

40. *Palouse City News*, January 2, 1890, Palouse City, Wash.

41. Amy M. Ryan, *The Sumner Story* (Sumner, Wash.: Sumner Historical Society, 1988), p. 103.

42. Elsie Frankland Marriott, *Bainbridge Through Bifocals* (Seattle: Gateway Printing Company, 1941), p. 60. The company operated a cook-house to provide meals for its employees. Most of them were single men.

43. Catharine Beecher, *Miss Beecher's Housekeeper and Healthkeeper* (New York: Harper & Brothers, Publishers, 1873), p. 66.

44. Blaine, *Letters and Papers of Rev. David E. Blaine and His Wife Catharine*, p. 44.

45. Elizabeth Gedney, "Cross-Section of Pioneer Life at Fourth Plain," *Oregon Historical Quarterly* 43:1 (March 1942): 26.

46. Sarah J. Hale, *Mrs. Hale's New Cook Book* (Philadelphia: J.B. Peterson and Brothers, 1857), p. 422.

47. Leta May Smith, *The End of the Trail* (Hicksville, N.Y.: Exposition Press, 1976), p. 124.

48. Smith, *Centralia The First Fifty Years*, p. 66.

49. Batter or dough-mixing machines came on the market around 1860. Universal claimed one of their machines made four loaves.

50. Jackson, Koontz, Glover Family Papers, MSS 078, Box 2: SLO.

51. Bryan, *The Kentucky Housewife*, p. 320.

52. J.H. Horner, "Early Wallowa Valley Settlers," *Oregon Historical Quarterly* 18:3 (September, 1942): 219.

53. Correspondence from Mrs. Tove Burhen to the author, August 31, 1994.

54. *New York Post*, Feb. 12, 1850.

55. Wilson and Dunlap Notebook, 1857, Box 3, Wilson and Dunlap, UWL/MUA. "Papers" were forerunners of the modern package.

56. Catharine Beecher, *Miss Beecher's Domestic Receipt Book* (New York: Harper & Bros., 1856), p. 130.

57. Smith, *Centralia The First Fifty Years,* p. 76.

58. Thornton McElroy to Sarah McElroy, April 3, 1853, Box 1/38, McElroy Family Papers, Acc. #27, 101, 169, UWL/MUA.

59. *Columbia*, October 23, 1852, Olympia, Wash. Terr.

60. Wilson and Hurd Journal, April 20, 1854, Box 3, Wilson and Dunlap, UWL/MUA.

61. *The Seattle Gazette*, April 12, 1864.

62. *Puget Sound Dispatch*, January 20, 1872, Seattle, Wash. Terr.

63. Sandra L. Oliver, *Saltwater Foodways* (Mystic, Conn.; Mystic Seaport Museum, Inc., 1995), p. 78.

64. *The Washington Standard*, June 8, 1872, Olympia, Wash. Terr.

65. Ladies of the First Presbyterian Church, *A Feast of Good Things* (Spokane: Quick Print Co., 1895), p. 44.

Notes for Chapter Five

1. *Told by the Pioneers*, 3 Vols. (Olympia, Wash.: Works Projects Administration, 1937), 3: 174

2. Herndon Smith, compiler, *Centralia The First Fifty Years, 1845-1900* (Centralia, Wash.: *The Daily Chronicle,* 1942), p. 76.

3. Mrs. Cecil Laramie Deutsch, compiler, *Family Records and Reminiscences of Washington Pioneers*, Vol. V (typewritten, no publisher, 1935), p. 110.

4. David Edwards Blaine, *Letters and Papers of Rev. David E. Blaine and his Wife Catharine: Seattle, 1853-1856, Oregon, 1856-1862* (Seattle: Historical Society of the Pacific Northwest Conferences of the Methodist Church, 1963), p. 144.

5. Michael Luark Diary, December 25, 1861, Box 1/10, Michael Luark Papers, Acc. #309, UWL/MUA.

6. Information supplied by David Hansen, Park Historian at Fort Vancouver. Source: Lester Ross "An Historical and Archaeological Investigation of Goods Imported and Manufactured by Hudson Bay Company," typescript, 1976. The Hudson's Bay Company, under the direction of Dr. John McLoughlin, was most generous in supplying emigrants, particularly those who came in the 1840s, with foods and seeds to plant. For more information on gardens and livestock at Fort Vancouver see *Cultural Landscape Report: Fort Vancouver National Historic Site* (Seattle: National Park Service, 1992).

7. Financial Record Book 1856-57, July 20, 1856, June 1857, Box 1, Elizabeth and Henry Roeder Papers, UWL/MUA. See also Oscar Osburn Winther, *The Old Oregon Country: A History of Frontier Trade, Transportation, and Travel* (Lincoln: University of Nebraska Press, 1950), for information about early roads and wagon trails.

8. Victor J. Farrar, "Diary Kept by Colonel and Mrs. I.N. Ebey," *The Washington Historical Quarterly* 8:2 (April 1917): 140.

9. Arthur A. Denny, *Pioneer Days on Puget Sound* (Fairfield, Wash.: Ye Galleon Press, 1979), p. 51.

10. Blaine, *Letters and Papers of Rev. David E. Blaine and his Wife Catharine*, p. 192.

11. Thomas W. Prosch, *McCarver and Tacoma* (Seattle: Lowman and Hanford Stationery and Printing Company, 1906), pp. 46-47.

12. Thornton McElroy to Sarah McElroy, January 11, 1853, Box 1/38, McElroy Family Papers, Acc. #27, 101, 169, UWL/MUA.

13. Lillian Schlissel, Byrd Gibbens, Elizabeth Hampsten, *Far From Home: Families of the Westward Journey* (New York: Schocken Books, 1989), p. 21.

14. Blaine, *Letters and Papers of Rev. David E. Blaine and his Wife Catharine*, pp. 82, 98.

15. Weldon Willis Rau, "Frontier Conflict," *Columbia* 7:1 (Spring 1993): 8.

16. Correspondence from Mrs. Tove Burhen to author, August 31, 1994.

17. Sarah Hunt Stevens, *Book of Remembrances of Marion County, Oregon Pioneers 1840-1860* (Portland: The Berncliff Press, 1927), p. 245.

18. Smith, *Centralia: The First Fifty Years 1845-1900*, p. 327.

19. Elizabeth Gedney, "Cross-Section of Pioneer Life at Fourth Plain," *Oregon Historical Quarterly* 43:1 (March 1942): 24-25.

20. *Oregon Spectator*, August 18, 1853, Oregon City, Oregon Terr.

21. Elof Norman, *The Coffee Chased Us Up: Monte Cristo Memories* (Seattle: The Mountaineers, 1977), p. 16.

22. Dorothy Koert, *The Lyric Singer: A Biography of Ella Higginson* (Bellingham, Wash.: Center for Pacific Northwest Studies & Fourth Corner Registry, 1985), p. 42.

23. Linda Deziah Jennings, compiler, *Washington Women's Cook Book* (Seattle: The Washington Equal Suffrage Association, 1909), p. 43.

24. Lois Barton, *Spencer Butte Pioneers: 100 Years on the Sunny Side of the Butte, 1850-1950* (Eugene, Oregon: Spencer Butte Press, 1982), p. 70.

25. Stevens, *Book of Remembrances of Marion County, Oregon Pioneers*, p. 245. Sorrel has been used as an ingredient in pies since at least the eighteenth century.

26. Correspondence from Erica Calkins to the author, November 23, 1994. Calkins is a historical gardener in Oregon City. The story is from Hunsaker family chronicles.

27. Karen Hess, correspondence with the author, March 19, 1996.

28. *Epworth Cook Book* (Spokane, Wash.: Arranged by the Ladies of the Epworth M.E. Church, 1910), p. 56.

29. *Told by the Pioneers*, Vol. 2, p. 188.

30. Edith Beebe Carhart, *A History of Bellingham* (Bellingham, Wash.: The Argonaut Press, 1926), p. 38.

31. *The Washington Standard*, May 30, 1874, Olympia, Wash. Terr.

32. Georgiana M. Blankenship, *Early History of Thurston County Washington: Together with Biographies and Reminiscences of Those Identified with Pioneer Days* (Olympia, Wash.: no publisher, 1914), p. 93.

33. Information about Pruitt family bee hunting came in a letter, Bob Pruitt to the author, October 26, 1995.

34. Oluf Olson, *History of Milwaukie, Oregon* (Milwaukie, Oregon: Federal Writers' Project, 1965), pp. 86-87.

35. *Ibid.*

36. *The Ladies' Aid Society First M.E. Church Cook Book of Tested Recipes* (Seattle: Covington & Jordon, 1906), p. 55.

37. *Baptist Ladies Aid Cook Book*, (Dayton: no publisher; no date, but approximately 1910), p. 42.

38. Gedney, "Cross-Section of Pioneer Life at Fourth Plain," p. 26.

39. Sarah J. Hale, *Mrs. Hale's New Cook Book* (Philadelphia: T.B. Peterson and Brothers, 1857), p. 334.

40. Jackson, Koontz, Glover Family Papers, MSS 078, Box 2/5, SLO.

41. Ladies of the Battery Street Methodist Church, *North Seattle Cook and Recipe Book* (Seattle: Acme Publishing Co., Press, 1904), p. 40.

42. Hale, *Mrs. Hale's New Cook Book*, p. 334.

43. Farrar, "Diary Kept by Colonel and Mrs. I.N. Ebey," p. 59.

44. *The Daily Pacific Tribune*, April 3, 1869, Olympia, Wash. Terr.

45. Gertrude Strohm, *The Universal Cookery Book* (New York: White, Stokes, & Allen, 1887), p. 172.

46. Leta May Smith, *The End of the Trail* (Hicksville, N.Y.: Exposition Press, 1976), p. 90.

47. William Weaver, *A Quaker Woman's Cookbook* (Philadelphia: University of Pennsylvania Press, 1982), p. lxxv.

48. Gedney, "Cross Section of Pioneer Life at Fourth Plain," p. 25.

49. Mary Randolph, *The Virginia House-wife* (Washington: Davis and Force, 1824), p. 201-202. Cited in Andrew F. Smith, *The Tomato in America: Early History, Culture, and Cookery* (Columbia: University of South Carolina Press, 1994), p. 187.

50. Victor J. Farrar, "Diary Kept by Colonel and Mrs. I.N. Ebey," p. 54.

51. Nancy Torgenson, *Food...Preservation...Before the Mason Jar* (Decatur, Ill.: Glimpse of the Past, 1994), p. 50.

52. Hale, *Mrs. Hale's New Cook Book*, p. 320.

53. Smith, *Centralia The First Fifty Years*, p. 339.

54. Jennings, *Washington Women's Cook Book*, p. 180.

55. *Told by the Pioneers*, Vol. 3, p. 116.

56. Blaine, *Letters and Papers of Rev. David E. Blaine and His Wife Catharine*, p. 78.

57. Mark D. Kaplanoff, ed., *Journal of The Brigantine Hope, 1790-92* (Barre, Ma.: Imprint Society, 1971), p. 149.

58. Barton, *Spencer Butte Pioneers*, p. 72.

59. Guy Waring, *My Pioneer Past* (Boston: Bruce Humphries Inc. Publishers, 1936), pp. 99-100.

60. *Told by the Pioneers*, Vol. 3, p. 156.

61. *Ibid.*

62. Lillian Miller Christiansen, "Memories of Jefferson County Washington, 1894," Acc. #1922, MOHI.

63. Charles M. Dwelley, ed., *Skagit Memories, Series #6* (Mt. Vernon, Wash.: Skagit County Historical Society, 1979), p. 26.

64. *The Morning Oregonian*, September 13, 1866, Portland, Oregon.

65. See Francis Fugate, *Arbuckles: The Coffee That Won the West* (El Paso: Texas Western Press, 1994) for an in-depth discussion of the rise of Arbuckle's coffee.

66. Norman, *The Coffee Chased Us Up*, pp. 3-4.

67. *Godey's Lady's Book and Magazine*, January 1861, p. 76.

Notes for Chapter Six

1. David Edwards Blaine, *Letters and Papers of Rev. David E. Blaine and his Wife Catharine: Seattle, 1853-1856, Oregon, 1856-1862* (Seattle: Historical Society of the Pacific Northwest Conference of the Methodist Church, 1963), p. 194.

2. *Ibid.*, p. 70.

3. Sarah McElroy to Mother, January 6, 1861, Box 1/40, McElroy Family Papers, Acc. #27, 101, 169, UWL/MUA.

4. *The Daily Pacific Tribune*, January 16, 1869, Seattle, Wash. Terr.

5. Elizabeth Gedney, "Cross-Section of Pioneer Life at Fourth Plain," *Oregon Historical Quarterly*, 43:1 (March, 1942): 17

6. *Ibid.*

7. David James, *From Grand Mound to Scatter Creek* (Olympia, Wash.: State Capitol Historical Association of Washington, 1980), pp. 36-37.

8. Thomas White, *To Oregon in 1852, Letter of Dr. Thomas White* (Indianapolis: Indiana Historical Society, 1964), p. 23.
9. Blaine, *Letters and Papers of Rev. David E. Blaine and his Wife Catharine*, p. 50.
10. Mary Hayden, *Pioneer Days* (Fairfield, Wash.: Ye Galleon Press, 1979), p. 37.
11. Bruce A. Wilson, *Late Frontier, A History of Okanogan County, Washington 1800-1941* (Okanogan, Wash.: Okanogan County Historical Society, 1990), p. 167.
12. Phoebe Goodell Judson, *A Pioneer's Search for An Ideal Home* (Bellingham, Wash.: Union Printing, Binding and Stationery Company, 1925), p. 105.
13. Edmund T. Becher, *Spokane Corona, Eras & Empires* (Spokane: C.W. Hill Printers, 1974), p. 244.
14. Judson, *A Pioneer's Search for An Ideal Home*, p. 105.
15. Jim Attwell, *Early History of Klickitat County* (Skamania, Wash.: Tahlkie Books, 1977), p. 82.
16. Victor J. Farrar, ed., "Diary Kept by Colonel and Mrs. I.N. Ebey," *The Washington Historical Quarterly* 8:2 (April 1917): 124-152.
17. Sarah McElroy, Journals, etc., Box 2-11, McElroy Family Papers, UWL/MUA.
18. Correspondence from Norma Lou Jones to author, January 26, 1995.
19. *The Daily Pacific Tribune*, April 3, 1869, Olympia, Wash. Terr.
20. Louise Swift to Mother, December 3, 1864, VF #40 Louise Swift Letters 1863-1869, UWL/MUA.
21. Lillian Schlissel, Byrd Gibbens, Elizabeth Hampsten, *Far From Home: Families of the Westward Journey* (New York: Schocken Books, 1989), pp. 29, 31.
22. *Told by the Pioneers*, 3 Vols. (Olympia, Wash.: Works Projects Administration, 1937), 2: 112.
23. Sheba Hargreaves, "The Letters of Roselle Putnam," *Oregon Historical Quarterly* 29:3 (September 1928): 262.
24. Don Raycraft and Carol Raycraft, *A Collector's Source Book* (Des Moines, Iowa: Wallace Homestead, 1980), p. 45.
25. Notebook, 1857, Box 3: Wilson and Box 3, Wilson and Dunlap Business Records, UWL/MUA.
26. Scarlet runner beans, winter keeper beets, Siberian kale, yellow plum tomato, and early rose potato are a few of the varieties grown in 1857 and still commercially available.
27. John Campbell Diary, May 22, 1870, John Campbell Papers, Box 1, UWL/MUA.
28. Michael Luark Diary, July 10, 1865, Michael Luark Papers, Box 2, Acc. #309, UWL/MUA.
29. Correspondence from Minerva W. Herrett to author, September 1994. Herrett grew up in a small town in eastern Washington.
30. Wilson, *Late Frontier, A History of Okanogan County*, p. 162.
31. Michael Luark Diary, Feb.?? 1864, Box 2/2, UWL/MUA.
32. Miles Hatch to Tamar Richardson, December 1876, Melvin F. Hawk Collection, MS7/15, WSHSL.
33. John Campbell Diary, January 9, 1871, UWL/MUA.
34. "Special Issue: The Life and Letters of Adelaide Sutton Gilbert, Spokane Pioneer," *The Pacific Northwest Forum* 5:1 (Winter-Spring 1992): 56.
35. Georgiana M. Blankenship, *Early History of Thurston County Washington: Together with Biographies and Reminiscences of Those Identified with Pioneer Days* (Olympia, Wash.: no publisher, 1914), p. 92.
36. Barbara Zimmerman and Vernon Carstensen, eds., "Pioneer Woman in Southwestern Washington Territory, The Recollections of Susanna Maria Slover McFarland Price Ede," *Pacific Northwest Quarterly* 67:4 (Oct. 1976): 142.

37. Eula Fisher, Tape 1, *Washington Women's Heritage Project*, Acc. #3416-13, UWL/ MUA.
38. *Told by the Pioneers*, 3: 96.
39. Mrs. Hugh Fraser and Hugh C. Fraser, *Seven Years On the Pacific Slope* (New York: Dodd, Mead and Company, 1914), p. 135.
40. Visit to Borst home by author, June 30, 1994.
41. Jackson, Koontz, Glover Family Papers, MSS 078, Box 2/5, SLO.
42. Catharine Beecher, *Miss Beecher's Housekeeper and Health Keeper* (New York: Harper & Brothers, Publishers, 1873), p. 104.
43. Arline Ely, *Our Foundering Fathers, The Story of Kirkland* (Kirkland, Wash.: Kirkland Public Library, 1975), pp. 3-4.
44. Michael Luark Diary, July 26, 27, 1865, UWL/MUA.
45. Sarah McElroy to brother, January 26, 1858, and 1880 (no specific date), Box 2/7; 2/9, McElroy Family Papers, UWL/MUA.
46. Blaine, *Letters and Papers of Rev. David E. Blaine and his Wife Catharine*, pp. 105, 70.
47. Herndon Smith, compiler, *Centralia, The First Fifty Years 1845-1900* (Centralia, Wash.: *The Daily Chronicle* and F.H. Cole Printing Company, 1942), p. 327.
48. Correspondence from Dale Rutledge to author, February 16, 1994.
49. Jackson, Koontz, Glover Family Papers, MSS 078, Box 2/5, SLO.
50. Smith, *Centralia, The First Fifty Years*, p. 328.
51. Sophie Frye Bass, *When Seattle was a Village* (Seattle: Lowman & Hanford Co., 1947), p. 173.
52. *Godey's Lady's Book and Magazine,* July 1861, p. 553.
53. Hargreaves, "The Letters of Roselle Putnam," p. 256.
54. R.D. Pitt, *Directory of the City of Seattle and Vicinity, 1879* (Seattle, Washington Territory: Hanford & McClaire Printers, 1879), p. 93.
55. *Clark County Register*, July 27, 1882, Vancouver, Wash. Terr.
56. Linda Franklin, *300 Years of Kitchen Collectibles* (Florence, Alabama: Books Americana, 1991), pp. 1-2, 42-48.
57. *Scientific American* 13 (April 24, 1858): 260.
58. John D. Unruh, *The Plains Across: The Overland Emigrants and the Trans-Mississippi West, 1840-60* (Urbana: University of Illinois Press, 1979), p. 391.
59. *Pioneer and Democrat*, March 11, 1853, Olympia, Wash. Terr.
60. "From Memory's Pages," Box 1/1A, Andrew Jackson Chambers Family papers, Acc. #939, UWL/MUA.
61. Farrar, "Diary Kept by Colonel and Mrs. I.N. Ebey," p. 134.
62. "The Life and Letters of Adelaide Sutton Gilbert," p. 75.
63. Laura Shapiro, *Perfection Salad* (New York: Farrar, Straus and Giroux, 1986), p. 99.
64. Ely, *Our Foundering Fathers, The Story of Kirkland*, p. 3.
65. Ladies of Steven's Relief Core #1, *Household CookBook* (Seattle: Metropolitan, 1910), p. 53.
66. James, *From Grand Mound to Scatter Creek*, p. 72.
67. Sarah McElroy, Journals, etc., Box 2-11, McElroy Family Papers, UWL/MUA.
68. Judson, *A Pioneer's Search for An Ideal Home*, p. 89.
69. "Reminiscence of Elizabeth Chambers Hunsacker," Box 1/1A, Andrew Jackson Chambers Family papers, Acc. #939, UWL/MUA.
70. Clareta Olmstead Smith, *The Trail Leads West* (Philadelphia, Dorrance & Company, 1946), p. 11.
71. Sarah J. Hale, *Mrs. Hale's New Cookbook* (Philadelphia: T.B. Peterson and Brothers, 1857), p. 375.

72. Beecher, *Miss Beecher's Housekeeper and Healthkeeper*, p. 108.
73. Lettice Bryan, *The Kentucky Housewife* (1839; reprint, Columbia: University of South Carolina Press, 1991), p. 346. A variation of this method continued into the 1850s and 1860s.
74. "Reminiscence of Elizabeth Chambers Hunsacker," Acc. #939, UWL/MUA.
75. Nancy Torgerson, *Food Preservation...Before the Mason Jar* (Decatur, Ill: Glimpse of the Past, 1994), p. 22.
76. Chauncey M. Depew, *One Hundred Years of American Commerce* (New York: no publisher, 1895), p. 258.
77. Hugo Zieman and Mrs. F.L. Gillette, *The White House Cookbook* (New York: The Saalfield Publishing Co., 1905), p. 126.
78. *Godey's Lady's Book and Magazine* April 1861, p. 366.
79. Laura M. House, "Eastern Washington Territory Pioneer," M-102, WSHSL.
80. Smith, *Centralia, The First Fifty Years*, p. 327.
81. Zimmerman and Carstensen, "Pioneer Woman in Southwestern Washington Territory," p. 140.
82. Nina L. Williamson, *Pioneer Stories of Linn County, Oregon* (Albany, Oregon: Early Pioneer Publications, 1984), p. 99.
83. *Ibid.*
84. "Reminiscence of Elizabeth Chambers Hunsacker," Acc. #939, UWL/MUA.
85. Torgerson, *Food Preservation...Before the Mason Jar*, pp. 35-36.
86. See Julian H. Toulouse, *Fruit Jars* (Camden, New Jersey: Thomas Nelson & Sons, 1969), for a discussion of the early patents, descriptions of jars, and the men who made them.
87. Amy M. Ryan, *The Sumner Story* (Sumner, Wash.: Sumner Historical Society, 1988), p. 48.
88. For more details about the errors of canning see Toulouse, *Fruit Jars*.
89. For more information on the canning industry see Hyla M. Clark, *The Tin Can Book* (New York: New American Library, 1977). For discussion about the acceptance of canned goods see Shapiro, *Perfection Salad*, pp. 199-208, and Susan Williams, *Savory Suppers and Fashionable Feasts: Dining in Victorian America* (New York: Pantheon Books, 1985), pp. 95-100.
90. *A. McDonald, L. Schwabacher v. William H. Watson,* District Court at Dayton, Columbia County, Washington Territory, Frontier Justice Case Files-Washington Territorial Court Records in *Frontier Justice 1853-1889: A Guide to Court Records of Washington Territory* (Olympia: State of Washington, Office of Secretary of State, Division of Archives and Records Management, 1987).
91. Leta May Smith, *End of the Trail* (Hicksville, N.Y.: Exposition Press, 1976), p. 125.
92. Wilson and Dunlap Notebook, September 26, 1856, Box 3, Wilson and Dunlap Business Records, UWL/MUA.
93. Mrs. William Gottstein, Mrs. Sigismund Aronson, Mrs. Salmon Spring, eds., *The Ladies' Auxiliary to Temple de Hirsch Famous Cook Book* (Seattle: Ladies' Auxiliary Temple DE Hirsch, 1916), p. 111.
94. Sandra Brightbill, "Mamie Sasse Growing Up in Pine Creek, Washington," *Pacific Northwest Forum* 7:3 (Summer-Fall 1982): 35.
95. Ryan, *The Sumner Story*, p. 104.
96. Wilson, *Late Frontier, A History of Okanogan County*, p. 173.
97. Beecher, *Miss Beecher's Housekeeper and Healthkeeper*, p. 52.
98. Ladies Aid Society of First Christian Church, *The Little Gem Cook Book* (Waitsburg, Wash.: Wheeler Publishing Co., 1909), p. 112.

99. *The Ladies' Aid Society First M.E. Church Cook Book* (Seattle: Covington & Jordon, 1906), p. 85.

100. *Citizen Cook Book* (Bothell, Wash.: no publisher; no date), p. 27.

101. *The Washington Standard* (Olympia) July 8, 1871.

Notes for Chapter Seven

1. David Edwards Blaine, *Letters and Papers of Rev. David E. Blaine and his Wife Catharine: Seattle, 1853-1856, Oregon, 1856-1862* (Seattle: Historical Society of the Pacific Northwest Conference of the Methodist Church, 1963), p. 109.

2. *Ibid.*, p. 109.

3. Amy M. Ryan, *The Sumner Story* (Sumner, Wash.: Sumner Historical Society, 1988) p. 47.

4. Sarah J. Hale, *Mrs. Hale's New Cook Book* (Philadelphia: T.B. Peterson and Brothers, 1857), p. 475.

5. Louise Swift to Mother, July 12, 1863; Aug. 3, 1863, VF #40 Louise Swift Letters 1863-1869, UWL/MUA.

6. Margaret Stevens to Mother, February, 18, 1855, Box 8/11, Issac Stevens Papers, Acc. #111, UWL/MUA.

7. David James, *From Grand Mound to Scatter Creek* (Olympia, Wash.: State Capitol Historical Association of Washington, 1980), p. 27.

8. Lillian Schlissel, Byrd Gibbens, and Elizabeth Hampsten, *Far From Home: Families of the Westward Journey* (New York: Schocken Books, 1989), p. 14.

9. Michael Luark Diary, June 12, 1862, Box 1/10, Michael Luark Papers, Acc #309, UWL/MUA.

10. Victor J. Farrar, "Diary Kept by Colonel and Mrs. I.N. Ebey," *The Washington Historical Quarterly* 8:2 (April 1917): 129.

11. Sheba Hargreaves, "The Letters of Roselle Putnam," *Oregon Historical Quarterly*, 29:3 (September, 1928): 256.

12. Phoebe Goodell Judson, *A Pioneer's Search for An Ideal Home* (Bellingham, Wash.: Union Printing, Binding and Stationery Company, 1925), p. 104.

13. Blaine, *Letters and Papers of Rev. David E. Blaine and his Wife Catharine*, p. 124.

14. Diaries and Letters, Henry Roeder, January 14, 1861, Box 1, Elizabeth and Henry Roeder Papers, UWL/MUA.

15. Oscar O. Winther, *The Great Northwest: A History* (New York: Alfred A. Knopf, 1952), pp. 77-78.

16. *Ibid.*

17. Mary Bozarth to Mary Beam, Oct. 6 (no year, probably 1860), Part 2, Box 4/12, Winfield Ebey Collection, UWL/MUA.

18. Judson, *A Pioneer's Search for An Ideal Home*, pp. 104-105.

19. *A Country Kitchen* (Maynard, Mass.: Chandler Press, 1987; reprinted from Mary Cornelius, *The Young Housekeeper's Friend*, 1850).

20. John Campbell Diary, May 22, 1870, John Campbell Papers, Box 1, UWL/MUA.

21. *Ibid.*, August, 1, 1869.

22. Farrar, "Diary Kept by Colonel and Mrs. I.N. Ebey," p. 129.

23. Caroline Gale Budlong, *Memories* (Eugene, Or.: The Picture Press Printers, 1949), p. 26.

24. Michael Luark Diary, October 25, 1861. "Looked for cattle" was a frequent entry in the Luark diaries.

25. Colville Mothers' Club and Stevens County Historical Society, *Tales of the Pioneers* (Colville, Wash.: Stevens County Historical Society, 1964) p. 4.
26. *Ibid.*, p. 30.
27. *Godey's Lady's Book and Magazine,* Jan. 1861, p. 76.
28. Bruce A. Wilson, *Late Frontier, A History of Okanogan County, Washington 1800-1941* (Okanogan, Wash.: Okanogan County Historical Society, 1990), p. 172.
29. Schlissel, Gibbens, and Hampsten, *Far From Home,* p. 14.
30. "Reminiscence of Elizabeth Chambers Hunsacker," Box 1/1A, Andrew Jackson Chambers Family, Acc. #939, UWL/MUA.
31. Bessie Wilson Craine, Squak Valley (Issaquah), VF 471, UWL/MUA.
32. Elof Norman, *The Coffee Chased Us Up: Monte Cristo Memories* (Seattle: The Mountaineers, 1977), p. 35.
33. Clareta Olmstead Smith, *The Trail Leads West* (Philadelphia: Dorrance & Company, 1946), p. 52.
34. Reprinted in *The Washington Standard*, August 28, 1869.
35. Hale, *Mrs. Hale's New Cook Book,* p. 476.
36. Smith, *The Trail Leads West*, p. 52.
37. Wilson, *Late Frontier, A History of Okanogan County,* p. 161.
38. Ryan, *The Sumner Story,* p. 103.
39. William S. Lewis, "Reminiscences of Delia B. Sheffield," *Washington Historical Quarterly* 15:1 (January, 1924): 60.
40. *Polk's Portland City Directory* (Portland: R.L. Polk & Co., 1865), p. 80.
41. *State of Washington Second Annual Report of the State Dairy Commissioner for the year 1896* (Olympia, Wash.).
42. *The Washington Standard*, August 7, 1864, Olympia, Wash. Terr.
43. Bessie Wilson Craine, Squak Valley (Issaquah), VF 471, UWL/MUA.
44. Leta May Smith, *The End of the Trail* (Hicksville, N. Y.: Exposition Press, 1976), p. 40.
45. This recipe appeared in *The Washington Standard*, December 15, 1860. It is almost identical to the one in *Peterson's Fashion Magazine,* May, 1858. Newspapers did not bother to give sources. Nancy Torgerson, author of *Food...Preservation...Before the Mason Jar* (Decatur, Ill.: Glimpse of the Past, 1994), p. 39, says that she tried this method and the butter in the flower pot "was only one degree cooler than the butter in a covered butter dish."
46. Lelah Jackson Edson, *Pioneers Along The Bend of The Nooksack* (Bellingham, Wash.: Office of County Superintendent, 1945), pp. 54, 151.
47. Charles Dwelley, ed., *Skagit Memories: Stories of the Settlement Years* (Mount Vernon, Wash.: Skagit County Historical Society, 1979), p. 75.
48. Michael Luark Diary, July 9, 1862.
49. Catharine Beecher, *Miss Beecher's Housekeeper and Healthkeeper* (New York: Harper & Brothers, Publishers, 1873), p. 73.
50. Guy Waring, *My Pioneer Past* (Boston: Bruce Humphries Inc., 1936), p. 98.
51. Colville Mothers' Club, *Tales of the Pioneers* (Colville, Wash.: Stevens County Historical Society, 1964), p. 145.
52. *Godey's Lady's Book and Magazine,* April 1861, p. 366.
53. Recipe Book, Box 2, McElroy Family Papers, Acc. #27,101,169, UWL/MUA.
54. Suggestions and hints are from Hale, *Mrs. Hale's New Cook Book,* and Beecher, *Miss Beecher's Domestic Receipt Book.*
55. *Pioneer Receipts, Facts, Fancies and Remedies,* Vol. 1 (Kelso, Wash.: Cowlitz County Historical Society, 1973), p. 15.

56. Lois Barton, *Spencer Butte Pioneers: 100 Years on the Sunny Side of the Butte, 1850-1950* (Eugene, Or.: Spencer Butte Press, 1982), p. 9.

57. Dwelley, ed., *Skagit Memories*, p. 75.

58. Beecher, *Miss Beecher's Housekeeper and Healthkeeper*, pp. 23, 25.

59. *The Washington Standard* (Olympia), July 24, 1869.

60. Luark Diary, December 9, 1862.

61. Laura M. House, "Eastern Washington Pioneer," M-102, Robert Hitchman Collection, WSHSL.

62. Dwelley, ed., *Skagit Memories*, p. 75.

63. House, "Eastern Washington Pioneer," WSHSL.

64. Herndon Smith, compiler, *Centralia, The First Fifty Years 1845-1900* (Centralia, Wash.: *The Daily Chronicle* and F.H. Cole Printing Company, 1942), p. 317.

65. Elizabeth Gedney, "Cross-Section of Pioneer Life at Fourth Plain," *Oregon Historical Quarterly* 43:1 (March 1942): 24.

66. Susanna Maria Slover McFarland Price Ede, "Pioneer Woman in Southwestern Washington Territory," *Pacific Northwest Quarterly* 67:4 (October, 1976): 142. This exact quote, attributed to another person, also appeared in *Incidents In the Life of A Pioneer Woman* (State Association of the Daughters of the Pioneers of Washington, no date), p. 133—one of the reasons history is so intriguing!

67. House, "Eastern Washington Pioneer," WSHSL.

68. Sue Robinson Dennis, *Growing Up in the Northwest* (Seattle, Wash.: Smuggler's Cove Publishing, 1991), p. 78.

69. Smith, *Centralia, The First Fifty Years*, p. 317.

70. Dennis, *Growing Up in the Northwest*, p. 78.

71. See Linda Franklin, *300 Years of Kitchen Collectibles* (Florence, Alabama: Books Americana, 1991), pp. 12-41 for a description of the numerous types of chopping, grating, and grinding implements.

72. Smith, *Centralia, The First Fifty Years*, p. 317.

73. Dennis, *Growing Up in the Northwest*, pp. 72-73.

74. *Puget Sound Dispatch*, January 20, 1872, Seattle, Wash. Territory.

75. Barton, *Spencer Butte Pioneers*, p. 68.

76. Eula P. Fisher, Tape 1, Washington Women's Heritage Project, Acc. #3416-13, UWL/MUA.

77. Kathryn Carlson, *Rich Heritage* (Colville, Wash.: *Statesman-Examiner*, 1979), p. 54.

78. Dennis, *Growing up in the Northwest*, pp. 72-73.

79. Jackson, Koontz, Glover Family Papers, MSS 078, Box 2/5, SLO.

80. Sarah Hale, *Mrs. Hale's New Cook Book*, p. 163.

81. This recipe is from *The Washington Standard*, January 13, 1872, but similar versions appeared in many mid-nineteenth century cookbooks.

82. Blaine, *Letters and Papers of Rev. David E. Blaine and his Wife Catharine*, pp. 104, 141.

83. Ryan, *The Sumner Story*, p. 47.

84. Blaine, *Letters and Papers of Rev. David E. Blaine and his Wife Catharine*, p. 104.

85. Dennis, *Growing up in the Northwest*, p. 73.

86. Recipe Book, Box 2, McElroy Family Papers, UWL/MUA.

87. Miscellaneous Writings, Box 4, Michael Luark Papers, Acc. #309, UWL/MUA.

88. *American Farmer* 3:2 (August, 1861).

89. Miscellaneous records, Letter to John Dunn, January 3, 1881, VF #30713, UWL/MUA.

Notes for Chapter Eight

1. John Campbell Diary, November 4, 1869, Box 1, John Campbell Papers, UWL/MUA. Though many pioneers wrote about shooting pheasants, the birds were probably grouse, a member of the *Tetraonidae* family. Pheasants, *Phasianos colchicus*, are not native to the Pacific Northwest or any other place in North America. The ring-necked pheasant was introduced into California in 1857 and Oregon in the 1880s, according to *The Audobon Society Encyclopedia of North American Birds*. There are several explanations for the misnomer. In the nineteenth century, "pheasant," which has been popular since antiquity, was the generic name for any flavorful, edible game bird. Or perhaps pheasants managed to make the Northwest home earlier than previously believed. At any rate, few pioneers wrote about shooting grouse; they believed they were shooting and eating pheasant.

2. David Edwards Blaine, *Letters and Papers of Rev. David E. Blaine and his Wife Catharine: Seattle, 1853-1856, Oregon, 1856-1862* (Seattle: Historical Society of the Pacific Northwest Conference of the Methodist Church, 1963), p. 77.

3. Louise Swift Letters, January 6, 1864, VF #40, Louise Swift Letters 1863-1869, UWL/MUA.

4. Bruce A. Wilson, *Late Frontier, A History of Okanogan County, Washington 1800-1941* (Okanogan, Wash.: Okanogan County Historical Society, 1990), p. 161.

5. Charles Prosch, *Reminiscence of Washington Territory: Scenes, Incidents and Reflections of the Pioneer Period on Puget Sound* (Seattle: no publisher, 1904), p. 25.

6. "Special Issue: The Life and Letters of Adelaide Sutton Gilbert, Spokane Pioneer," *The Pacific Northwest Forum* 5:1 (Winter-Spring 1992): 16.

7. Herndon Smith, compiler, *Centralia, The First Fifty Years 1845-1900* (Centralia, Wash.: *The Daily Chronicle* and F.H. Cole Printing Company, 1942), p. 327.

8. Sarah J. Hale, *Mrs. Hale's New Cook Book* (Philadelphia: T.B. Peterson and Brothers, 1857), p. 182.

9. "Reminiscence of Elizabeth Chambers Hunsacker," Box 1, Andrew Jackson Chambers Family, Acc. #939, UWL/MUA. Mrs. Hunsacker wrote her reminiscences after pheasant had been introduced to the Pacific Northwest.

10. John Campbell Diary, Dec. 21, 1870, UWL/MUA.

11. Hale, *Mrs. Hale's New Cook Book*, p. 227.

12. Victor J. Farrar, ed., "Diary of Colonel and Mrs. I.N. Ebey," *The Washington Historical Quarterly* 8:2 (April, 1917): 132.

13. James Swan, *Almost Out of the World: Scenes from the Washington Territory* (Tacoma: Wash.: State Historical Society, 1971), p. 82.

14. Edmund T. Becher, *Spokane Corona, Eras & Empires* (Spokane: C.W. Hill Printers, 1974), p. 245.

15. Clareta Olmstead Smith, *The Trail Leads West* (Philadelphia: Dorrance & Company, 1946), p. 11. Prairie chickens are related to grouse; people often interchange the names.

16. Smith, *Centralia, The First Fifty Years*, p. 327. Beavers are members of the amphibious rodent family *(Castoridae)*.

17. Robert Emmett Hawley, *Skqee Mus or Pioneer Days on the Nooksack* (Bellingham, Wash.: Self published, 1945), p. 33.

18. Thornton McElroy to Sallie (Sarah) McElroy, April 3, 1853, Box 1/38, McElroy Family Papers, Acc. #27,101, 169, UWL/MUA.

19. Sarah McElroy to brother, October 17, 1875, Box 2/8, McElroy Family Papers, UWL/MUA.

20. Gary Fuller Reese, ed., *They Came to Puget Sound: Reminiscences of Pioneer Women as Published in the Tacoma Daily and Weekly Ledger, 1892-1893* (Tacoma, Wash.: Tacoma Public Library, 1984), p. 3.
21. *Seattle Post Intelligencer*, January 22, 1905, Seattle.
22. *Told by the Pioneers*, 3 Vols. (Olympia, Wash.: Works Projects Administration, 1937), 2: 52. Also see: Kathy Neustadt, *Clambake: A History and Celebration of an American Tradition* (Amherst, Mass.: University of Massachusetts Press, 1992).
23. Scrapbook, clipping, June 9, 1887, Box 3/3, Granville Owen Haller Papers, Acc. #3437-3, UWL/MUA.
24. *The Columbian*, August 6, 1853, Olympia, Wash. Terr.
25. Dunbar Scrapbook, #55. p. 46, UWL (Special Collections).
26. See Neustadt, *Clambake,* for a discussion of the origins and customs of the New England clambake.
27. "Special Issue: The Life and Letters of Adelaide Sutton Gilbert, Spokane Pioneer," p. 93.
28. Ladies of Church of the Holy Family, *The Auburn Cookbook* (Auburn, Wash.: no publisher, 1909), p. 66.
29. Henry T. Finck, *My Adventures in the Golden Age of Music* (New York: Funk and Wagnals Company, 1926), p. 27.
30. Waverly Root, *Food* (New York: Simon & Schuster, 1980), p. 311.
31. E.N. Steele, *The Rise and Decline of the Olympia Oyster* (Elma, Wash.: Fulco Publications, 1957), p. 33.
32. See Jan Longone, "From the Kitchen," *The American Magazine and Historical Chronicle* 4:1 (Spring-Summer 1988), for a discussion of the oyster's popularity throughout history. See Willard R. Espy, *Oysterville* (New York: Clarkson N. Potter, Inc. 1977), for the history of Oysterville.
33. Martha Wiley, "Mrs. Hugh Wiley: Pioneer Mother," *Northwest Legacy* 2:2 (December 1976): 147.
34. *The Townsend Cook Book: Choice and Tested Recipes Furnished by the Ladies of Port Townsend, Washington* (Port Townsend, Wash.: Ladies' Society of the Presbyterian Church, 1905), p. 2.
35. Goldie Robertson Funk, "Captain Doane's Oyster Pan Roast," *Pacific Northwest Quarterly* 43:2 (April, 1952): 154-155.
36. Recipe and information concerning early days in Oysterville from Lucille Wilson to the author, May 26 and June 9, 1986.
37. Saint Peter's Guild, *The Saint Peter's Cook Book* (Pomeroy, Wash.: Saint Peter's Guild of the Episcopal Church, 1904), p. 41.
38. *The Ladies' Aid Society First M.E. Church Cook Book* (Seattle: Covington & Jordon, 1906), p. 31.
39. *The Washington Standard*, April 16, 1870, Olympia, Wash. Terr.
40. *The Oregonian*, December 20, 1885, Portland, Oregon.
41. Leta May Smith, *The End of the Trail* (Hicksville, N.Y.: Exposition Press, 1976), p. 180.
42. Elizabeth Gedney, "Cross-Section of Pioneer Life at Fourth Plain," *Oregon Historical Quarterly* 43:1 (March 1942): 24.
43. *The Washington Republican*, June 12, 1857, Steilacoom, Wash. Terr.
44. *Ibid.*
45. *The Washington Standard*, August, 13, 1870, Olympia, Wash. Terr.
46. Laura Virginia Wagner, *Through Historic Years with Eliza Ferry Leary* (Seattle: Dogwood Press, 1934), pp. 17-18.

47. Sarah McElroy, Journals, etc., Box 2-11, McElroy Family Papers, UWL/MUA.

48. Bessie Wilson Craine, Squak Valley (Issaquah), VF 471, UWL/MUA.

49. Gedney, "Cross-Section of Pioneer Life at Fourth Plain," p. 24.

50. Sarah Willoughby to Oliver L. Willoughby, August 1887, Box 2, Charles and Sarah Willoughby Papers, UWL/MUA.

51. Ladies Aid Society of First Christian Church, *The Little Gem Cook Book* (Waitsburg, Wash.: Wheeler Publishing Co. Printers, 1909), p. 30.

52. *The Saint Peter's Cook Book*, p. 42.

53. Information about early canneries and labels is from John N. Cobb, *Pacific Salmon Fisheries* (Washington D.C.: U.S. Government Printing Office, Bureau of Fisheries, 1930).

54. *Tacoma Ledger*, December, 25, 1892, Tacoma, Wash.

Notes for Chapter Nine

1. Foster Rhea Dulles, *A History of Recreation: America Learns to Play* (New York: Appleton-Century-Crofts, 1965), pp. 148-150.

2. John Campbell Diary, December 10, 1872, Box 1, John Campbell Papers, UWL/MUA.

3. Matthew P. Deady, *Pharisee Among Philistines: The Diary of Judge Matthew P. Deady, 1871-1892* (Portland: Oregon Historical Society, 1975), p. 242.

4. Edmund T. Becher, *Spokane Corona, Eras & Empires* (Spokane: C.W. Hill Printers, 1974), p. 263.

5. Dan E. Clark, "Pioneer Pastimes," *Oregon Historical Quarterly* 57:4 (December, 1956): 338.

6. *Told by the Pioneers*, 3 Vols. (Olympia, Wash.: Works Projects Administration, 1937), 3: 156.

7. Thornton McElroy to Sallie (Sarah) McElroy, December 18, 1853, Box 1/38, McElroy Family Papers, Acc. #27, 101, 169, UWL/MUA.

8. Sarah McElroy to Brother, January 26, 1858, Box 2/7, *ibid.*

9. See Simon R. Charsley, *Wedding Cakes and Cultural History* (London: Routledge, 1992) for a fascinating discussion about wedding cakes.

10. Ladies of the Battery Street Methodist Church, *North Seattle Cook and Recipe Book* (Seattle: Acme Publishing Co. Press, 1904), p. 32.

11. *The Daily Pacific Tribune*, Dec. 21, 1870, Olympia, Wash. Terr.

12. *The Washington Standard*, March 29, 1873, Olympia, Wash. Terr.

13. Sarah McElroy, Journals, etc., Box 2-11, McElroy Family Papers, UWL/MUA. McElroy's comments about recipes are in parentheses.

14. See John L. Hess and Karen Hess, *The Taste of America* (Columbia: South Carolina, University of South Carolina Press, 1989) for discussion of the rise of sugar in American baking.

15. *The Washington Standard*, May 4, 1872, Olympia, Wash. Terr.

16. Sarah McElroy, Journals, etc., Box 2-11, McElroy Family Papers, UWL/MUA.

17. *The Washington Standard*, May 4, 1872, Olympia, Wash. Terr.

18. Laura Shapiro, *Perfection Salad: Women and Cooking at the Turn of the Century* (New York: Farrar, Straus and Giroux, 1986), pp. 115-117.

19. Sarah McElroy, Journals, etc., Box 2-11, McElroy Family Papers, Acc. #27, 101, 169, UWL/MUA.

20. Becher, *Spokane Corona, Eras & Empires*, p. 262.

21. Women's Home Missionary Society, *Ostrander Methodist Church Women's Home Missionary Society Cookbook* 1909; reproduced by the Cowlitz County Historical Museum, 1994), pp. 35-36.

22. *The Territorial Republican*, August 2, 1869, Olympia, Wash. Terr.

23. Charles Prosch, *Reminiscences of Washington Territory: Scenes, Incidents and Reflections of the Pioneer Period on Puget Sound* (Seattle: no publisher, 1904), p. 42.

24. "Special Issue: The Life and Letters of Adelaide Sutton Gilbert, Spokane Pioneer," *The Pacific Northwest Forum* 5:1 (Winter-Spring 1992): 14.

25. *Ibid.*, p. 18.

26. Joan Curtis, Alice Watson, Bette Bradley, eds., *Town On The Sound: Stories of Steilacoom* (Steilacoom, Wash.: Steilacoom Historical Museum Association, 1988), p. 60.

27. *The Territorial Republican*, November 16, 1868, Olympia, Wash. Terr.

28. Becher, *Spokane Corona, Eras & Empires*, p. 263.

29. Memorabilia: Dance programs, 1872, Box 3/14, Eliza Ferry Leary Papers, UWL/MUA.

30. Susan Williams, *Savory Suppers and Fashionable Feasts* (New York: Pantheon Books, 1985), pp. 113-114.

31. Sarah McElroy, Journals, etc., Box 2-11, McElroy Family Papers, UWL/MUA.

32. *The Daily Pacific Tribune*, March 11, 1870, Olympia, Wash. Terr.

33. *The Washington Standard,* June 26, 1869, Olympia, Wash. Terr.

34. *The Daily Pacific Tribune*, July 16, 1864, Olympia, Wash. Terr.

35. *Ibid.*, Dec. 24, 1870, Olympia, Wash. Terr.

36. J.K. Prior, *Portland Directory* (San Francisco: S.J. McCormick, 1865), p. 64.

37. *The Palouse Gazette,* Oct. 17, 1879, Colfax, Wash. Terr.

38. *The Washington Standard*, Dec. 23, 1871, Olympia, Wash. Terr.

39. *Ibid.*, Dec. 30, 1871.

40. *Seattle Post-Intelligencer*, Sept. 15, 1883, Seattle, Wash. Terr.

41. Addie Jensen Hazel, *Across The Years: Pioneer Story of Southern Washington* (no publisher, 1951), p. 21.

42. Bessie Wilson Craine, Squak Valley (Issaquah), VF 471, UWL/MUA.

43. *Baptist Ladies Aid Cook Book* (Dayton, Wash.: no. publisher, no date but probably around 1906).

44. *The Washington Standard*, May 4, 1872, Olympia, Wash. Terr.

45. M.A. Gerrish to Eliza Ferry, Dec. 1879, Box 2/1, Eliza Ferry Leary Papers, UWL/MUA.

46. *The Morning Oregonian*, March 18, 1861, Portland, Oregon.

47. *The Palouse Gazette*, January 5, 1878, Colfax, Wash. Terr. Miners coined the term slumgullion during the 1849 California gold rush period.

48. *The Washington Standard*, December 25, 1871; May 14, 1870, Olympia, Wash. Terr.

49. Becher, *Spokane Corona, Eras & Empires*, p. 262.

50. *Ibid.*

51. *Ibid.*

52. Louise Swift to Mother, August 3, 1863, VF #40, Louise Swift Letters 1863-1869, UWL/MUA.

53. Diary of Mary (Ebey) Wright, January 22, 1866, Box 2 #7, Part 1, Winfield/Ebey Collections, UWL/MUA.

54. R. D. Pitt, Compiler, *Directory of City of Seattle and Vicinity-1879* (Seattle: Hanford & McClaire, 1879), p. 17.

55. Williams, *Savory Suppers and Fashionable Feasts*, p. 137.

56. Edmond S. Meany, ed., *A New Vancouver Journal On The Discovery of Puget Sound* (Seattle: University of Washington Press, 1915), p. 7. Also see: Jacqueline Williams, "Spruce Beer: In Lieu of Their Grog," *British Columbia Historical News* (Winter 1991-92): 2-3.

57. Sarah Hale, *Mrs. Hale's New Cook Book* (Philadelphia: T.B. Peterson and Brothers, 1857), p. 443.

58. Becher, *Spokane Corona, Eras & Empires*, p. 272.

59. *The Washington Standard*, July 6, 1872, Olympia, Wash. Terr.

60. *Told by the Pioneers*, 3 Vols. (Olympia: Works Projects Administration, 1937), 3: 165.

61. Michael Luark Diary, July 2, 3, 4, 1865, Box 2/3, Michael Luark Papers, Acc, #309, UWL/MUA.

62. *The Washington Standard*, July 18, 1873, Olympia, Wash. Terr.

63. *Ibid.*, June 4, 1870.

64. Deady, *Pharisee Among Philistines*, p. 169.

65. Becher, *Spokane Corona, Eras & Empires*, p. 272.

66. *Spokane Falls Review*, May 25, 1890, Spokane, Wash.

67. Amy M. Ryan, *The Sumner Story* (Sumner, Wash.: Sumner Historical Society, 1988), p. 63.

68. Luark Diary, Dec. 25, 1861, Box 1/10, UWL/MUA.

69. David Edwards Blaine, *Letters and Papers of Rev. David E. Blaine and his Wife Catharine: Seattle, 1853-1856, Oregon, 1856-1862* (Seattle: Historical Society of the Pacific Northwest Conference of the Methodist Church, 1963), p. 49.

70. Lettice Bryan, *The Kentucky Housewife* (1839; reprint, Columbia: University of South Carolina Press, 1991), p. 391.

71. Brother to Eliza Ferry, November. 28, 1870, Box 1/3, Eliza Ferry Leary Papers, UWL/MUA.

72. *Vancouver Register*, March 12, 1875, Vancouver, Wash. Terr.

73. Dorothy Koert, *The Lyric Singer: A Biography of Ella Higginson* (Bellingham Wash.: Center for Pacific Northwest Studies, 1985), pp. 37-38. Advertisements announcing the sale of turkeys appeared in *Daily Oregonian*, Dec. 14, 1866.

74. *Told by the Pioneers*, 2: p. 189.

75. Sarah Willoughby to Oliver Willoughby, Nov. 1886, Box 2/15, Sarah and Charles Willoughby Papers, UWL/MUA.

76. "The Life and Letters of Adelaide Sutton Gilbert, Spokane Pioneer," p. 22.

77. Polly McKean Bell, "Christmas In The Eighties," *Oregon Historical Quarterly*, 44:4 (December, 1948): 295.

78. *The Palouse Gazette*, Dec. 27, 1878, Colfax, Wash. Terr.

About the Author

Jacqueline Williams researches and writes about the daily life of those who traveled the Oregon Trail and settled in the Pacific Northwest. Reviewers have acclaimed her award-winning book *Wagon Wheel Kitchens: Food on the Oregon Trail*, writing that it has "an immediacy and freshness that most writers only hope for." She contributes frequently to historical journals and newspapers, lectures widely about Pacific Northwest foodways, and is co-author of the cookbooks, *No Salt, No Sugar, No Fat; Hold the Fat, Sugar, and Salt;* and *Lowfat American Favorites*. Williams lives in Seattle where she collects early Pacific Northwest cookbooks.

Index